# INHERITING ABRAHAM

**LIBRARY OF JEWISH IDEAS**
Cosponsored by the Tikvah Fund

The series presents engaging and authoritative treatments of core
Jewish concepts in a form appealing to general readers who are curious about Jewish treatments of key areas of human thought and
experience.

# INHERITING ABRAHAM

## THE LEGACY OF THE PATRIARCH IN JUDAISM, CHRISTIANITY, AND ISLAM

*Jon D. Levenson*

PRINCETON UNIVERSITY PRESS

Princeton and Oxford

Copyright © 2012 by Princeton University Press
Published by Princeton University Press,
41 William Street, Princeton, New Jersey 08540
In the United Kingdom: Princeton University Press,
6 Oxford Street, Woodstock, Oxfordshire OX20 1TW

press.princeton.edu

Library of Congress Cataloging-in-Publication Data
Levenson, Jon Douglas.
    Inheriting Abraham : the legacy of the patriarch in Judaism, Christianity, and Islam / Jon D.
Levenson.
        p. cm.
    Includes bibliographical references and index.
    ISBN 978-0-691-15569-2 (cloth : alk. paper)   1. Abraham (Biblical patriarch)   2. Abraham
(Biblical patriarch)—In rabbinical literature.   3. Bible. O.T. Genesis—Criticism, interpretation,
etc.   4. Abraham (Biblical patriarch) in the New Testament.   5. Abraham (Biblical patriarch)—
In the Koran.   I. Title.
    BS580.A3L483 2012
    222′.11092—dc23      2012013158

British Library Cataloging-in-Publication Data is available

Publication of this book has been aided by the Tikvah Fund

This book has been composed in Minion Pro

Printed on acid-free paper ∞

Printed in the United States of America


10  9  8  7  6  5  4  3  2  1

For Lila Ruth Levenson and Eliana Rose Levenson,
two new daughters of Abraham

[1]Listen to Me, you who pursue justice,
You who seek the Lord:
Look back to the rock from which you were hewn,
To the quarry from which you were dug.
[2]Look back to Abraham your father
And to Sarah who brought you forth.
For he was only one person when I called him,
But I blessed him and made him many. (Isa 51:1–2)[1]

# Contents

# Acknowledgments

THE SUBJECT OF THIS BOOK is the biblical narratives about Abraham and their appropriation into Judaism, Christianity, and Islam, with the major emphasis falling on the Jewish material. It is a subject on which I have lectured for more than three decades, not only in my own classrooms but also in colleges, universities, seminaries, conferences, synagogues, churches, clergy associations, and interreligious gatherings too numerous to list here. I am thankful not only to those who have hosted me but also to all those who have sharpened and expanded my thinking with their questions and suggestions. The students at Harvard who have taken the seminars I have offered on various aspects of the subject over the years have, needless to say, helped me greatly. My one regret in this connection is the number of topics addressed in those seminars (such as Abraham as apocalyptic seer and as culture hero) that could not receive proper treatment in a book with the comparative focus and limitations of length of this one.

A number of scholars read all or parts of my manuscript at various stages or otherwise responded graciously and learnedly to my inquiries. I owe special thanks to Ellen Birnbaum, Diana Lobel, Kevin Madigan, Laura Nasrallah, David Powers, Michael Pregill, Bernard Septimus, Suzanne Smith, and Andrew Teeter. I must also thank the two anonymous readers whom Princeton University Press engaged for helping me avoid some mistakes and misstatements. Needless to say, I alone am responsible for the errors that remain.

Two expert editors were also of invaluable assistance. Neal Kozodoy, the creator of the Library of Jewish Ideas, was enormously helpful to me at every stage; the beneficial effects of his renowned editorial acumen can be seen throughout the book. Fred Appel of Princeton University Press also proved consistently helpful and accommodating, as did three other individuals associated with the Press, Sarah David, Beth Clevenger, and my expert copyeditor, Cathy Slovensky.

I did much of the work for this volume during research leaves from Harvard Divinity School, to which I am therefore grateful. My work would have been vastly harder were it not for my faculty assistant, Felicia Share, and the research assistants with whom I have been blessed in recent years, Maria Metzler, Keith Stone, Mary Ruth Windham, and Jonathan Kaplan.

All translations from the Hebrew Bible/Old Testament in this book are taken from *Tanakh*, except for those cited within an excerpt from another source. (Reprinted from the *Tanakh: The Holy Scriptures* by permission of the University of Nebraska Press. Copyright 1985 The Jewish Publication Society, Philadelphia.) Unless otherwise noted, the quotations from the New Testament and the Apocrypha that appear herein are from the New Revised Standard Version Bible. (Copyright © 1989, Division of Christian Education of the National Council of the Churches of Christ in the United States of America. Used by permission. All rights reserved.) All translations from the Qu'ran are taken from *An Interpretation of the Qu'ran: English Translation of the Meanings*, translated by Majid Fakhry (Washington Square, N.Y.: New York University Press, 2000. © courtesy of Garnet Publishing Ltd.). An earlier version of chapter 5 was first published by Marquette University Press as *Abraham between Torah and Gospel: The Père Marquette Lecture in Theology 2011*, vol. 42. Milwaukee, Wisconsin: Marquette University Press, 2011. http://www.marquette.edu/mupress/PM2011Levenson.shtml. A brief form of chapter 6 can be found in "The Idea of Abrahamic Religions: A Qualified Dissent," *Jewish Review of Books*. (Used by permission of the *Jewish Review of Books*.)

# A Note on Transliteration from Hebrew

THIS IS A BOOK WRITTEN for both general and scholarly readers. Some of the general readers will have knowledge of Hebrew, and some will not. The former and perhaps even the latter will be interested on occasion in knowing the key Hebrew words that are the focus of discussions. Scholarly readers, or at least those in the fields of Hebrew Bible and Jewish Studies, will have the same interest. The goal, then, is to present Hebrew terms in a way that is accessible to both sets of readers. To do this, I have refrained from providing scientific transliteration, with all its diacritical marks that so confuse and frustrate the nonspecialist. I trust my fellow specialists will forgive my foray into accessible communication.

Alephs and ayins are used throughout the book. Neither consonant is pronounced in the Ashkenazic tradition or by large numbers of speakers of Modern Hebrew, perhaps most. For those with some knowledge of Hebrew, I simply note that *aleph* is rendered as ' but ayin as '. As for the consonant *vav*, which was once pronounced like the English *w* (hence, scholars sometimes call it *waw*), in this book it appears as a *v*, the way it is almost always pronounced in Modern Hebrew. That is also the way the letter *bet* sounds when it is aspirated and thus called *vet*, and so it, too, appears as *v*.

Two other consonants, also once distinguished, that today are generally pronounced identically, include *kaf* and *qof*. Here, following convention, the first is rendered as *k* and the second as *q*. Sometimes *kaf* is aspirated so that it sounds like the *ch* in the German *Bach*. When that is the case, many Jews (including many Israelis) today articulate it exactly as they do another letter, *chet*. To avoid confusion, I render *chet* as *ch* and the aspirated *kaf* (or *khaf*) as *kh*. The letters *samekh* and *sin*, similarly once but no longer distinguished in pronunciation, I render respectively, as *s* and as *ś*. *Tet* and *tav*, too, are now generally pronounced identically; the former appears with a subdot (*ṭ*), and the latter always as a simple *t*. The letter *tsadi* appears here as *ts*, just as it is usually pronounced today. I have not employed diacritics with Hebrew vowels, trusting that here, too, any confusion that might result will be negligible.

# Abbreviations

## Books of the Hebrew Bible

| | |
|---|---|
| Chr | Chronicles |
| Dan | Daniel |
| Deut | Deuteronomy |
| Esth | Esther |
| Exod | Exodus |
| Ezek | Ezekiel |
| Gen | Genesis |
| Hab | Habakkuk |
| Isa | Isaiah |
| Jer | Jeremiah |
| Josh | Joshua |
| Judg | Judges |
| Kgs | Kings |
| Lev | Leviticus |
| Mic | Micah |
| Num | Numbers |
| Prov | Proverbs |
| Ps | Psalms |
| Sam | Samuel |
| Zech | Zechariah |

## Books of the New Testament

| | |
|---|---|
| Cor | Corinthians |
| Eph | Ephesians |
| Gal | Galatians |
| Heb | Hebrews |
| Matt | Matthew |

Pet          Peter
Rom          Romans
Thes         Thessalonians

## Ancient Jewish Works (Other than the Hebrew Bible)

Apo Abr      Apocalypse of Abraham
*b.*         Babylonian Talmud
*Gen. Rab.*  *Genesis Rabbah*
Jub          Jubilees
*m.*         Mishnah
Mac          Maccabees
*Rosh. Hash.*  *Rosh Hashanah*
*Sanh.*      *Sanhedrin*
*Shab.*      *Shabbat*
Sir          Wisdom of Joshua ben Sira
*t.*         *Tosephta*

## Other Abbreviations

JA           *Jewish Antiquities*
NRSV         New Revised Standard Version
NJPS         *Tanakh: The Holy Scriptures; The New Jewish Publication Society*

# INHERITING ABRAHAM

## Who Was (and Is) Abraham?

> On the day when Our Father Abraham passed away from the
> world, all the great people of the nations of the world stood in a
> line and said, "Alas for the world that has lost its leader, and alas
> for the ship that has lost its pilot!"
>
> —Talmud[1]

THE OLDEST SOURCE for the story of Abraham is in the biblical book
of Genesis, where it occupies about fourteen chapters, or roughly
twenty pages. Readers who are unfamiliar with the story would be well
advised to read it now, and in a modern, accessible translation.[2] When
they do, they will see that it is the deceptively simple tale of a person
to whom God, suddenly and without preparation, makes some rather
extravagant promises. This childless man (whose wife is infertile) is to
be the father of a great nation; he will become famous and blessed, in
fact a source or byword of blessing for many; and his descendants will
be given the land of Canaan, to which he is commanded to journey,
leaving his homeland in Mesopotamia (today, Iraq) and his family
of origin behind. Much of the drama in these early chapters of the
story derives from the question, how will this man whose wife has
never been able to conceive a child and is now advancing in years
ever beget the great nation that is at the center of the promise? The
wealth associated with that promise comes quickly, but the son who
will be Abraham's heir and continuator does not, and this casts into
doubt both the reliability of the promise and the God who made it.

When at long last Abraham does gain a son, it is not through
his primary wife, but, at her suggestion, through an Egyptian slave
who serves as a surrogate mother for her mistress. The resolution
is short-lived. For no sooner is Abraham's ostensible heir (Ishmael)
born than God makes the astounding promise that the infertile wife,

Sarah, now eighty-nine years old, will give birth to the promised son after all, and that this son will inherit not only the promises of blessing and great nationhood, as does Ishmael, but, unlike Ishmael, the covenant as well. Much of the second half of the story of Abraham focuses on the relationship of these two sons (and that of their mothers as well), until finally Ishmael and his mother Hagar are removed from the household and Hagar procures an Egyptian wife for her son, confirming, as it were, the divine prediction that his would not be Abraham's prime lineage. That status has been reserved for Sarah's son Isaac, who is born not through the course of nature but through nothing less than a miracle. But this time, too, the happy resolution is short-lived, for soon after it is established that Sarah's son Isaac is the promised offspring, God again, suddenly and without warning, commands Abraham to sacrifice this child, the son he loves and on whom he has staked his life, as a burnt offering on an as-yet-unspecified mountain in a distant land.

And yet, once again, Abraham obeys God's inscrutable will. At the last minute, God interrupts the sacrifice, having determined that Abraham obeys even when that means acting against his own self-interest and paternal love. Isaac survives. Abraham, before he dies, succeeds in buying a gravesite for Sarah, his only acquisition of real estate in the land promised his descendants. He also arranges a marriage for Isaac within his extended family back in Mesopotamia, ensuring that the promise will not die in his generation but extend into the next, as Isaac and Rebekah succeed Abraham and Sarah as the progenitors of the special nation. The promise secured—and to some extent realized—Abraham passes away at a ripe old age, contented.

So much for Abraham in the Jewish Bible, the subject of our first two chapters and part of the third (and to be treated at greater length later in this introduction). What is too easily missed is that in the Jewish tradition, the Bible comes bundled with a rich body of interpretation that has grown over many centuries. This makes it inadequate to restrict a discussion of Abraham in Judaism to the figure who appears in Genesis. Rather, the story continued to grow even after the biblical texts became fixed, and expanded versions of the story in Genesis—along with some that seem to have no or only slight rooting there—became plentiful among Jews living under various forms of Greek or Roman domination. In fact, as Judaism changed under the impact of fresh challenges and resources, the conception of Abraham changed as well. Much richer and more variegated portraits of him emerge, along with new conceptions of his significance and his legacy. The evolution of the figure of Abraham in Jewish sources reflects the evolution of Judaism itself over the centuries.

In the Jewish tradition, Abraham is known as *'Avraham 'Avinu*, "Our Father Abraham." As the father of the Jewish people, he is not simply their biological progenitor (and, as the tradition would have it, the father of all who have converted to Judaism as well); he is also the founder of Judaism itself—the first Jew, as it were—and the man whose life in some mysterious ways pre-enacts the experience of the Jewish people, who are his descendants and who are to walk in trails he blazed. The major way in which they are to do so is by serving and worshipping the God whom, according to those postbiblical but still authoritative traditions, Abraham rediscovered. To this day, the Jewish liturgy speaks of God as "the God of Abraham, the God of Isaac, and the God of Jacob," referring in the last two phrases to the special son and grandson through whom, according to the biblical narrative, the Jewish people came into existence.

That Abraham should have assumed such prominence is more than a little surprising, and for at least two reasons. The first is that so little of what the tradition instructs Jews to practice can be found in the biblical narratives about Abraham. Neither he nor anyone else in Genesis, for example, observes the Sabbath (*Shabbat*), a central focus of Jewish life from antiquity till the present. True, God "ceases" (Hebrew, *shavat*) from his labors on the seventh day of creation, but, as the Torah's story has it, he does not disclose Shabbat itself or command any human beings to keep it until the time of Moses, long after the death of Abraham. The same can be said about the great bulk of the commandments of the Torah. The opposition to idolatry and the insistence on the one God who has created the world, the characteristic ethical and legal norms, the laws governing sacrificial worship, the dietary laws, the festivals—Abraham is involved with none of these, the single, glaring exception being circumcision. But in time all this changes, as Abraham the father becomes Abraham the founder as well—the man who heroically stands up for the one invisible and transcendent God, who created the world, guides and governs it through his providence, and gave the Torah and its commandments to the Jewish people.

To historians, this postbiblical reconception of Abraham as the founder of Judaism is, of course, problematic, and not simply because it fails to reflect the earliest surviving sources about him. To the modern historian, the whole concept of a single person founding a great religion is too simplistic to account for the complex cultural and social dynamics by which any religious tradition comes into being. There is ample room to reject the notions, for example, that the tradition Westerners call "Confucianism" was founded by Confucius and that Christianity was founded by the man its adherents called "Jesus Christ" (who was, in fact, an observant Jew). In both those cases, however, the putative founder is revered and viewed as a paradigm for the adherents to follow, and no later figure in the tradition even begins to equal him. The same can be said for the Buddha and Muhammad. Abraham as he appears in the Torah is arguably (but not indisputably) presented as worthy of reverence, but little of what he is reported to have done is directly amenable to imitation. On the basis of the biblical traditions, if the problematic title of "founder" must be invoked at all, Moses would seem to have a much better claim to it than Abraham.

This brings us to the second reason that the reconception of Abraham in Jewish tradition is surprising. It is not simply that in Genesis, Abraham does not teach what Moses is said to have taught; it is that he does not teach anything at all. In this, too, he distinguishes himself radically from other putative founder-figures, like the Buddha, Confucius, Jesus, and Muhammad. Genesis, like the entire Jewish Bible, is extraordinarily reticent about providing editorial evaluations of Abraham. The same reticence also partly accounts for the occasional willingness of the Jewish tradition to find serious fault with Abraham.[3] In this, too, Judaism seems radically different from the way most religious traditions treat their founders, who are regarded as models for emulation and, in the case of orthodox Christianity, as the very incarnation of God himself.

In the later part of the Second Temple period (roughly 200 B.C.E.–70 C.E.), when the latest compositions in the Hebrew Bible were being finished, Judaism faced one of those challenges to its conception of Abraham alluded to above and found the resources to deal with it. The challenge lay in the advance of scientific thinking in the Greco-Roman world and the philosophical claims on behalf of naturalism with which it was associated. In particular, the discovery of mathematically predictable regularities inscribed in the motion of the heavenly bodies posed a formidable challenge to the traditional Jewish belief in a personal God who created the world (including the planets and stars) and actively governs it through his providence. As we shall see in chapter 4, one way in which Judaism sought to meet the new challenge was by finding in Abraham the man who had seen through astrology/astronomy (the two were not yet distinguished) and discovered the God who is above nature and not wholly immanent in it or constrained by it. The traditional absence of an icon of the Deity in Jewish worship lent itself to making a similar point. Whereas in the Abraham narratives of Genesis, there is no notion at all of idolatry or of false gods, late Second Temple Jewish literature exhibits an Abraham who, strikingly, not only intuits the non-corporeal nature of God but also sets himself courageously against the regnant idolatry. In the manner of biblical prophets like Elijah and Jeremiah, or of Jewish martyrs of the late Second Temple period itself, this Abraham is willing to witness to the highest truth with, if need be, his very life. This idea of Abraham's uncompromising opposition to idolatry carries over into rabbinic and later Jewish sources; it is familiar to many Jews today, some of whom are surprised to learn that there is not a word to that effect in Genesis. Appearing prominently in the Qur'an as well, it becomes an important part of the common heritage of Judaism and Islam.

Judaism, Christianity, and Islam are often described as the monotheistic religions, meaning those that insist there is but one God (though the one God of Christian tradition is believed to exist in three equally divine "persons"). Although in the Middle Ages the oneness of God becomes a focus of important philosophical reflection, monotheism among the Jews of biblical, Second Temple, and rabbinic times (the last period runs roughly from about 70 C.E. to 500 C.E.) was not focused primarily on the number of deities but on the transcendence of the true God over nature and humankind, which are his handiwork and ultimately dependent upon him and his generosity. Importantly, there was also a pagan monotheism in the Greco-Roman world ("pagan" in this usage is not derogatory but simply designates someone whose identity did not in any way derive from ancient Israel). But the one God in whom the Stoic philosophers believed, to use them as an example, was not the creator of the world and did not transcend the natural order, as did the creator God of the Jews and the Christians (and later, the Muslims). At least just as important is the crucial fact, too often overlooked, that Jewish, Christian, and Muslim monotheism focuses not only on the one God but also on the special human community to whom he has graciously revealed himself and his will in sacred scripture—another aspect unparalleled in pagan (or, philosophical) monotheism.

In the context of Judaism, one thus cannot speak very long or very adequately about God without speaking about the people Israel, the people descended from Abraham, Isaac, and Jacob; conversely, one cannot speak very long or very adequately about the people Israel without speaking about the God of Israel. Something analogous can be said about Christianity and Islam, but not about pagan monotheism. In Second Temple and rabbinic tradition, Abraham is not just the man who rediscovered the one God; he is also, as in the Hebrew Bible, the forefather of the Jewish people, who, like him, are witnesses to that God.

The rise of Christianity in the first century of the Common Era posed a different sort of challenge to Judaism and elicited a different sort of response. In this case, the central issue was twofold: Which community today can lay just claim to the promises made to Abraham's descendants, and what is that community obligated to practice? For the Christian apostle Paul, Abraham was "the father of all who have faith without being circumcised and who thus have righteousness reckoned to them, and likewise the father of the circumcised who are not only circumcised but who also follow the example of the faith that our father Abraham had before he was circumcised" (Rom 4:11–12).[4] Here, the key thing is not birth but faith, and Gentiles and Jews—the uncircumcised and the circumcised—qualify equally for "descent" from Abraham if they have faith. That Abraham lived before

Moses's reception of the Torah and, according to Genesis, was pronounced righteous by God because of his faith proved to Paul, himself once a practicing Jew, that the commandments of the Torah were not necessary for a right relationship with God.

Even the *mitsvah* (commandment) of ritual circumcision, which Abraham and his descendants were categorically commanded to practice, was no exception, for, as Paul sees it, Abraham was pronounced righteous because of his faith *before* that commandment was ever given.[5] And so, ritual circumcision, a requirement for men converting to Judaism, would not be required of Christians at all. The faith of Abraham the Gentile made him righteous in God's eyes even before circumcision made him into Abraham the first Jew. In Paul's theology, the community for which Abraham served as a paradigm was thus a mixed group of Gentiles and Jews, a community created by God and founded upon faith in the gospel of Christ crucified and risen from the dead. It was, in other words, the Church, and so it remains in the minds of most Christians to this day.

The precise innovation brought about by the Jewish response to Paul's and kindred early Christian theologies is difficult to establish, since we cannot easily distinguish between a response to a Christian challenge and the natural unfolding of Jewish theology and biblical interpretation. (The current Jewish Bible, give or take a few books, was the only Bible the earliest Christians knew.) A good case in point is the issue of the dispensability of ritual circumcision for men of Abrahamic descent. When the Talmudic sages, who refer to the circumcision ceremony as inducting the boy into "the covenant of Abraham Our Father," also devised a liturgy that proclaims, "Were it not for the blood of circumcision, heaven and earth would not endure!" (Babylonian Talmud [*b.*], *Shabbat* [*Shab.*] 137b), were they responding to the contrary Christian theology; to long-standing, in fact pre-Christian, Gentile contempt for the practice; to the great emphasis the Torah itself places upon the ritual; or to some combination of these three possibilities? Whatever the answer, it is certainly the case that the rabbis refused to dispense with circumcision or to subordinate it or the rest of the *mitsvot* (commandments) of the Torah to faith.

Indeed, in a number of places in rabbinic literature, we find Abraham practicing other mitsvot as well, even those undisclosed until after his death. "Thus," a rabbinic text reports, "we find that Our Father Abraham practiced the whole Torah, in its entirety, before it was given" (Mishnah [*m.*] *Qiddushin* 14:4). It is tempting to view this as a response to Paul's insistence that the case of Abraham shows the Torah and its commandments are not necessary and that it is faith that determines who belongs to the people of God and who does not. This may well be so, though, as we shall see in chapter 5, the idea that Abraham, Isaac, and Jacob observed the Mosaic Torah is also pre-Christian. The rabbis continued this idea but did not originate it. They also challenged it on occasion.

Islam (which arose in the seventh century C.E.) focuses on Abraham more than does either Judaism or Christianity.[6] Like Christianity, it seeks to detach Abraham from the flesh-and-blood Jewish people. But there is an extremely important difference between the Christian and the Muslim cases. Christianity has historically taught that descent from Abraham is essential; it differs from Judaism in holding that one becomes a descendant of Abraham through Christian faith and not through natural birth as a Jew or conversion to Judaism. Islam, on the other hand, beginning in the Qur'an itself, has taught that descent is insignificant. Abraham, in other words, is not the father of the believing community—neither "Our Father Abraham" nor "the father of all who have faith"—but rather a link in the chain of prophets that begins with Adam and culminates in the greatest of all prophets, Muhammad. As we shall see in chapter 6, the Qur'an conceives of Abraham as submitted to God (Arabic, *muslim*) and believes that those worthy of him are the followers of the man he foreshadowed, Muhammad, "Seal of the prophets" (33:40).[7] Alongside Abraham the Jew and Abraham the Christian (or at least the man who foreshadowed Christian faith), we thus must also reckon with Abraham the Muslim, or, to put the same point differently, with the Muslim claim that Islam is the restoration of "the religion of Abraham" (Qur'an 2:135), a religion long distorted and misinterpreted by Jews and Christians alike.

Given these conflicting interpretations of the supposedly common figure, the claim that Abraham is a source of reconciliation among the three traditions increasingly called "Abrahamic" is as simplistic as it is now widespread. Historically, Abraham has functioned much more as a point of differentiation among the three religious communities than as a node of commonality. The assumption that we can recover a neutral Abraham that is independent of Judaism, Christianity, and Islam—yet authoritative over them—is, as we shall see in chapter 6, quite unwarranted. Any argument that the Abraham of one of these three religions is the real Abraham will necessarily be fatally circular and privilege the scriptures and traditions of the very religion it seeks to validate. Thus, our concentration on the Jewish Abraham in this book implies no claim that the rival Abrahams of Christianity and Islam lack a parallel integrity of their own. On the contrary, the distinctive character of Abraham in Judaism—and to a large degree the distinctive character of Judaism itself—can be best understood through an honest and nonapologetic comparison and contrast with Abraham as he appears in the other two traditions now conventionally termed Abrahamic. It is surely the case that Jews, Christians, and Muslims have more in common than most of their adherents recognize, and one important item they have in common is a tendency to reflect on the figure of Abraham as he appears in their respective collections of authoritative literature. But those collections differ, the Abraham who appears in each of them is distinctive in important ways, and, although interreligious concord is devoutly to be desired, the patriarch is less useful to that end than many think.

The separation of Abraham from the subsequent history of the Jews and Judaism that Christianity and Islam brought about has, over the centuries, served as a sign of a potent challenge to traditional Jewish identity. In response, the Jewish tradition, building on certain clues in Genesis itself, has connected Abraham's experience to that of the people Israel over the centuries. Thus, when he is instructed to take a certain set of animals to use in the covenant-making ceremony, a midrash (an imaginative rabbinic interpretation of biblical verses) sees the animals as symbolizing the sequence of empires that ruled over the Jewish people, culminating in Rome, which dominated in the rabbis' own time.[8] The implication is that the covenant with Abraham will outlast those who have triumphed over his descendants (including the increasingly Christianized Roman Empire), and the Jewish people will outlive each of their vanquishers and reclaim the land that God solemnly covenanted with their father to give them.

Another midrash relates to the near-sacrifice of Isaac—the Aqedah, or "Binding," as it is known in rabbinic literature. The midrash dwells on a verse that has God showing Abraham the Temple: "built, destroyed, and rebuilt" (*Genesis Rabbah* [*Gen. Rab.*] 56:10). Developing a late biblical identification of the mountain in the land of Moriah,[9] on which the Binding took place, with the Temple Mount in Jerusalem, this midrash makes Abraham a sign of eventual Jewish restoration but only after unspeakable travail—travail that he already pre-enacted.

The story of the Aqedah is the subject of chapter 3. We turn to that episode now because it points to a critical dimension of the development of Jewish reflection on Abraham that is too often missed. It is not the case that as new challenges arose, the Jewish tradition responded to them by merely rejecting the new thinking out of hand and restating the old theology. Rather, the new challenges prompted Jewish thinkers to delve deeper, probing and adjusting the contours of their own tradition. The Aqedah represents a case in which a passage that is almost never referred to again in the Hebrew Bible grew in importance in the late Second Temple period and became central to the theology of the rabbis in the first several centuries after the birth of Christianity. Was this last turn just the natural continuation of an evolutionary process? Or was it a response to the Christian story of the father who was willing to sacrifice his beloved son and the son who was willing to lay down his own life in obedience and love—a story that had itself developed in part with the Aqedah as a template?

As so often in the relationship of Judaism with Christianity (and later with Islam as well), we are not dealing with a straightforward instance of mother-religion and daughter-religion, but rather with complex patterns of dependence and mutual influence in traditions that change over time. Whatever the case may be with regard to the Aqedah, the fact remains that this text, though commonly and indeed drastically misinterpreted today, is extremely important for understanding the role Abraham plays in Judaism—and for understanding Judaism itself. Something similar can be said about the important role of this same highly enigmatic and brilliantly narrated story in Christianity and Islam. Against these traditional readings, in modern times there has emerged an interpretation of the Aqedah that sees in Abraham not a man who passed the most demanding of tests but rather one who failed it by his willingness to murder an innocent person in response to a voice that could not possibly have been God's. In chapter 3, we will explore not only the various religious contexts in which the Aqedah has been read but also this modern assault on the story itself and seek to uncover the deeper issues at work.

So far, we have spoken of Judaism, Christianity, and Islam as if they all have a common Abrahamic legacy, but with some important differences along the way. One difference, so far unmentioned but very fundamental, divides the first two traditions from the third.

However much Judaism and Christianity may diverge, they agree on the canonical status of Genesis. With the rendition in that book of the story of Abraham, the question of which son and grandson inherit the patriarchal promise is acute. Is the son Ishmael or Isaac? Is the grandson Esau or Jacob/Israel? From the biblical standpoint, then, the Muslim dismissal of this issue of chosenness or election seems absurd. But Jews and Christians need to remember that Islam does not regard Genesis as canonical scripture, a status that the Qur'an holds uniquely. So, although the Qur'an exhibits wide and deep indebtedness to the Hebrew Bible and the New Testament (and affirms respect for the antecedent scriptures), as well as to postbiblical Jewish and Christian traditions, it omits passages that Jews and Christians consider essential, and it encompasses materials those two communities lack.

Nonetheless, it remains fair to say that the Jewish response to Christianity served the Jews against the challenge of Islam as well. For, despite the enormous differences between them, both challengers sought to detach Abraham from the Jewish people, and in the face of both challenges, the Jewish people in the aggregate clung stubbornly to the man they called Our Father Abraham.

The competition among Jews, Christians, and Muslims over the question of which community is truly Abrahamic, fascinating as it may be in itself, clearly leaves a sour taste in the mouths of many Westerners.

For, the thinking goes, how can we hope to understand Abraham before we have recovered the historical individual from the millennia of traditions that have accumulated around his name, progressively obscuring his identity and co-opting him for various agendas? To the modern Western mind, with its characteristic suspicion of tradition and its keen sense of historical change, the real question is not how this figure has been appropriated in Judaism, Christianity, and Islam over the centuries but rather, "Who was the *real* Abraham?" Without answering that all-important question, so the thinking goes, we have no basis to assess the relative value of those appropriations.

The question, it turns out, is considerably more complicated than most people think. One reason is that we have no contemporaneous references to Abraham whatsoever,[10] despite the discovery of thousands upon thousands of documents from the ancient Mesopotamian, Syro-Palestinian, and Egyptian cultures in which Genesis reports him to have lived. To be sure, the recovery of those long-lost cultures over the past century and a half has enabled us to understand many aspects of Genesis much better than we did, though in a way that also challenges interpretations provided by the postbiblical traditions. Forty years ago, American scholars (Europeans tended to be more skeptical) often thought they could accurately date Abraham to the first half of the second millennium B.C.E., when names and legal institutions appear that are reminiscent of some in the patriarchal narratives. Beginning in the 1970s, this line of thought received a solid drubbing, as scholars pointed out that the names and institutions in question, even when properly interpreted (as had not always been the case), tended to be more general and more enduring than had been assumed.[11]

Indeed, evidence from the ancient Near East (including other biblical evidence) and from the field of anthropology has increasingly suggested that the quest for the historical patriarchs may be a wild goose chase. "Abraham," "Isaac," and "Jacob," so the reasoning goes, may have been names of tribes or tribal confederations whose experiences over the centuries came to be expressed in stories about their putative ancestors. If so, "Abraham" may have been analogous to the American "Uncle Sam" or the English "John Bull" (whose activities have similarly become the objects of tales). In any event, even if Abraham was a "real" individual, he seems to have left a vastly smaller impression on his contemporaries than the ongoing traditions of the Jews, Christians, and Muslims (including biblical traditions) later imagined. Indeed, the very idea that he had a connection with those subsequent traditions—even those of biblical Israel—is open to doubt in the minds of most historians who seek to be intellectually honest.

To many religious traditionalists, of course, these findings of historical research matter not a whit. To them, the mere fact that their respective scriptures tell us of Abraham, Isaac, and Jacob means these men must not only have existed but must also have done what the canonical narratives say they did.

In the Jewish case, such an affirmation of historical accuracy often goes beyond the biblical accounts, incorporating the midrashim of the Talmudic rabbis into the historical picture as well. This stance produces the figure of an Abraham who preached monotheism, destroyed his father's idols, survived lethal persecution by an idolatrous king, and, what is more, practiced the whole Torah—both the Written (biblical) and Oral (rabbinic)—before it was given on Sinai or otherwise made publicly available. In the Christian case, an analogous traditionalism of roughly the same period yields, for example, an Abraham who talked with Jesus.[12] In Muslim tradition, it produces an Abraham who, together with his son Ishmael, purified the *ka'ba*, the building in Mecca that is the holiest site in Islam, for proper worship.[13] This sort of traditionalism fits well with the high esteem for tradition (one's own, but not that of others) and the weak or nonexistent sense of historical change characteristic of pre-Enlightenment thinking everywhere.

The modern suspicion of tradition, especially on questions of scripture, draws added strength from the slogan of the Protestant Reformation that theology should be governed *sola scriptura*, "by scripture alone," and not by the accumulated teachings of the Church over the centuries. Applied to our subject and detached from Protestant theology, this idea leads to the claim that the exclusive key to the "real" Abraham is Genesis itself, and not later elaborations of its narratives, no matter how hallowed or even authoritative they have become. But tradition is not so easily eliminated, and, in the case of biblical literature, what was thrown out through the front door has quietly reentered through the back. In particular, the assumption that the oldest narratives about any person or event must convey authentic historical information has been cast into grave doubt. In the case of the Abrahamic narratives in Genesis, the current consensus among historians is that the material dates to the first millennium B.C.E. (some of it even to the second half) and is thus centuries removed from the supposedly historical figure it renders. To reconstruct the traditionary process that predates these literary compositions is at best exceedingly speculative and impossible to do with any certainty.

In sum, scripture is itself partly a product of tradition. Anyone inclined to doubt that new material about a revered figure like Abraham could come into existence in a religious tradition and be readily accepted need only consult the examples cited above from Second Temple and rabbinic Judaism, as well as Christianity and Islam, to grasp how general that process is. What is not so general—and, in fact, almost limited to the modern West—is the familiar idea that the significance of a foundational figure is limited to the historical period in which he or she lived and is undermined by introducing new, historically implausible material. The profoundly antitraditional idea that the "real" Abraham is the original Abraham undercuts all three traditions and, effectively, leaves us with no Abraham at all.

Modern biblical historians have likewise challenged another familiar idea—the notion that the biblical text is unitary and therefore lacking the internal diversity characteristic of tradition everywhere else. Even a cursory reading of the Abraham story in Genesis reveals features that suggest either that the received text made use of diverse and not altogether consistent sources or that massive interpretive imagination is necessary to provide the astute reader with a sense of narrative harmony. For example, in Genesis 21, as Abraham expels Ishmael and his mother Hagar from his household at his wife Sarah's insistence, he seems to place his son on Hagar's shoulder, along with some food and water, and send them on their way (v. 14). When the water runs out in the desert, the distraught mother leaves her son under a bush and moves some distance away, saying, "Let me not look on as the child dies" (v. 16).

All this makes a great deal of sense if Ishmael is a baby or a toddler, but according to the chronological information Genesis provides, he is actually well into his teens! For he was thirteen when the miraculous birth of his brother Isaac was announced, and Isaac has now already been weaned.[14] It is no easy thing for a mother to carry her teenaged son on her shoulder on a trek into the desert or to leave him crying under a bush with certainty that he will not move away.

From the standpoint of modern historical scholarship, the answer to this problem is that we are dealing with diverse sources that may not know of each other and that were combined by an editor (redactor) who did not feel free to eliminate the inconsistencies by dropping or changing his sources.[15] A traditional answer to the same problem, though, appears in a midrash that tells us that Sarah had cast the evil eye on Ishmael (whose age is there given as twenty-seven), rendering him too ill to walk on his own.[16] The midrash may seem fanciful and intrusive, but without it, the smoothly unitary quality of the narrative vanishes, and we are left with differing narratives—even differing Abrahams.

The same sort of resolution of the text as we now have it into antecedent sources can be invoked to explain a host of other curious features of the Abraham narratives, especially texts that seem to be doublets. It explains, for example, why Abraham twice passes his wife off as his sister, why God twice (and under different names) makes a covenant with him, why explanations of the origin of Isaac's name appear twice (once in relation to the father and once in relation to the mother), and why, for that matter, Hagar and Ishmael are twice expelled.[17] Contrary to what is sometimes asserted, the goal of these historical-critical explanations is not to atomize the text as an end in itself but, instead, to understand better the process by which the text over time came to assume the shape it now has. The identification of sources (or source criticism, as the activity is called) is in the service of reconstructing the history of the religion of ancient Israel. In the case at hand, the goal is to reconstruct the earliest surviving literary traditions about the figure of Abraham by putting the biblical evidence we have into chronological order. When we do so, we see that the growth of the Abraham tradition is actually internal to the book of Genesis itself; it is not the creation of postbiblical Jewish (or Christian or Muslim) figures who were insufficiently attentive to the text of Genesis.

To many Jewish traditionalists (and not a few traditional Christians as well), historical-critical analysis of the Pentateuch is unacceptable on principle, since, by impugning the traditional doctrine that the author of those books is Moses, it undermines the divine origin of the five books and treats them merely as contingent products of human culture. This objection, on the one hand, is based on some confusions and misunderstandings, but, on the other, does raise an important point too little attended to by historical scholars.

The first confusion is the identification of Mosaic authorship with divine revelation. It implies that God could not speak through other individuals as well, in a more complicated historical process of revelation than the traditional image suggests. Yet the historical evidence, unknown until modern times and thus unavailable to those who formulated the doctrine of Moses's authorship, now points to the need to develop a model of revelation that can deal with the new challenge.[18] A second confusion is the assumption that the classic (i.e., premodern) Jewish tradition adhered without dissent to the doctrine of Mosaic authorship of the Torah, an assumption that cannot withstand scrutiny.[19] On both these points, traditionalists miss the mark.

The important question to which they do properly point, however, is this: How do we perceive God within, and receive instruction from, texts that we interpret only as artifacts of human culture? Within the paradigm of the historical-critical scholar of religious literature, there is no immediate need to face this issue. Indeed, biblical scholars who are not only secular themselves but utterly uninterested in normative theological questions have become a familiar presence in recent decades.[20] By treating only the historical dimension of the text, they imply, whether intentionally or not, that the larger, transhistorical meanings either do not exist or are not of central importance.

From the perspective of the classical Jewish tradition, however, holiness pervades all the authoritative texts, even those openly acknowledged to have human authors who were teaching, at one level, within the limits of their historical culture. The elucidation of historical context—surely a great boon to interpretation—must not be allowed to distract us from seeking to identify and develop the larger theological claims that the texts made in their own time and that, for committed Jews, they continue to make today. An analogous point about the Christian and Muslim traditions can be easily made.

The appropriate goal, then, is, on the one hand, to be open to instruction from history and aware of the cultural embeddedness of the texts about Abraham and, on the other hand, to be equally open to the transcendent and enduring religious messages these texts convey. As we are about to see, one of the central claims of the biblical tradition about Abraham from the earliest we can probe it is that the very particular, historical people known as Israel carries nonetheless a transhistorical, indeed, everlasting identity and message.

## CHAPTER ONE

## Call and Commission

> For it is hard for a person to leave the land in which he dwells
> and in which his friends and companions are found. All the
> more so if it is the land in which he was born, and all the more
> so if his whole family is there. That is why it was necessary to tell
> him to leave everything for the sake of his love for the Holy One
> (blessed be He!).
>
> —Nachmanides[1]

WITH THE INTRODUCTION of Abraham (called "Abram" until Genesis 17), the narrative of the Torah subtly yet momentously changes direction. The first eleven chapters of Genesis are marked by a pattern of human rebellion followed by divine punishment, which is then tempered by divine forbearance. By the end of chapter 11, the high hopes that God had held for the human race seem dashed. He had created them in his image and charged them with worldwide dominion under his sovereignty, yet they had repeatedly disobeyed him—in the Garden of Eden, with Cain's murder of Abel, with the evil that had brought on the great flood, and now with the Tower of Babel, with which they arrogantly hoped to reach the heavens and "make a name for [themselves]"—but with the result that the various nations were instead deprived of the ability to understand one another and were scattered "over the face of the whole earth" (Gen 11:4, 9). In the cases of Adam, Eve, and Cain, however, grace tempers the divine judgment, as the miscreants are sentenced to exile but not to the immediate death that had been expected. And in the case of the flood, God lowers his expectations of humanity, promising not to destroy it—though the human inclination to evil remains intact—and solemnizing his gracious promise in a covenant with all mankind and even with the animals as well (Gen 8:21–9:17). Humanity shall endure in spite of itself.

With the Tower of Babel, the last narrative before the introduction of Abram, the pattern breaks. Here, there is no note of grace to leaven the dire sentence of international incomprehension and universal exile with which the story of the tower concludes.[2] What follows, rather, is a new beginning, focused on a man whose promised destiny turns out to be not simply a tempering of the note of judgment but a reversal of it:

> [1] The LORD said to Abram, "Go forth from your native land, from your kin-group, and from your father's house to the land that I will show you.
>     [2] I will make of you a great nation,
>     And I will bless you;
>     I will make your name great,
>     And you shall be a blessing.
>     [3] I will bless those who bless you
>     And curse him that curses you;
>     And all the families of the earth
>     Shall bless themselves by you." (Gen 12:1–3)[3]

The command to separate himself from his country and kinfolk suggests that Abram, too, is going into exile, and yet only a few verses later, when he has dutifully obeyed the mysterious command to journey to the unnamed land, God tells him that he will grant that land (which turns out to be Canaan) to his offspring (v. 7).

In context, the gift of the land to the descendants of Abram forms a counterpoint to the universal exile that concludes the previous narrative. Similarly, the theme of blessing, underscored fourfold in the little poem above, reverses the theme of punishment and curse that dominates from the story of Adam and Eve through that of the Tower of Babel. What is more, God promises to do for Abram what the builders of that tower catastrophically failed to do for themselves—to grant him a great name (compare 11:4). Moving farther back in the narrative, we can also see the conjoining of blessing to the promise of land as a reversal of the cursing of the ground that was the punishment for Adam's disobedience in the Garden of Eden (3:17–19). And the promise to make of Abram "a great nation," that is, a man with a multitude of descendants, is quite possibly a reversal of Eve's punishment, which involved intense pain in childbirth (v. 16).[4] As I have observed elsewhere, "Abram, the tenth generation from Noah, who, in turn, is tenth in descent from Adam, is, no less and, in fact, more than Noah himself, the realization of the hoped-for reversal of the curses on Adam. The man without a country will inherit a whole land; the man with a barren wife will have plenteous offspring; and the man who has cut himself off from kith and kin will be pronounced blessed by all the families of the earth."[5]

In sum, a close reading of the initial call of Abram drives us to but one conclusion: with this act, God is no longer engaging in damage control, as he was in the first eleven chapters of the Torah. He is making a new beginning. Abram, and the as-yet-unnamed people promised to derive from him, represent a fundamentally different relationship between God and human beings from that which characterized primordial humanity. This new beginning, this new relationship, is found in the "great nation" that will, according to God's remarkable promise, descend from Abram through (as Genesis later is at pains to point out) his son Isaac and grandson Jacob, whose very name becomes that of the promised people, "Israel."

Why did God single out the people Israel and their ancestor Abram? Our first impulse is to answer by reference to the mission with which they were charged. And indeed, as we shall see, the Jewish tradition not infrequently attributes a lofty mission to Abram and his descendants. The Torah itself, by contrast, offers little by way of explanation for God's great act of choosing Israel. One text in which it does, in fact, cites no mission but only God's inexplicable love:

> [6] For you are a people consecrated to the LORD your God: of all the peoples on earth the LORD your God chose you to be His treasured people. [7] It is not because you are the most numerous of peoples that the LORD took a passion for you (*chashaq*) and chose you—indeed, you are the smallest of peoples; [8] but it was because the LORD loved you and kept the oath He made to your fathers that the LORD freed you with a mighty hand and rescued you from the house of bondage, from the power of Pharaoh king of Egypt. (Deut 7:6–8)[6]

According to this theology, the chosenness of Israel derives from an act of passion, God's passion for them or for their forefathers Abraham, Isaac, and Jacob, to whom he swore an inviolable oath. That oath, and nothing that Israel had done or would do, accounts for the exodus from Egypt.

Not surprisingly, Jewish sources generally suggest that God's singling out of the Jews, foreshadowed in the call of Abram, is, in fact, irrevocable. Nor do the Jews' specialness and uniqueness in the eyes of God *depend* on their fulfilling any mission. Nevertheless, many of the sources insist they do have a mission to fulfill: to share the universal and transcendent truth to which they have graciously been made privy. In this thinking, the blessing of Abram and the blessing of all the peoples of the earth are not at odds with each other. They are related parts of the same divine initiative.

The man whom God summons with the lofty call of Genesis 12:1–3 is an exceedingly unlikely candidate to father the "great nation" therein promised. For Abram's wife, Sarai (not yet called "Sarah"), is barren and childless, as the narrator explicitly notes (11:27). It is striking that Abram nonetheless obeys the directive to leave homeland and kinfolk and does so without questioning the extravagant promise with which it is bound. His obedience foreshadows a key fact about the "great nation" that will emerge from him: namely, that in this and other biblical texts, its existence is due to the special providence of God rather than the natural processes of human reproduction and population growth. The barrenness of the other two generations of matriarchs (Rebecca, Rachel and Leah) underscores this key theological point, one that will be echoed throughout the history of Judaism. An ancient Hebrew couplet, ascribed to the Gentile seer Balaam, puts it best: "There is a people that dwells apart / Not reckoned among the nations" (Num 23:9). And closely associated with this special identity is Israel's status as a blessed nation, very much as in the call of Abram. "How can I damn whom God has not damned?" asks Balaam, who has been hired specifically to curse this unique people, "How doom when the LORD has not doomed?" (v. 8).

Another factor, already mentioned in passing, speaks to the same point but from a different angle. Just before the story of the Tower of Babel, we find a table listing the seventy peoples who emerged from Noah's three sons.[7] That Israel, which emerges only afterward, is not one of these early nations is a matter of the highest significance, underlining the fundamentally different character of the new nation, not only born later but emerging as a result of a highly unlikely promise. As Genesis would have it, Israel is not a nation like any other. There is no genus of which God's chosen people is a species. Rather, the new people comes into existence only through God's promise to Abram, a childless man with a barren wife. Israel was never secular, so to speak; it never had an identity unconnected to the God who called it into existence in the beginning and who has graciously sustained it ever after. As the philosopher Saadya (Egypt and Iraq, 892–942) put it, "Our people is not a people except by virtue of its Torahs" (that is, the two Torahs of rabbinic Judaism, the Written and the Oral Torah).[8]

It might be argued that this particular expression of Jewish uniqueness does not reflect the course of historical events; that this theology of divine election is, rather, itself a later phenomenon, appearing only after the nation had long been in existence. Historically, this is quite plausible, and, given the likely date of the patriarchal narratives, it may even be probable. Even in the Hebrew Bible, indeed, there are other models of Israel's origin. For example, the prophet Ezekiel (early sixth century B.C.E.) presents an allegory of the history of Jerusalem, in which this capital city of the kingdom of Judah results from the mixed marriage of an Amorite and a Hittite (Ezek 16). The God of Israel adopts the newborn baby, abandoned by her parents, and, when she has reached puberty, marries her: "I entered into a covenant with you by oath—declares the Lord GOD; thus you became Mine" (v. 8). If we may extrapolate from Jerusalem, in Ezekiel's time the capital of the sole remaining Israelite commonwealth, to the whole people Israel, the prophet is here suggesting that the chosen people emerged not from a prior promise to a childless ancestor but from the adoption of an existing child of undistinguished, even shameful origins.

Still, whether speaking of an antecedent promise or of the adoption of an existing child, the Hebrew Bible consistently assumes a unique dependence of the special people upon God. In each case, moreover, it speaks of a radical discontinuity starting with the biological ancestor—Abram leaving his "father's house" in Genesis, the Amorite father and the Hittite mother abandoning their newborn daughter in Ezekiel. And in each case, it is God who takes the place of the lost parent.[9] No wonder converts to Judaism to this day take "Abraham" as the name of their father. The man who left his "father's house" to obey the command of God becomes the father of all who make the same journey.

The variant tradition in Ezekiel is illuminating for another reason as well. It draws attention to the fact that the difference between the chosen people and the rest of humanity is not genetic (a concept itself unknown in biblical times). In Ezekiel, the child who probably represents the whole chosen people, and who certainly represents their capital city, site of God's very palace, has emerged from two idolatrous peoples whom Israel supplanted long ago—and, according to the dominant biblical narrative, justly so. In Genesis, analogously, the childless man from whom the promised nation will emerge is one of three brothers; like them and every other human being, he is descended not from the gods or from a master race or the like ("race" being another modern concept unattested in the Hebrew Bible) but from Noah and his wife and from Adam and Eve before them. As the Mishnah famously observes, God created humanity from one man so that no one would say to his fellow, "My father is greater than your father!" (*m. Sanhedrin* [*Sanh.*] 4:5). Given this fundamental belief in the equality of all human beings, the doctrine of the chosen people cannot be equated with racism. Abram was not chosen because he was in any biological way superior to his contemporaries, and neither is the difference between Abram and his descendants, on the one hand, and the rest of humanity, on the other, a biological one.

The subtle concept of peoplehood underlying the call and commission of Abram is thus not easily accommodated by any of the models that come most readily to the modern mind, emphatically including the biological one. Rather, it rests on a seeming paradox. That Abram is commanded to break with his father at the beginning of his story—and to give up his son at the end of it, as we shall see in chapter 3—tells us that the "great nation" of which he is the promised progenitor is not simply another ethnic group, to be added to the seventy nations cataloged in Genesis 10.[10] Instead, it is something more like a religious community, a collectivity founded on shared faith rather than on descent. Yet the fact that the promised heir, from whom this nation is to descend, comes into being not from Abram's preaching—for he preaches nothing in Genesis—but from his own loins suggests something very different.[11] It suggests that the "great nation" is *not* a community founded upon a creed or a religious experience. Rather, it is a natural family.

So conceived, the people Israel is neither a nationality in the conventional sense nor a churchlike body composed of like-minded believers or practitioners of a common set of norms. Having something in common with both of these more familiar identities, it reduces to neither of them. Rather, as the call and commission of Abram already indicate, it is a natural family with a supernatural mandate.

Probably the most controversial clause in the call and commission of Abram is Genesis 12:3b, rendered in the King James Version, "And in thee shall all families of the earth be blessed." What, precisely, does it mean?

Here is the comment of the best-known medieval Jewish commentator, Rashi (Rabbi Shlomo Yitschaqi, northern France, 1040–1105):

> There are many freer interpretive traditions, but according to its contextual sense, it means this: A man says to his son, "May you be like Abraham!" And this is so in every case of those words, "shall bless themselves *by you*" [emphasis added] in the Bible, and here is the proof: "By you shall Israel invoke blessings, saying, 'May God make you like Ephraim and Manasseh.'" (Gen 48:20)

Rashi, in short, thinks the Hebrew preposition in question here does not mean "in" or "through," as the King James Version and many other translations render it, but rather "by." This traditional Jewish reading can be seen in the New Jewish Publication Society translation: "And all the families of the earth / Shall bless themselves by you." Christian translations, by contrast, often read something more on the order of the King James Version. Underlying the translation that we have been using (and Rashi's interpretation) is also the notion that the form of the verb indicates reciprocity or reflexivity: the families of the earth shall bless themselves or one another. Translations like the King James Version presuppose, instead, that the verb is simply passive: the families shall be blessed.[12]

Taking these two grammatical points into consideration, we reach the conclusion that according to its plain sense, what Genesis 12:3b actually promises Abraham is that he shall become a byword of blessing.[13] It is by reference to him that members of the families of the earth/land shall give blessings. To use modern analogies, it is as if someone were to say, "May you make money like Rockefeller!" or "May you dunk like Michael Jordan!"

Rashi's astute citation of Genesis 48:20, in which we are told that Israel shall give blessings by reference to the good fortune of the tribes of Ephraim and Manasseh, provides solid support for this understanding of our verse. A contemporary scholar, R.W.L. Moberly, finds further evidence for it in the book of Jeremiah. There we find the prophet condemning two other prophets with whom he has come into conflict over their optimistic view of the immediate future. They will, Jeremiah says, be handed over to the Babylonian king and put to death in the very sight of the Babylonian Jewish community, whose imminent redemption from exile they seem to have predicted:

> And the whole community of Judah in Babylonia shall use a curse derived from their fate: "May God make you like Zedekiah and Ahab, whom the king of Babylon consigned to the flames!" (Jer 29:22)

The two prophets, then, are the mirror image of the two tribes of Ephraim and Manasseh. Whereas according to Genesis 48:20 Israel *blesses* by reference to Ephraim and Manasseh, those in Babylonia, Jeremiah predicts, will *curse* by reference to Zedekiah and Ahab.

Moberly associates this latter prediction with another text in which Jeremiah attacks the Jews who have remained in the land instead of going into exile in Babylonia:

> I will make them a horror—an evil—to all the kingdoms of the earth, a disgrace and a proverb, a byword and a curse in all the places to which I banish them. (Jer 24:9)

To Moberly, that those not exiled become a curse recalls the end of Genesis 12:2, in which Abram is told, "you shall be a blessing," or, perhaps more literally, "be a blessing!" Individuals can surely pronounce a blessing, but how can they become one? The answer, he writes, is that "someone is a blessing or a curse if something happens to them such that when people formulate blessings and curses, their name is regularly used as an example of the desired outcome."[14] In sum, Abram will be a blessing because people will bless themselves by reference to him, just as Rashi thought.

What I have been describing—chosenness, in a word—is a concept essential to the traditional view of Jewish peoplehood, and also one of the least understood or most misunderstood. Among the impediments to understanding, the most readily available and one of the least helpful is the traditional Christian belief that the Jewish people are—or, to be more precise, were—a prototype for another body, namely, the Church. This statement necessitates a brief bit of background before returning to our narrative.

For many Christians—as well as those non-Christians influenced by the Christian interpretation of Genesis—the new relationship initiated with God's call and commission of Abram involves a dramatic movement away from particularism toward universalism. The mysterious singling out of Abram is thus not so mysterious after all, for the new beginning that it represents finds its proper fulfillment only in the eventual emergence of a *universal* community, much larger than and very different from the Jewish nation.

This reading places great emphasis on that key clause: "And all the families of the earth / Shall bless themselves by you" (Gen 12:3b). Starting already in an early letter of Paul, the Jewish contemporary of Jesus who after the latter's death became his "Apostle to the Gentiles," these words become the prooftext for a theology that insists that the blessing in question falls on the Gentiles and not only (or perhaps not at all) on the Jews:

> [6]Just as Abraham "had faith in God, and it was reckoned to him as righteousness" [Gen 15:6], [7]so, you see, those who have faith are the descendants of Abraham. [8]And the scripture, foreseeing that God would justify the Gentiles by faith, declared the gospel beforehand to Abraham, saying, "All the Gentiles shall be blessed in you" [Gen 12:3]. [9]For this reason, those who have faith are blessed with Abraham who had faith." (Gal 3:6–9)[15]

Like Paul, the rabbis of the Talmudic period, too, would quote Genesis 15:6 (the fascinating verse to which we shall devote more attention in chapter 5). But for them it provided evidence that the Jewish people are "people of faith and the descendants of people of faith."[16] The difference between their theology and Paul's does not lie in the question of whether faith is or is not important; it was highly important in both theologies. The essential difference, rather, lies in the question, faith in what?

For the rabbis, the faith in question is faith in the promises that God had given the Jewish people, first conveyed to their ancestor Abram, the archetypical man of faith. For Paul (whose thinking on this issue has dominated Christian tradition over the centuries), it is faith in Jesus, who he believed had definitively broken the power of human sinfulness and thus fulfilled the promise to Abram given in Genesis 12:3b. As Paul goes on to say in the same chapter of Galatians, "The scripture has imprisoned all things under the power of sin, so that what was promised through faith in Jesus Christ might be given to those who have faith" (Gal 3:22).[17]

We must be clear, however. It is not the case—though many Christians make the mistake of thinking otherwise—that Paul himself redirected the interpretation of Genesis 12:3b from a particularistic one centered on the Jewish people to a truly universal one centered on all humanity. In point of fact, Paul saw the promise to Abraham as applying only to the Church: that is, to the mixed group of Jews and Gentiles constituted by their faith in Jesus. A Gentile's conversion to Judaism (meaning the religion centered on observing the commandments of the Torah)—a possibility that Paul, curiously, seems not to mention—would not make him or her a beneficiary of the Abrahamic promises; only the Gentile's inclusion in the Church could do that.

It bears underscoring that in the middle of the first century C.E. when Paul wrote, the Church was a *smaller* group than the Jewish people. Contrary to the common misperception, Paul did not expand the circle of "those who have faith." He contracted it—with the goal, of course, of diffusing the particularistic community that was the Church throughout the world. And here is the point with which the familiar depiction of Judaism as particularistic and Christianity as universalistic fails to reckon, with drastic consequences: for Paul, the Church is not just a particularistic community; *it is made up exclusively of descendants of Abraham*. "And if you belong to Christ," the Apostle to the Gentiles declares, "then you are Abraham's offspring, heirs according to the promise" (Gal 3:29). Conversion to Christianity (to use terminology that did not exist in Paul's time), then, gives Gentiles the status that Jews claimed for themselves: it makes them descendants of Abraham and thus heirs to the promise given him. It does this, moreover, while bypassing the laws of Moses and even the law of circumcision, given to Abraham himself six generations before Moses (Gen 17:3–14). Baptism, not circumcision, makes a Gentile, as it were, into a Jew. In Paul's theology, this is the blessing signaled in Genesis 12:3b.

Where does this leave those who have been Jews all along and who are not persuaded by the new phenomenon that will come to be called Christianity? On this critical question, Paul's thought shows development over time but never breaks free of a nagging ambivalence. On the one hand, in a long reflection on this issue written at the end of his apostolate (Rom 9–11), he expresses great concern for his Jewish "kindred according to the flesh," declares that traditional theological goods such as the covenant and the patriarchs belong to them, and explicitly denies that God has rejected his people (9:1–5; 11:1). He also warns Gentile Christians against boasting at the expense of the Jews (11:17–24). On the other hand, in the same passage he reiterates his view that since the promise trumps the flesh (that is, birth), "not all of Abraham's children are his true descendants," and he declares that the Jews are branches that have been broken off the tree because of their unbelief and replaced by Gentiles who have been grafted in "in their place" (9:6–8; 11:17–20). To complicate the picture still further, the latter affirmation closes with what seems to be a prediction that "these natural branches [will] be grafted back into their own olive tree" (11:24).

This last turn, it would appear, relates to Paul's expectations for the end-time, when he thought Jesus would return. Today, many of those involved in interfaith dialogue see in Romans 9–11 a theology in which Judaism and Christianity are equal, but, given Paul's belief about the end-time and the intense Christocentrism of his theology, it is much more likely that he thought the Jews, like the rest of the world, would turn to Jesus, and as a consequence God would lift his punishment on them for their disbelief and restore them to their prior and ultimately irrevocable glory.

Unfortunately, even Paul's ambivalence about Jews who did not become Christians was largely lost in subsequent Christianity, and the putative blessing for the nations turned into a curse for the Jews. Already, for example, the unknown author of the early Christian work known as the Epistle of Barnabas (about 100 C.E.), commenting on God's declaration that Abram, still uncircumcised, is righteous on the basis of his faith (Gen 15:6), interprets it thus: "Behold, I have made thee, Abraham, the father of the Gentiles . . . who believe in God in uncircumcision" (13:7). The same author declares, as Jeffrey S. Siker puts it, that "God has abandoned the Jews for the Gentiles."[18] The apologist Justin, who wrote after the Roman Empire had brutally defeated the Jews in the Bar Kokhba War (132–135 C.E.), took the next step. He transformed circumcision from a sign of God's enduring and unbreakable covenant with the people he has promised to bless, as it is in Genesis, into exactly the opposite, a sign of divine rejection and Jewish suffering, especially the loss of the Land of Israel. Justin's Christian spokesman addresses his Jewish interlocutor thus:

> Indeed the custom of circumcising the flesh, handed down from Abraham, was given to you as a distinguishing mark to set you off from other nations and from us Christians. The purpose of this was that you and only you might suffer the afflictions that are now justly yours; that only your land be desolate, and your cities ruined by fire; that the fruits of your land be eaten by strangers before your very eyes; that not one of you be permitted to enter the city of Jerusalem.[19]

By this strange route, the contempt in which the world of Greco-Roman paganism had long held circumcision and sometimes (but not always) the Jews themselves rapidly made its way into Christianity. It has colored for millennia the way even Abraham himself has been perceived in the Christian and post-Christian worlds.[20]

In this notion that the singling out of Abraham never referred to the Jews, or no longer refers to the Jews but applies only to the

Church, God's choice of Abraham is seen as purely instrumental: God did not fall in love with Abraham and with the nation that would descend from him for their own sake. Rather, he singled them out strictly for the purpose first declared in Genesis 12:3b: "And in thee shall all families of the earth be blessed" (to revert to the King James rendering). The characteristic effort of Christians to convert all nations, and the lack of just such an effort among the Jews, could then be interpreted as further proof that the Church, not the people Israel, carried on the Abrahamic legacy.

Consider, for example, the words of H. H. Rowley (1890–1969), one of the more prominent Old Testament scholars of the twentieth century:

> That Judaism has cared so little for the One [that is, Jesus] who, on lowest count, is the greatest of her sons, and the One who has most powerfully influenced the world, is a singular fact. . . . If, then, the first element of the service of the elect was to receive and cherish the revelation of God given to Israel, then the church performed it more fully than did Judaism.

For Rowley, the "service of the elect" (or "chosen") involves an obligation "to mediate to all men the law of her God, and to spread the heritage of her faith through all the world."[21] It is not hard to see here a particular Christian construction of Genesis 12:3b, the half verse that speaks of the blessing that "all the families of the earth" would know. By not accepting the claims made for Jesus, and by declining as well to preach to others the law of God and faith in him, the Jews have proven unworthy of the Abrahamic legacy. With regard to the Jews, the distance from Justin in the second century C.E. to Rowley in the twentieth is not so great after all.

Now we must return to Rashi and those "freer interpretive traditions" (Gen 12:3b) that he mentions. The term alludes to a crucial aspect of the Jewish heritage: the plain sense of the verses does not control the rabbinic understanding of the Bible. Rather, along with the plain sense (known in medieval times as *peshat*), the tradition values a less contextual but more expansive and imaginative sense (*derash*, related to the word *midrash*). For that very reason, simply accepting that our verse means "And all the families of the earth / Shall bless themselves by you"—that Abram, that is, will be a byword of blessing, as Rashi and others argue—does not identify that meaning as the sole Jewish interpretation. Although many Jews and Christians imagine that Judaism adheres exclusively to the simple sense of the Hebrew Bible whereas Christianity does not, the truth is that over time both traditions came to recognize a plurality of senses in scripture.

An ancient midrash, in fact, offers an alternative reading to Rashi's: "Rain comes through your merit; dew comes through your merit" (*Gen. Rab.* 39:12). The implications of this interpretation are enormous, not only for the understanding of Abraham but for the understanding of the Jewish people as well.

To be sure, the notion of the "merit" of Abraham (and of Isaac and Jacob, the other two patriarchs) is not biblical but rabbinic. In the Hebrew Bible, the point is not that these men were righteous but that they were the recipients of God's gracious promise, and the Jewish people benefit not from any merit they supposedly accrued but from the irrevocable promise to them that centers on their descendants.[22] That allowance having been made, the gloss of Genesis 12:3b in our midrash is still very valuable, for it shows that the blessing on Abram has positive consequences for "*all* the families of the earth," whose prosperity is owing to him through the benefits conferred by his descendants, the Jewish people.

In this interpretation, Abram is thus not simply a byword of blessing, as Rashi was to think; he is a universal *source* of blessing. The midrash that offers this reading supports it with intriguing examples of Gentiles who prosper because of the interventions of Jews: the pharaoh to whom Joseph revealed the coming famine and how to survive it and whom Jacob later explicitly blesses; the Babylonian king Nebuchadnezzar, to whom Daniel conveys important revelations; and the Persian king Ahasuerus, whose life Mordecai and Esther save from an assassination plot.[23]

This ancient midrashic notion that God will bless "all the families of the earth" because of Abram was developed much further in the Middle Ages. Rabbi David Qimchi (Provence, 1160–1235), for example, finds here God's promise to send his blessing to all the peoples in whose lands Abram will sojourn so that they will be favorably disposed to him. This makes Abram not only the recipient but also the mediator of blessing and binds his fortune—and by implication that of his promised descendants—tightly to the nations among whom he dwells. An even more expansive understanding of the clause appears in the works of the philosopher, commentator, and statesman Isaac Abarbanel (Portugal, Spain, and Italy, 1437–1508):

> The goal of his journeying is hinted at in the expression, "you shall be a blessing" (Gen 12:2), for He commanded him that when he would journey, there would be a blessing among the peoples because he would teach them and make them know the true faith in such a way that the world would be perfected by means of him. And He (may He be blessed!) informed him that His providence would adhere to those people who accept his teaching and learn his faith.[24]

True, Abarbanel's interpretation depends on an idea, already ancient in his time but unattested in Genesis or anywhere else in the Hebrew Bible, that Abraham had a distinctive theological teaching and sought to make the world aware of it. We shall explore this dramatic transformation of the Abraham tradition at length in chapter 4. Here, what is germane is that Abarbanel draws a tight connection between the directive to Abram to journey forth, conveyed at the beginning of God's initial charge to him ("Go forth from your native land," Gen 12:1), and the enigmatic blessing at its end ("And all the families of the earth / Shall bless themselves by you," v. 3). In the passage quoted above, Abarbanel does not (at least primarily) address the question of why Abram was chosen but rather why he must travel about through Canaan, Egypt, and Philistia. As much of a hardship as the journeys were on him—travel was vastly harder in antiquity and the Middle Ages than it is now—they were inextricably associated with the blessing that he would receive and, in turn, impart to others, the incomparable blessing of the knowledge of God and subjection to his providence.

With this, we revert to the predominating Christian view of the election of Israel and specifically to Rowley's insistence that "the first element of the service of the elect was to receive and cherish the revelation of God given to Israel" and that this "service of the elect" involves an obligation "to mediate to all men the law of her God, and to spread the heritage of her faith through all the world." In the view of Abarbanel and the traditions on which he relies, this is precisely what Abram did and, by implication, what the Jewish people are to do, so far as they can. But this could not be farther from Rowley's restatement of the traditional Christian claim that the failure of the Jews to follow Jesus led to their replacement by the Church in the role of the elect.

In the thinking of Abarbanel and all the other Jewish sources we have quoted, God's singling out of the Jews, foreshadowed in the call of Abram, is irrevocable. To say it again, their specialness and uniqueness in the eyes of God do not depend on their fulfilling any mission, but they do have a mission to fulfill nonetheless—namely, to share the universal and transcendent truth that has graciously been disclosed to them alone. The blessing of Abram and the blessing of all the peoples of the earth are not in opposition. They are related parts of the same divine initiative.

Another interpretation of chosenness, also popularized by Christianity and accepted even by many who think of themselves as unaffected by Christianity, equates the chosen with the saved, and the unchosen therefore with the damned, as the English term "election" can suggest. In some (but not all) currents of Christian theology, there is a notion that salvation is only for the elect, and the rest of humanity is destined for perdition. In its most extreme version, this doctrine denies all hope to non-Christians, as implied by one interpretation of the ancient formula, *extra Ecclesiam nulla salus*— "outside the Church there is no salvation." At times, something very close to this highly exclusive theology has appeared in Judaism, too, but so has the position that "there are righteous people among the Gentiles who have a portion in the World-to-Come" (*Tosephta* [*t.*] *Sanh.* 13:2), with the "World-to-Come" serving as the Jewish equivalent of Christian "salvation." In general, it is this more inclusive position that comes to dominate in rabbinic tradition. The great legal authority, philosopher, and communal leader Maimonides (Spain, Morocco, and Egypt, 1138–1204), for example, explicitly adopts it in his law code.[25]

As for the book of Genesis, it not only lacks any notion of a World-to-Come; it also lacks any notion that the singling out and blessing of Abram imply the rejection of everyone or anyone else. Indeed,

Genesis 12:2–3 explicitly connects his call and commission with the possibility of a wider blessing, one that involves "all the families of the earth." It is thus a capital error (though, sadly, a familiar one) to treat the biblical and rabbinic theology of chosenness as encompassing only two categories, the chosen and the unchosen, like the intensely exclusivistic stream in Christian theology that speaks only of the elect and the damned. It is much more accurate to follow the lead of Joel S. Kaminsky, who speaks of three categories: the elect, the non-elect, and the anti-elect. The last—and they alone—are the enemies of Israel and her God.[26] Within the non-elect, one may further identify a subcategory that can be called the pro-elect: Gentiles who, like the Canaanite prostitute Rahab (Josh 2), actively affirm the God of Israel and come to the aid of his chosen people.[27] These, to revert to the language of Genesis 12:3, are those whom God blesses because they bless Abram.

Ironically, the dualism of the exclusivist stream in Christian theology reappears in the tendency of many contemporary secular intellectuals to speak of identity in general as inevitably bound up with animosity for the outsider, or "the Other." "The Other against whom Israel's identity is forged is abhorred, abject, impure, and in the 'Old Testament' vast numbers of them are obliterated," writes a contemporary scholar of English literature. "The very idea that identity is constructed 'against' suggests scarcity, as though there were a finite amount of identity itself, and so a space must be carved out for it and jealously guarded, like finite territory."[28] But the call of Abram in Genesis 12:1–3, like many other passages in the Tanakh, speaks powerfully to the diametrically opposite point: identity need not be forged in opposition, outsiders need not be identified with impurity and the like, and the blessings of a particular identity are not restricted to those defined by it but can extend generously outward.

All this requires us to challenge the convenient dichotomy between the Jewish and the Christian understandings of Genesis 12:3b. For the Jews, if we rely on Rashi and the apparent plain sense of the verse alone, it is about Abram and tells how blessed he—and, by implication, the "great nation" that will derive from him—will be. For Christians, if we rely on Paul (whose interpretation, as we have seen, has been enormously influential), Genesis 12:3b is principally about the families or nations of the world—the "Gentiles," in the translation of Galatians 3:6–9 given earlier in this chapter—and the blessing they will receive through Abram. But now we see why the distinction is *too* convenient. Although the Christian interpretation of Genesis 12:3b is widespread and often simply assumed today (again, even by people who pride themselves on their secularity), it turns out that traditional Jewish interpretations of the verse include more than Rashi's reading, to the point where at times, as in the case of Abarbanel, it approximates the universal aspiration evident in the Pauline reading. In so doing, it falsifies the convenient dichotomy, along with the equally wrongheaded stereotype that Judaism is tribalistic and inward-looking (or even misanthropic), while Christianity is universal and outward-looking.

In much of the classical Christian tradition, Abram and the Jews were only instrumental to the emergence of the gospel and its exportation to all the nations of the world. For the classical Jewish tradition (and many contemporary Christians), Abram and the people who descend from him have full importance in their own right; their election, God's mysterious singling out of them from among all the families of the earth, is not canceled when they fail at the lofty ethical and theological missions that come to be associated with their first father. The promises endure, despite appearances to the contrary. And as we shall see in chapter 2, the tension between promises and empirical realities becomes intense already in Abram's own life.

## CHAPTER TWO

## Frustrations and Fulfillments

> There are three attributes that characterize this nation: They are
> merciful, modest, and charitable. . . . "Charitable," as it is writ-
> ten, "in order that [Abraham] may instruct his children and his
> posterity to keep the way of the LORD by doing what is just and
> right." Anyone who has these three attributes is fit to become at-
> tached to this nation.
>
> —Talmud[1]

ONE OF THE MOST extraordinary aspects of the story of Abraham in
Genesis is the long, circuitous, and difficult route that lies between
the LORD's initial promises to him and their fulfillment in the emergence of a great nation descended from him and in possession of
the land of Canaan. Indeed, though aspects of those promises are
fulfilled in Abraham's own lifetime—in most cases, only after enormously discouraging and painful delays—the promise in its fullness
is not realized until long after his life has come to an end and, even
more, after the Torah story itself comes to an end in the book of
Joshua, when Israel finally conquers the land.

Already in the first narrative after it is given, the promise seems
to be derailed. Under the pressure of an intense famine, Abram and
Sarai (as they are called until Genesis 17) leave Canaan for Egypt.
Worried that the Egyptians, reputed elsewhere in the Bible to be
sexually deviant, will put the husband of such a beautiful woman
to death, Abram asks his wife to do him the favor of claiming she is
actually his sister. As he feared, the natives notice Sarai's beauty, and
soon she is taken to Pharaoh's palace. The result for Abram, though,
is highly positive: he not only escapes murder but "because of her,
it went well with Abram; he acquired sheep, oxen, asses, male and
female slaves, she-asses, and camels" (Gen 12:16).

And so, the promise of blessing (of which wealth is usually a component in the Hebrew Bible) has already come about. But Abram's marriage seems over and with it the chance of his becoming "a great nation," and no sooner has he been promised a land than he finds himself in exile. Just as things seem hopeless, though, "the LORD afflicted Pharaoh and his household with mighty plagues on account of Sarai" (Gen 12:17), and Pharaoh, not before rebuking the mendacious patriarch-to-be, sends him off with his wife and his possessions (vv. 18–20).

This little narrative (Gen 12:10–20) is so compressed and so cryptic that it is susceptible to many interpretations, some diametrically opposite to others. In one popular modern reading, Abram is a rank cad who subjects his wife to sex with other men—foreigners to boot—just to save his own skin. The most extreme version of this negative interpretation sees in Abram's acquisition of great wealth "because of her" evidence that he was, as one scholar indecorously puts it, "pimping his wife," getting rich from the services she was forced to perform in Pharaoh's palace.[2] But, as has often been noted, it is possible to read the same verse (v. 16) as the fulfillment of Abram's hope that "I may remain alive thanks to you" (v. 13). On that understanding, it was because of Sarai's willingness to pass herself off as his sister that Abram remained alive and thus was able to experience the promised blessing in the form of the unexpected wealth he amasses even in the land of his exile.

But the deepest challenge to the negative view of Abram's stratagem can be expressed in one simple question: How would Sarai have been better off with her husband dead? For surely, if Abram's anxiety about the Egyptians is valid (and one does not hear Sarai disputing it), then his wife would have ended up in an Egyptian harem either way. Anyone who faults Abram's stratagem—and Sarai's willingness to implement it—needs to explain how that outcome would have been to her advantage.

There is, however, another and more subtle approach that again casts doubt on the appropriateness of Abram's behavior in Genesis 12:10–20. If one reads the narrative of Abram and Sarai in Egypt in conjunction with the promises to Abram that precede it in the same chapter, then a case might be made that having been commanded

to enter the land and then promised it would be given to his descendants, he should not have abandoned it on his own initiative—or
have feared that he would be put to death before his childlessness had
come to an end. For leaving the Promised Land suggests disobedience to the command to go there, and Abram's fear that he, though
still childless, would be killed signals a lack of faith in the promise
that he will be blessed himself and become a byword or source of
blessing for others as well, and that his descendants will be given the
land he now abandons. Add to this the fact that in the process he ex-
poses his marriage to destruction, and Abram's stratagem is exposed
as all the more heinous.

This is essentially the interpretation given by the great theologian
and commentator Ramban (Rabbi Moses ben Nachman, also known
as Nachmanides, Spain, 1194–1270), who wrote that Abram "committed a great sin inadvertently" by leaving the land promised him
and "[bringing] his righteous wife to a stumbling-block of sin" in
Egypt—so great a sin that, by the karmic process that Ramban saw
operating in the Torah, Abram's unintended sin caused the exile in
Egypt that his descendants would later suffer. Instead, Abram "should
have trusted that the LORD would rescue him and his wife" and not
allow them to die in the famine.[3]

Ramban's harsh judgment raises a large theological question that
we shall see again and again in the story of the patriarch, one that is,
in fact, intrinsic to the very nature of ancient Israelite religion and its
Jewish, Christian, and Muslim successors. Does faith in God and his
promises require in the beneficiaries a stance of quietism and passiv-
ity, or does it, rather, require the opposite stance of human initiative
and activism to help bring about the promised result? The question
can be illustrated with the old joke about the man informed by God
that he will win the state lottery. After years of failing to win, the un-
happy man finally musters the courage to confront the Almighty. The
answer: "It would help if you bought a ticket!" In Genesis 12:10–20,
Abram buys a ticket that he hopes will secure his and his wife's life in
the famine and protect him from the lecherous, murderous people
whom he expects to encounter in Egypt. In Ramban's mind, Abram's
activism signals a lack of faith and a correlative moral failure. And
yet, as the joke implies, it can be argued that it was precisely Abram's

activism that enabled him and Sarai to survive and God's promise to begin its long and excruciating process of fulfillment.

The modern recovery of the ancient Near Eastern world in which narratives like this one were written adds valuable new light to their interpretation and raises novel interpretive possibilities less likely to occur to the traditional commentators. A particularly interesting example is a study by Assyriologist Barry L. Eichler that finds evidence that "in Mesopotamia, a woman's brother is often documented in his capacity as the legal representative of the fatherless sister, who arranges for her marriage and receives her bride-price." Eichler states the implications of this for our narrative:

> Now, with the help of the above-cited biblical and ancient Near Eastern materials and supplementary anthropological data, the realistic reader is able to explore once again the purport of Abram's stratagem with greater critical control and less subjectivity. It is now clear that by assuming the status of Sarai's brother, Abram not only removes the threat to his life posed by being the husband of a beautiful woman in a foreign land but also enhances his chances for survival by being identified as her irreplaceable brother. Furthermore, it is also clear now that, as her brother, Abram would be recognized as the protector and legal guardian whom one would approach to negotiate Sarai's marriage. Thus, based on evidence external to the narrative, the reader can now appreciate the twofold purpose of Abram's ploy: the preservation of his life and the protection of his wife. But alas, Abram never anticipated Pharaoh's swift abduction of Sarai, which suddenly rendered him so powerless.[4]

To be sure, we must resist the tendency to regard this very modern interpretation as telling us what the story *really* means, as if all the ambiguities could be resolved if only we had more data. And, truth to tell, the legal institution that Eichler reconstructs, though not without resonance in biblical and Talmudic literature, is still a reconstruction, and its applicability to our narrative is not beyond doubt. His interpretation does suggest that even those who are determined to resist traditional pieties and apologetics would do well to think again before interpreting Abram as a cad. What it cannot resolve, however, is the larger question of whether the promises made by God absolve human beings from taking measures that seem necessary to bring about the promises.

Before we leave the story of Abram and Sarai in Egypt to explore another case involving the same theological question, it is worthwhile to say something about the role the story plays when understood in the context of the entire Torah, the first five books of the Bible. Salient aspects of the story should sound familiar: famine drives a couple out of the Promised Land to seek food in Egypt. There the fear emerges that the man will be killed and the woman alone allowed to live, but despite the danger, the man survives. The LORD afflicts Pharaoh and his household with great plagues, a confrontation with the king ensues, and Pharaoh sends the couple off with all the great wealth that they amassed during their exile in his kingdom. Put this way, it is not hard to hear in this tale an adumbration of the story of the Exodus, when famine drives the people Israel into Egypt, Pharaoh orders their newborn boys but not their girls killed, Moses and Aaron confront him and then call down mighty plagues from the LORD, and Pharaoh at long last releases his Israelite slaves, who go out with gold and silver that they have taken from their accommodating neighbors.[5]

In sum, apart from all the moral, psychological, and theological complexities and ambiguities evident in the little tale that is Genesis 12:10–20, a larger perspective reveals a meaning not apparent when the story is interpreted as a self-contained unit. This larger perspective sees in Abram and Sarai's experience a pre-enactment of the fate of their descendants undergoing the foundational experience of the people Israel that was the Exodus from Egypt. This is not to second Ramban's view that Abram's behavior here served as the *cause* of the exile and enslavement his descendants would endure, but it is to suggest that reading the story without any awareness of the larger national dynamics and the providential plan is sadly inadequate. There is an essential dimension to this tale that those who condemn Abram and those who defend him both miss. For, when the text is viewed as part of Jewish scripture, we are not talking about just any childless couple and the nature of their relationship in a difficult time and the painful ethical conundrum they faced. We are talking about Our

Father Abraham and Our Mother Sarah, the first parents of the promised nation.

Back in Canaan, Abram faces a new problem. This one involves his orphaned nephew Lot, whom he took with him in response to God's command to go forth from his native land and his father's household. Whether he was right to have brought along his late brother's son is unclear. Given Sarai's barrenness and the promise centering on Abram's childlessness, he perhaps thought of his orphaned nephew as his heir. If so, Lot is the first of the three men who initially seem to be the heir to the patriarchal promise but then turn out not to be. In the case of Lot, the problem is that the flocks and herds of the two kinsmen have grown so large that the land can no longer support them all, and this leads to quarrels between the respective herdsmen.

Abram resolves the conflict by proposing a separation, doing so with the generosity and modesty that tradition has come to associate with his name.

> [8]Abram said to Lot, "Let there be no strife between you and me, between my herdsmen and yours, for we are kinsmen. [9]Is not the whole land before you? Please separate from me: if you go north, I will go south; and if you go south, I will go north." (Gen 13:8–9)[6]

Lot's response suggests that he serves here, as he will serve later,[7] as a foil for Abram. For, showing none of his uncle's liberality, he chooses for himself what he judges to be the best land, the "well watered . . . plain of the Jordan," which was "like the garden of the LORD, like the land of Egypt." Ironically, Lot fails to perceive (as Abram too failed to do) that the LORD would render the area bone-dry and utterly infertile when he punished its residents for their egregious sins (13:10; 19:23–28). Lest the reader imagine that the loss of this sole representative of the next generation means that the land will not be given to Abram's descendants after all, or that Lot will end up inheriting his uncle's portion after the latter's death, Genesis 13 closes with the LORD's promise that he will deed all the land that Abram can see to him and his offspring in perpetuity and make his offspring as numerous as the innumerable "dust of the earth." Abram is then to walk the length and breadth of the land in what seems to be a legal ceremony by which he takes possession of it (vv. 14–17). Whereas Lot "chose for himself" the territory he wanted (v. 11), Abram, having waited patiently for God's instruction, is given the land "forever" and is promised progeny as well.

Lot's separation from Abram does not mean his disappearance from the story, at least not yet. In the next, very atypical episode, Abram takes on a coalition of four foreign kings who have made war against five rebellious Canaanite vassal kings and captured his hapless nephew Lot in the process. Appearing here not as a vulnerable if wealthy migrant but as an important figure in international politics, with a private army of 318 men, Abram campaigns all the way from his residence in the south of Canaan to the extreme north, defeats the four kings, and rescues his nephew (Gen 14:13–16). The same dynamic appears a few chapters later, when, Abram's repeated pleas to the LORD to spare Sodom for the sake of the putative righteous minority within it having failed, "God was mindful of Abraham"—his name had been changed by then—"and removed Lot from the midst of the upheaval" (19:29). After that, Lot leaves the story of Abraham.

The figure of Lot represents in a nutshell an important but much misunderstood aspect in the dynamic of the figure of Abraham in the book of Genesis. On the one hand, Lot separates from Abram, at the latter's suggestion. He is not part of Israel but instead fathers (however inadvertently) two nations of his own, Moab and Ammon.[8] Whereas the story of Abram's migrations begins with Lot's inclusion, by the end the latter has been excluded; he is not the heir to the promise after all, or even a member of the chosen family. But his exclusion does not imply his rejection. He is not among the family of the elect, but neither is he among the damned, as if those were the only two categories. Though an outsider to the Abrahamic lineage, Lot twice benefits from his connection to the patriarch-to-be; in the second instance, that of Sodom, his Abrahamic connection saves his very life.

On the one hand, as we saw in chapter 1, the story of Abraham reaches out beyond the borders of Israel, much to the benefit of outsiders. On the other hand, its central concern is the emergence of the people Israel, and the outsiders remain outsiders, with no expectation that they should or ever will become Israelites. The story of Lot illustrates nicely why any convenient dichotomy of inclusiveness versus exclusiveness is woefully inadequate to elucidate the subtle theological dynamics of the biblical story of Abraham—and of the relationship of the Jewish people to the nations ever after.

Lot's separation from Abram only underscores the glaring deficiency in the latter's otherwise astoundingly blessed life—namely, his childlessness. Now that it is clear that his nephew will not be the next generation in the lineage that will result in the promised "great nation" (Gen 12:2), the patriarch-to-be voices his frustration, even his doubts, directly to the LORD. When the LORD assures him after his battle with the foreign kings, from whom he refused to take booty, that nonetheless "Your reward shall be very great," Abram answers, "O Lord GOD, what can You give me, seeing that I shall die childless, and . . . my steward will be my heir" (15:1–4). Here, the reference is to the otherwise unknown Eliezer, whom Abram may perhaps have adopted in order to have someone to take care of him and Sarai in their old age, with the provision that Eliezer would inherit their estate. And so, briefly, Eliezer serves as the next contender to be second patriarch of Israel.

The divine response to Abram's plaint arrives swiftly:

> ⁴The word of the LORD came to him in reply, "That one shall not be your heir; none but your very own issue shall be your heir." ⁵He took him outside and said, "Look toward heaven and count the stars, if you are able to count them." And He added, "So shall your offspring be." ⁶And because he put his trust in the LORD, He reckoned it to his merit. (Gen 15:4–6)

Now the "offspring" who have been promised the land are explicitly identified as Abram's biological issue—the biological issue, that is, of an old man with an elderly and infertile wife. The unlikelihood that the promise would come true is patent and so, by implication, is the exceptional nature of the offspring to come. All this makes verse 6 the more striking. Abram trusts in the promise despite its apparent improbability, and God reckons that powerful faith to the credit of the promised patriarch. It is not surprising, then, that in postbiblical Jewish tradition, Abraham becomes a paradigm of faith, and his descendants, the Jewish people, come to be called "people of faith who are descendants of people of faith,"[9] based on this memorable and influential verse. As we shall see in chapter 5, however, the translation of the verse is not altogether clear, and the theological conclusions explicitly drawn from it will later stand at the center of disputes between Judaism and Christianity and within Christianity itself.

Abram follows up God's assurance by asking for a sign: "O Lord God, how shall I know that I am to possess it?" (Gen 15:8). The answer comes in the form of a special covenant-making ceremony, one in which one of the parties to the pact passes through the cut-up remains of animals. The parallels from Mesopotamia and in Jeremiah 34:17–22 suggest that the ritual is one of self-cursing: the one who passes between the cut-up pieces is solemnly affirming that if he violates the covenant, he will be like them—dead. What is especially important in the covenant-making ritual of Genesis 15 is that it is not Abram (who has been placed in a trance) but rather "a smoking oven" (or, brazier) and "a flaming torch" that pass between the pieces, as God promises to give the land to Abram's offspring (v. 17). Whether the reference is to one item or two (or one described in two different phrases that have both been incorporated into the verse), it certainly seems to represent the divine presence.

The covenant, then, is strictly promissory. No obligations are imposed on the human partner. God, as it were, curses himself should he fail to grant the land to Abram's future offspring. While Abram (together by implication with his descendants) is once again the recipient of God's gracious gift, that gracious promise has now been solemnized by covenant.

Not typical of covenant-making ceremonies, however, is a curious passage that interrupts the account of the ceremony:

> [13]And He said to Abram, "Know well that your offspring shall be strangers in a land not theirs, and they shall be enslaved and oppressed four hundred years; [14]but I will execute judgment on the nation they shall serve, and in the end they shall go free with great wealth. [15]As for you,
>    You shall go to your fathers in peace;
>    You shall be buried at a ripe old age.

[16]And they shall return here in the fourth generation, for the iniquity of the Amorites is not yet complete. (Gen 15:13–16)

Historians attempting to reconstruct the documents that have been combined to make the Torah as we have it usually ascribe this passage to another source than the one responsible for the covenant ceremony within which it now appears.[10] The passage presents Abram as a kind of prophet (the same source calls him exactly that in 20:7), vouchsafed a vision of his descendants' painful future but also the redemption that will follow. The troubling interruption of the covenant-making ritual corresponds to the interruption of the promise that the covenant seals. Abram's offspring shall not immediately take possession of their deeded patrimony but shall, like their father himself, live long as aliens and, worse, as slaves in a land that is not theirs. This detour frustrates the promise but does not defeat it, for when the evil of the Amorites—used in verse 16 as a synecdoche for all the Canaanite nations—reaches completion, Abram's descendants shall at long last return to the Promised Land.

Earlier, we saw that Abram and Sarai's experience in Egypt serves as a kind of pre-enactment of the experience of their Israelite descendants before and during the Exodus. Here, too, in the eerie little interruption of the covenant-making ceremony, Abram becomes involved in the suffering of the nation he will eventually father, but with a critical difference. In Genesis 15:13–16, the emphasis is on the contrast between their suffering and his good fortune to die "in peace . . . at a ripe old age" before the bad times come about. Abram has, in other words, become a symbol of God's fulfillment of his irrevocable promise despite the horrific and seemingly interminable parenthesis in history that is the oppression and enslavement in Egypt.[11] The patriarch-to-be will die in peace, though not without the troubling foreknowledge of the misery his descendants must endure before they legitimately take possession of their promised patrimony.

Correlatively, even though the covenant is in effect—this type of covenant is indefeasible—it does not guarantee freedom from adversity or a life without suffering for the vassal who has been granted it. To the contrary, the adversity and suffering are now included within the dynamics of the covenantal relationship. They do not defeat God's purpose; God has foreseen them. Perhaps he has even foreordained them for some unspecified reason (the mention of the "iniquity of the Amorites" explains why Israel cannot legitimately take the land earlier, but it does not explain why they endure enslavement and oppression). In any event, the horrific experiences of the people Israel in Egypt do not mean God has abandoned them or forgotten his covenantal promise. The experiences are, rather, a counterpart on the national level to the frustrations that, at the individual level, Abram their father must endure before the promised fulfillment comes about.

Abram's nonexistent descendants dominate Genesis 15, first through the question of whether they will exist at all (vv. 1–6) and then through the covenant by which God deeds the land to them yet predicts their continued landlessness, oppression, and even bondage before they take possession of it (vv. 7–20). That Eliezer, like Lot, will not be Abram's heir only underscores the magnitude and improbability of the promise. If "your very own issue shall be your heir" (v. 4), what does that imply about Abram's wife Sarai, long barren and surely getting no younger?

The attentive reader will have noticed that nothing in the several iterations of the promise of descendants has addressed in any way the question of who the matriarch of the future nation will be. At no point has it been promised that Abram's barren and aging wife will bear him the promised heir. Indeed, those inclined to righteous indignation over his treatment of Sarai as the couple approached Egypt need to ask themselves why Abram stayed with his barren wife all those years, even after the promises centering on his descendants— now further specified as his "very own issue"—were made. Given the ready availability of divorce and the legal and moral acceptability of polygamy at the time, why has he not availed himself of one of those mechanisms in order to bring about the promised result?

If we accept the quietist theology mentioned earlier in connection with the Egyptian sojourn, we have a ready answer: the promised child will be born because of God's promise alone, and no human assistance is necessary or even permissible. To revert to the old joke about the lottery, Abram will win it without buying a ticket. In fact, in this theology, were he to seek out a fertile woman to bear the heir, the very act of doing so would demonstrate a lack of faith in God's power to overcome adversity. But as in the case of Abram and Sarai's sojourn in Egypt, we cannot simply assume that, in the biblical view, the existence of a promise from God means its recipient must remain passive in the face of challenges to it.

As it turns out, Sarai resolves the crisis of Abram's childlessness in a way that is anything but quietist. Speaking of her Egyptian slave woman Hagar, she takes the initiative: "Look, the LORD has kept me from bearing. Consort with my slave woman; perhaps I shall have a son through her" (Gen 16:2).[12] The word rendered as "I shall have a son" (*'ibbaneh*) plays on the similarity in sound between the verb "to build" (*banah*), from which this word is formed, and the noun "son" (*ben*). Perhaps, Sarai is suggesting, she will acquire her own household, her own lineage, through the good services of Hagar when the latter bears the son promised to Abram but not to her.

Indeed, it may be that the son whom Hagar is to bear will actually be Sarai's in a legal, though not biological, sense. Evidence for this can be found in the only other biblical instances of slave women serving as surrogate mothers. This is the case of the two slaves who bear children to Jacob's wives, Rachel and Leah, during their periods of infertility.[13] In each case, it is the mistress and not the biological mother who names the child, and Rachel actually declares that "God has . . . given me a son" (Gen 30:6).

The basis for this idea that an infertile woman could become a mother through her slave probably lies in the legal institutions of ancient Israel. According to the law of the Hebrew slave as it appears in Exodus 21:2–6, "If his master gave him a wife, and she has borne him children, the wife and her children shall belong to the master" (v. 4). True, the analogy of the case at hand to the law of the Hebrew slave is not exact, since Abram—to name but one difference among several—is not Sarai's slave. But Hagar is, and this allows the suggestion that in giving Hagar a husband, Sarai entertains the thought that any resulting children will likewise belong to her, the slave's mistress. If so, then at long last the House of Abram and Sarai will be built because the barren wife will have a son. Whether the suggestion is valid or not, it is surely no wonder that Abram immediately accepts his wife's proposal, for it obviates his childlessness and does so not only with her consent but at her very initiative.

And so Abram marries Hagar. Whereas in his own Egyptian sojourn his wife "was taken into Pharaoh's palace" (Gen 12:15), now his wife brings an Egyptian into Abram's marriage chamber. For as the language of 16:3 indicates, he does not simply make use of her as a surrogate mother; rather, Sarai "took" her and "gave her to her husband Abram as a wife."[14] It has been said that whereas monogamy works to the advantage of high-status women and low-status men, polygamy has the opposite effect, advantaging low-status females and high-status males. In this instance, that is surely how the arrangement works. The slave (and foreigner) Hagar, unlikely to find a husband, has now become a wife, and to a very rich man. The freeborn Sarai, heretofore Abram's sole consort, now must share him with a co-wife—her own Egyptian slave, no less! Making things still worse, Hagar succeeds where Sarai has failed all those years; the text seems to imply that she becomes pregnant immediately after the marriage is consummated. Consequently, "her mistress was lowered in her esteem" (v. 4), as indeed it was in the objective fact of the inverse transformations in status that the two women have undergone.

As a result, Sarai angrily demands that Abram do something about the indignity she is suffering, and he responds by turning the matter over to her, in effect reclassifying Hagar as once more only a slave and no longer a wife: " 'Your slave woman is in your hands. Deal with her as you think right.' Then Sarai treated her harshly, and she ran away from her" (Gen 16:6). Those who think only in terms of contemporary liberation theology, with its belief that God invariably takes the side of the victimized, will expect him to respond as he does when the enslaved and badly mistreated Israelites run away from their Egyptian masters in the book of Exodus—that is, with miraculous and gracious succor. Here, however, when the mistreated slave is an Egyptian and her mistress is one of the mothers of Israel, God's response, given through an angel, is the opposite: "Go back to your mistress, and submit to her harsh treatment" (v. 9).

But that is not the end of God's dealings with Hagar, for in the very next verse, he makes a promise that resonates unmistakably with his repeated promise to Abram: "I will greatly increase your offspring, / And they shall be too many to count" (v. 10; cf. 13:16; 15:5). The implication is clear: the lineage that derives from Hagar is indeed Abrahamic, and their first mother, though a slave and properly subordinate to Sarai, will also be the matriarch of a great nation. God makes a promise to Hagar that he never makes directly to Sarai, "for," as the angel puts it, "the LORD has paid heed (*shamaʻ*) to your suffering" (v. 11). Indeed, the child's very name, Ishmael ("God has paid heed"), testifies simultaneously to the shameful mistreatment his mother endured and to God's refusal to allow it to be the last word.

With the birth of Ishmael, the problem posed by Abram's childlessness and God's promise of progeny seems solved. At last, Abram has the son he and Sarai have wanted. To be sure, the son's birth to a slave and, more important, to a foreigner casts a shadow of sorts over the fulfillment. In addition, although Hagar receives the promise of countless progeny, absent from Genesis 16 is the correlative promise that the land would be deeded to those descendants, and so is any mention of covenant. Still and all, now the question of whether Abram will have an heir at all yields to the question of which son will be the heir—until Abraham's great test in chapter 22, that is, when he is commanded to offer back to God the son he had been promised.

In Genesis 17, we find another account of God's covenant-making with Abram, but with significant differences from the one in chapter 15. Here the focus is not on his descendants taking over the land from various nations, but rather on the patriarch as a kind of international figure himself.[15] He is to become "the father of a multitude of nations" and the ancestor of kings. In fact, his very name is now lengthened from Abram to Abraham, to capture the sense of "father of a multitude" (*ʼav hamon*, v. 4) and perhaps also to suggest the fulfillment of the promise in his initial call, "I will make your name great" (12:2).[16] The longer name befits the greater figure that Abraham is to become.

And there is another difference between the account of the Abrahamic covenant in Genesis 15 and that in chapter 17: in the latter passage, the covenant has acquired a "sign," the circumcision of all boys in the covenant community at the age of eight days, and the relationship itself is now explicitly declared to be unbreakable: "I will maintain My covenant between Me and you, and your offspring to come, as an everlasting covenant throughout the ages, to be God to you and to your offspring to come." Accordingly, the land of Canaan becomes the "everlasting holding" of the heirs of the covenant with Abraham (17:7–14).

Then comes the most shocking difference between the two accounts of the covenant with Abram/Abraham:

> [15]And God said to Abraham, "As for your wife Sarai, you shall not call her Sarai, but her name shall be Sarah. [16]I will bless her; indeed, I will give you a son by her. I will bless her so that she shall give rise to nations; rulers of peoples shall issue from her." (Gen 17:15–16)

The change of Sarai's name to Sarah (probably meaning "princess" or the like) seems to reflect the promise that royalty shall descend from her. The promise that Sarah will bear Abraham a son at all, however, is not only highly unlikely in light of the future matriarch's lifelong infertility and her advanced age; it also renders Ishmael's very existence problematic. Hence, Abraham's less than enthusiastic response:

> [17]Abraham threw himself on his face and laughed, as he said to himself, "Can a child be born to a man a hundred years old, or can Sarah bear a child at ninety?" [18]And Abraham said to God, "O that Ishmael might live by Your favor!" [19]God said, "Nevertheless, Sarah your wife shall bear you a son, and you shall name him Isaac; and I will maintain My covenant with him as an everlasting covenant for his offspring to come. [20]As for Ishmael, I have heeded you. I hereby bless him. I will make him fertile and exceedingly numerous. He shall be the father of twelve chieftains, and I will make of him a great nation. [21]But My covenant I will maintain with Isaac, whom Sarah shall bear to you at this season next year." (Gen 17:17–21)

Is Abraham's laughter one of joy, thus reflecting the man of faith we saw in 15:6? Or is it one of disbelief, reflecting his doubts in that same chapter? And does his plea for Ishmael express his humble acknowledgment that he does not need the son whom God now solemnly contracts to give him or, rather, his fear that, Ishmael's conception having turned out to be unnecessary, God will kill Abraham's older son to make room for the younger one who is to be the true ancestor of the covenanted people?

Whatever the answer to these questions, God's response in Genesis 17:19–21 is so finely calibrated that it has often been misunderstood. On the one hand, it upholds the new promise without compromise, insisting that the covenant will be with the second son, adding only that the boy's name will be Isaac, taken from the verb "to laugh." On the other hand, once again playing on the meaning of Ishmael, God insists that he has heard Abraham's plea and will not only keep his older son alive but also confer the Abrahamic blessing of fertility upon him, making him the father of twelve tribal chieftains (the Israelite counterpart will come into existence only in the generation of Isaac's son Jacob/Israel, who engenders the eponymous heads of the twelve tribes of Israel). More than that, Ishmael shall be the father of a "great nation," again picking up the language of the original call to Abram in Genesis 12:2. The implication is clear: Ishmael inherits the Abrahamic promise but not the Abrahamic covenant. Isaac inherits both. That the covenant will be with Isaac and his descendants alone, and not with Ishmael and his progeny, is especially important because the gift of the land now nests within the covenant.[17] As in Genesis 16 (and as will be the case with its parallel text in 21:9–21), Ishmael has not been disowned and, in fact, has been given a great promise of his own. But the status of the two sons will not be identical. Though Ishmael receives a promise, Isaac will be, and remain, the promised son.

Ishmael, it turns out, is the last of the three figures who the reader suspects may fill the role of the promised heir but are then precluded from doing so. Yet unlike Lot and Eliezer, he represents an authentic realization of the Abrahamic promise, even as the fullness of the promise will be found in Isaac alone. In the version of the Abrahamic covenant that appears in Genesis 17, the existence of multiple Abrahamic nations is, in fact, an important aspect of God's gracious promise to the patriarch. Perhaps the prediction that "You shall be the father of a multitude of nations" (v. 4) is the equivalent—or, alternatively, an important clarification—of the earlier promise that "all the families of the earth / Shall bless themselves by you" (12:3). In any event, here, too, the promise looks both inward, toward the destined birth of Abraham's uniquely precious son, and outward, toward a larger community of nations who are Abrahamic in a way that is less immediate, if no less real.

But what nationalities make up that multitude of Abrahamic peoples? In answering this ancient and still pressing question, it will be helpful if we leave the biblical narrative to look briefly at its later history of interpretation.

The traditional Christian answer to the question is well known: Abraham is "the father of all who have faith," and it is through "Christ Jesus [that] the blessing of Abraham might come to the Gentiles" (Rom 4:11; Gal 3:14).[18] In other words, Abraham becomes the father of a multitude of nations when peoples of many diverse ethnic origins enter the Church.

This Christian interpretation has its Jewish analogies and perhaps antecedents as well. For in Jewish tradition, the idea that Abraham is the ancestor of all authentic proselytes is well attested. As the great legal authority and philosopher Moses Maimonides wrote, "Ever since then [i.e., the time when Abraham taught peoples about the true God] whoever adopts Judaism and confesses the unity of the Divine Name, as it is prescribed in the Torah, is counted among the disciples of Abraham our Father."[19] On this understanding, the wide variety of racial types that have come to make up the Jewish people testifies to Abraham's having become the father not only of a single "great nation" but of "a multitude of nations" as well.

The long-standing popular association of Abraham's promised fatherhood of "a multitude of nations" with conversion to Judaism, Christianity, or simply belief in the one incorporeal Deity subtly plants the idea that his descendants must be found everywhere, even as Jews, Christians, and other monotheists (especially Muslims) have spread out to the four corners of the earth. But the problem with this interpretation as biblical exegesis is that it renders Abraham's fatherhood metaphorical: it conflates "disciples of Abraham our Father" with the nations of whom, according to the promise, Abraham will be the *father*, and not the teacher. Indeed, though the notion that Abraham taught about the one true God becomes enormously important in postbiblical Judaism (as we saw in chapter 2 and shall see at length in chapter 4), it does not appear in the Bible at all. Nor, for that matter, does the idea of conversion as Maimonides and others in the same tradition conceive it. At the level of the plain sense of Genesis 17 and within the limited context of the Hebrew Bible, then, we must interpret the prediction that Abraham will father a multitude the way we interpret the promise in the same chapter that he will father Isaac—as referring unequivocally to biological fatherhood.[20]

But this only raises our question anew: Who are these other Abrahamic nations?

Within the context of Genesis, it is likely that the reference is to groups within the purview of the author and his audience. The group most central to the Israelite author and his audience is, of course, Israel itself, and we must not rule out the possibility that "multitude of nations" (*hamon goyim*) here means the same thing as "community of peoples" (*qehal 'ammim*) in Genesis 48:4, which describes those who God promised would come forth from Jacob.[21] Since what comes forth from Jacob is the twelve tribes of Israel, it could be that the promise to Abraham in chapter 17 comprehends only the populous confederation of tribes that was early Israel, and not some larger international fraternity of Abrahamic nations after all. Here it also bears mentioning that the term translated as "nation" (*goy*) may perhaps, if rarely, refer to an individual person.[22] If that is the meaning in 17:4, then Abraham is once again being informed simply that his descendants shall be very numerous; he is told nothing about their ethnic composition.

More likely, in its original meaning the multitude of nations refers to different nationalities, though not on a global scale but only within the world of the Levantine author. If we add up the nations to whom Genesis ascribes Abrahamic descent, we come to nine—Ishmaelites, Edomites (through Isaac's son, Esau/Edom), Israelites, and the descendants of the six sons that Abraham is said to have fathered through his otherwise unknown wife, Keturah.[23] Note that one of these six is Midian, ancestor of a large and extremely widespread tribal confederation. If it be protested that only the Edomites and Israelites descend from Sarah, it can immediately be retorted that the covenantal promise that Abraham will be "the father of a multitude of nations" makes no reference to Sarah and precedes the surprising announcement that she will bear a son.[24] There is no reason to believe that the nations and rulers descending from her will likewise constitute a "multitude."

Did the various nations to whom Genesis, on this interpretation, ascribes Abrahamic origins see themselves as cousins within a larger Abrahamic family? We have no evidence whatsoever that they did. To be sure, much later, in the fifth century of the Common Era, a Christian historian mentions cryptically an Abraham-centered cult located near Hebron in which (in his terminology) Phoenicians, Palestinians, and Arabs all took part.[25] Whether this was a survival of an ancient interethnic institution or the result of centuries of Jewish and Christian focus on Abraham (with important implications for the eventual emergence of Islam) is impossible to say with any certainty; the latter possibility seems more likely. What we can say is that even if the notion of an Abrahamic multitude of nations began as only the Israelites' way of describing certain ethnopolitical relationships, it still implies both the election of Israel, on the one hand, and the larger, extra-Israelite significance of their father Abraham, on the other. Again, the Abrahamic tradition as it is conceived in Genesis 17 looks both inward, toward the emergence of the unique inheritor of the patriarch's covenant, his grandson Jacob/Israel, and outward, toward a larger fraternity of peoples whose very existence testifies to the reliability of God's promise to Abraham.

We have seen that in contrast with the first account of the covenant with Abraham (Gen 15:7–19), the second (chapter 17) underscores the unbreakability of the relationship (which now becomes "an everlasting covenant," 17:19), provides a powerful and enduring explanation of ritual circumcision (*berit milah*) by associating it with the revered figure of Abraham, and ensures that the covenant devolves only upon Abraham's son by Sarah and their mutual descendants. To judge from this second account, we would never have guessed the existence of the first, to which it makes no allusion.

Historians of biblical literature have usually concluded that these two passages come from different antecedent documents that went into the making of the Torah, and if so, it would seem quite plausible that the second account originated as a revision of the first.[26] If the intention was to *replace* the earlier passage, however, the editorial process has frustrated that intention, since, it turns out, both passages remain in the Torah as we have received it. Read in its current location, chapter 17 not only augments the two preceding chapters but also clarifies the status of Ishmael and Sarah in an essential way. (By never mentioning Hagar, the passage leaves room to wonder what narrative about Ishmael's origins it may originally have presumed.) Lest one think of Abraham as having disowned and expelled Ishmael from the family—the sense one certainly gets from Genesis 16 and again, as we shall see, in Genesis 21—the clarification goes out of its way to stress Ishmael's rightful inheritance of the Abrahamic promise of blessing, fertility, and great nationhood, but *not* covenant itself.[27] Whatever the other antecedent documents may have said, Genesis 17 now establishes emphatically that Ishmael holds a special place amidst the multitude of Abrahamic peoples, albeit not the same place as Isaac. Its presence requires that chapters 15, 16, and 21 be read differently from the way we would naturally read them were it not present. In the case of literature as complex as the Torah, the whole is more than the sum of the parts.

Whatever their differences, both versions of the Abrahamic covenant present it as unconditional. That is, the existence of the pact and the promises it makes to the human partner and his descendants (or, in Genesis 17, his descendants through Isaac alone) are not dependent on the fulfillment of any conditions. God pledges to carry out his promises regardless of the conduct of the human parties. To be sure, in chapter 17, God commands Abram to "Walk in My ways and be blameless" and to institute circumcision as a continuing sign of the new relationship (vv. 1, 9–14), but there is no indication that his failure to do so would imperil the covenant itself or the fulfillment of its blessings. Note that "if any male who is uncircumcised fails to circumcise the flesh of his foreskin, that person shall be cut off from his kin; he has broken My covenant" (v. 14); but, despite the grave sin of omission that this individual has committed, the covenant remains in effect with the kin-group collectively.

The covenant with all Israel that Moses will broker on Mount Sinai stands in marked contrast to this Abrahamic pattern. For there the requirements upon the human party are legion—rabbinic tradition will come to number them as 613—and the failure to carry them out ensures catastrophe, as long lists of curses underscore in frightening detail.[28] As the narrative of the Torah goes, the Sinaitic covenant thus nests within the Abrahamic, or patriarchal one. For when Israel comes to Sinai and unanimously accepts the covenant that God offers them,[29] they are already in a covenantal relationship that was never brokered but simply announced to their father Abraham generations earlier. The overall effect of this arrangement is to preserve the notes of both conditionality and unconditionality: Israel's willingness to obey God's laws and commandments, now presented as stipulations of covenant, is indispensable, and yet when the Israelites fall into disobedience, the antecedent Abrahamic covenant (reiterated to Isaac and Jacob) remains in effect and offers a reservoir of grace for the errant people.

More than a theoretical implication, this dynamic interaction of the covenants appears in several key passages. Consider the episode of the Golden Calf. There the LORD proposes to replace the idolatrous people with a new one for whom Moses will serve as their Abrahamic father: "Now, let Me be, that My anger may blaze forth against them and that I may destroy them, and make of you a great nation" (Exod 32:10). One of Moses's counterarguments, and the one that immediately precedes the LORD's relenting, is to remind him of his unbreakable pledge to the patriarchs: "Remember Your servants, Abraham, Isaac, and Israel, how You swore to them by Your Self and said to them: 'I will make your offspring as numerous as the stars of heaven, and I will give to your offspring this whole land of which I spoke, to possess forever'" (v. 13). In other words, however much the LORD punishes the idolaters themselves, he has precluded himself from replacing Abraham with Moses or anyone else. The people Israel can be punished, even severely, but they cannot be annihilated, and their title to the land cannot be set aside.

One passage in Leviticus explicitly evokes the patriarchal covenant as setting a limit on the punishment Israel will receive and ensuring the covenanted people will be restored to their patrimony:

[39]Those of you who survive shall be heartsick over their iniquity in the land of your enemies; more, they shall be heartsick over the

iniquities of their fathers; [40]and they shall confess their iniquity and the iniquity of their fathers, in that they trespassed against Me, yea, were hostile to Me. [41]When I, in turn, have been hostile to them and have removed them into the land of their enemies, then at last shall their obdurate heart humble itself, and they shall atone for their iniquity. [42]Then will I remember My covenant with Jacob; I will remember also My covenant with Isaac, and also My covenant with Abraham; and I will remember the land.

[43]For the land shall be forsaken of them, making up for its sabbath years by being desolate of them, while they atone for their iniquity; for the abundant reason that they rejected My rules and spurned My laws. [44]Yet, even then, when they are in the land of their enemies, I will not reject them or spurn them so as to destroy them, annulling My covenant with them; for I the Lord am their God. [45]I will remember in their favor the covenant with the ancients, whom I freed from the land of Egypt in the sight of the nations to be their God: I, the Lord. (Lev 26:39–45)

This passage concludes one of those long lists of horrific curses mentioned above, and specifically the prediction that "[you] shall perish among the nations; and the land of your enemies shall consume you" (26:38). It now emerges, though, that some Israelites will survive in exile, and for them the experience of hardship will induce remorse, confession, and a softening of the hard hearts that brought them and their forebears into the pattern of sin. The change of heart and the act of confession that it prompts yield atonement for the offenses, thus exhausting the punishment and, most important for our purposes, motivating God to remember and reactivate his unbreakable covenant with the patriarchs. Here, the operative contrast is not between the individual who has broken the covenant and the nation whose covenant is unbreakable, as in the hypothetical case of the man who does not submit to circumcision in Genesis 17. Rather, the contrast is between the nation whose covenant has been suspended because of their sins and the nation whose unbreakable covenant will be reinstituted when they—or their members who survive the exile—have at long last repented of those sins. The two nations are, of course, the same, the people Israel, whose sins can temporarily disable the covenant but never destroy it.

The interplay of the Abrahamic and Sinaitic covenants thus yields a theology in which human deeds are critical to the divine-human relationship and yet not exhaustive of it. If the human community—in this case, the people Israel—obeys their divine Lord's commands, they will flourish. If they disobey and are "hostile" to him, then they will suffer. But the relationship transcends their obedience and their disobedience. The covenant does not reduce simply to the sum total of the human partner's deeds. It has a dimension of grace and mercy to it that allows, even necessitates, a second chance for the sinning nation. Indeed, God's willingness to allow repentance and confession to effect atonement is itself a concession for which strict justice cannot account.

And so, in the interaction of the Abrahamic and Sinaitic covenants we find a dynamic expressed that will become highly characteristic of the ensuing Jewish tradition. It is a dynamic in which well-being does not exist, to use Luther's term, *sola gratia*, "by grace alone." Rather, human actions are of infinite importance. At the same time, the divine-human relationship is not in the nature, let us say, of a bank account from which one withdraws only what he deposited. Rather, the relationship comes about and endures by God's grace. That human effort and divine grace are not inevitably opposed to each other but can operate in tandem (even if at times at cross-purposes) is one of the most characteristic aspects of Judaism. It is thus not surprising that the disputations about grace and works, or faith and works, so divisive of Christian communities over the centuries and so typical of the history of Christian thought into our own time find scant parallel in the Jewish tradition.

As is typical of the Abraham narrative in Genesis, there is a suspenseful lag between the promise and the fulfillment—in this case, the promise in chapter 17 of a son, to be named Isaac, who will be born to Sarah, and the joyous birth itself. The first fifteen verses of Genesis 18 are parallel to chapter 17 in announcing the same joyous event; but here the announcement comes through "three men"—two of them surely angels but one of them apparently the Lord himself—who visit the couple's tent. In Genesis 19, the two angels in human form will go on to Sodom to urge Lot to leave it before they destroy the city and its twin, Gomorrah, and rescue Abraham's nephew with no great assistance, alas, from the hapless beneficiary of the deliverance.

The contrast between Abraham and Lot is an important structural feature in Genesis 18–19, but only a few examples of it need be given here. One place where it can be detected is in the responses of the two men to the appearance of the supernal visitors. First Abraham:

> ²Looking up, he saw three men standing near him. As soon as he saw them, he ran from the entrance of the tent to greet them and, bowing to the ground, ³he said, "My lords, if it please you, do not go on past your servant. ⁴Let a little water be brought; bathe your feet and recline under the tree. ⁵And let me fetch a morsel of bread that you may refresh yourselves; then go on—seeing that you have come your servant's way." (Gen 18:2–5)

Now Lot:

> ¹The two angels arrived in Sodom in the evening, as Lot was sitting in the gate of Sodom. When Lot saw them, he rose to greet them and, bowing low with his face to the ground, ²he said, "Please, my lords, turn aside to your servant's house to spend the night, and bathe your feet; then you may be on your way early." (Gen 19:1–2)

Abraham runs; Lot only rises. Abraham offers water and food; Lot does not. And the food that Abraham actually provides—"a calf, tender and choice . . . curds and milk" as well as the cakes that he bids Sarah to rush to bake—contrasts with Lot's "feast," of which the only item mentioned is mere "baked unleavened bread" (18:6–8; 19:3). It is Abraham's exemplary eagerness to welcome his guests and his generosity to them that accounts for his having become the paradigm of *hakhnasat 'orechim*, the weighty and ancient Jewish practice of welcoming guests and travelers.

But the largest contrast lies in the initial purpose of the visitations to the two men. The one to Abraham is for the purpose of announcing a birth; the one to Lot, for the purpose of announcing impending death.

The announcement of the birth in Genesis 18:9–15 shows no awareness of the same event in the previous chapter, and this, together with other features, has once again led historical scholars to see the two accounts as originally variants of the same tradition, with chapter 17 perhaps originally intended as a rewriting of chapter 18.[30] In Genesis 18, it is not Abraham who laughs but Sarah, and the text lacks all notion of an Abrahamic covenant (which has already been established for this source in chapter 15). Here the birth of a son to the aged couple comes not as evidence of the LORD's reliability as a covenant partner but as a proof of his ability to work miracles— "Is anything too wondrous for the LORD?" he answers Sarah's laugh (18:14)—and thus of the miraculous nature of the nation to descend from the promised son.

In this, the birth of Isaac not only contrasts markedly with that of Ishmael, born through the very nonmiraculous mechanism of surrogate motherhood, but at the end of the next chapter, it also contrasts with the birth of Lot's two sons, conceived when their mothers— his own daughters—get their father drunk in order that they "may maintain life" after the mass death that has befallen Sodom and Gomorrah (Gen 19:32). Thus, Moab and Ammon, the ancestors of two neighboring nations with whom Israel had relations of various sorts for centuries, are both Lot's sons and his grandsons. The unseemly circumstances in which they are conceived highlight, by way of contrast, the lofty origin and larger meaning of Sarah's own coming pregnancy.

Between the announcement of Isaac's conception at the beginning of Genesis 18 and the account of Moab's and Ammon's conception and birth at the end of chapter 19 falls the story of Sodom and Gomorrah (18:16–19:29). The two stories about birth, the first of high seriousness (though with a comic touch) and the second of low comedy, serve as bookends for the story of death and destruction. That story begins with the LORD's disclosure of his plans to Abraham:

[16]The men set out from there and looked down toward Sodom, Abraham walking with them to see them off. [17]Now the LORD had said, "Shall I hide from Abraham what I am about to do, [18]since Abraham is to become a great and populous nation and all the nations of the earth are to bless themselves by him? [19]For I have singled him out, that he may instruct his children and his posterity to keep the way of the LORD by doing what is just and right, in

order that the LORD may bring about for Abraham what He has promised him." (Gen 18:16–19)

The LORD's inner need to share his plans with Abraham strikingly recalls the institution of prophecy. A passage from the book of Amos, in fact, nicely parallels the one above:

> [6]When a ram's horn is sounded in a town,
> Do the people not take alarm?
> Can misfortune come to a town
> If the LORD has not caused it?
> [7]Indeed, my Lord GOD does nothing
> Without having revealed His purpose
> To his servants the prophets. (Amos 3:6 7)

In this passage, the prophet serves as a kind of watchman, warning miscreants of the catastrophic consequences of their misdeeds.[31] In Genesis 18, however, Abraham does not confront the Sodomites; instead, he confronts the LORD:

> [23]Abraham came forward and said, "Will You sweep away the innocent along with the guilty? [24]What if there should be fifty innocent within the city; will You then wipe out the place and not forgive it for the sake of the innocent fifty who are in it? [25]Far be it from You to do such a thing, to bring death upon the innocent as well as the guilty, so that innocent and guilty fare alike. Far be it from You! Shall not the Judge (*shophet*) of all the earth practice justice (*mishpat*)?" (Gen 18:23–25)[32]

At first glance, it seems as though the patriarch is protesting the element of indiscriminate destruction in the LORD's plan and asking that it be replaced by a surgical strike against the offenders alone. Anything short of that would be unworthy of the justice (*mishpat*) that the Judge (*shophet*) of the world ought to practice. A closer look, however, reveals that Abraham is actually asking that the existence of a righteous minority stave off destruction for the *entire* town, sinners included. Here, too, the Abrahamic narrative finds a parallel attested, though much more rarely, among the prophets of Israel. Shown a plague of locusts about to descend, our prophet Amos exclaims, "O Lord GOD, pray forgive. How will Jacob survive? He is so small." The next verse tells us the result of the prophet's intercession: "The LORD relented concerning this. 'It shall not come to pass,' said the LORD" (Amos 7:2–3). The prophet, in short, does not simply confront the human community with God's demand for justice; he also confronts God with the urgent need for mercy. And, like Amos, Abraham succeeds up to a point, for the LORD agrees: "If I find within the city of Sodom fifty innocent ones, I will forgive the whole place for their sake" (Gen 18:26). But, alas, the righteous minority turns out not to exist, and Lot and his family alone escape the conflagration, and then only because "God was mindful of Abraham and removed Lot from the midst of the upheaval" (19:29).

God's soliloquy before disclosing his concerns to Abraham addresses not only the latter's special status but also one key aspect of the mission of the nation to descend from him, namely, that they are "to keep the way of the LORD by doing what is just and right" (Gen 18:19). It might at first seem that nothing is intended here other than the expectation that the nation-to-be will give everyone exactly what he deserves, neither more nor less. Modern research on the expression "just and right" (*tsedaqah umishpat*), however, suggests that something much different from bland moralism is intended, something that, in fact, corresponds to Abraham's plea that *all* the Sodomites be spared the punishment most of them deserve.

Examining the idiom "just and right" in its various forms in the Bible and in Mesopotamian literature, the Israeli scholar Moshe Weinfeld argues that it refers to acts of kindness and mercy, most specifically to enactments of law that grant an amnesty, reprieve, forgiveness of debts, and the like.[33] Applying Weinfeld's findings to this text, we should conclude that Abraham is to instruct the chosen nation in the ways of grace and mercy that characterize his God—and, it turns out, their father Abraham's own intense interaction with his God in our passage. It is not social justice as understood in modern secular terms that is mandated here; it is the intensely religious understanding of justice that characterizes the relationship of God and the prophet who recognizes the gravity of sin yet pleads for mercy for the sinners. No wonder the Talmud defines mercy, along with modesty and charitableness, as one of the three attributes that characterize the Jewish people and those fit to join them.[34]

Abraham's challenge to God is the first text we meet in the Bible in which someone dares to accuse the Deity himself of injustice. But others follow, not only in scripture but in the subsequent Jewish tradition as well, into modern times. Given how foreign and unjust so many of the biblical norms seem, it is not surprising that many in our time should draw comfort, even inspiration from the patriarch's courageous challenge. What is less often celebrated is his profound deference to God, his keen sense that he speaks not by right but by his Lord's sufferance only—"Here I venture to speak to my Lord, I who am but dust and ashes . . . Let not my Lord be angry if I go on . . . I venture again to speak to my Lord . . . Let not my Lord be angry if I speak but this last time" (Gen 18:27, 30, 31, 32). And that *is* his last time. Having persuaded God to spare the city for just ten innocent Sodomites, down from the sum of fifty with which he began, Abraham dares go no further. His challenge to God, like that of Jewish traditionalists who followed in his footsteps, takes place within a relationship of profound submission to the LORD's inscrutable judgments. The challenge would be altogether different without it. Abraham is not Prometheus.

After the episode of Sodom, there follows the second of the three stories in which a patriarch passes his wife off as his sister.[35] The last time it was Abram and Pharaoh. This time it is Abraham and Abimelech, king of Gerar, perhaps a Philistine town in the Negev. Read in its literary context, the story raises the question of why Abraham has not learned from the last time he tried the same move. Historical scholars have argued in reply that the two stories stem from different sources. The first is responsible for the accounts involving Abram and Pharaoh and Isaac and Abimelech (Gen 26:6–11). The second is responsible for the present account, whose protagonists are Abraham and Abimelech.[36] If this analysis is correct, then originally no source involved any figure in more than one wife-sister episode, and the question of why Abraham—or, for that matter, Abimelech—did not learn from his prior experience becomes an illusion deriving from an editor's combination of once disparate sources.

If this prehistory of the text be granted (along with the possibility that the variant accounts are refractions of the same earlier, perhaps oral story), one must still reckon with the effect of the stories in their present locations, whatever their prehistory may be. In the case of Genesis 20, it is significant that God acts in advance to make sure that Abimelech does not have sex with Sarah (v. 6). It will be recalled that he took no such action toward Pharaoh; the text of Genesis 12:10–20 leaves open the question of whether any sexual relationship took place while Sarai was in the palace. Given its placement within the story of Abraham and Sarah, whose fertility, it has been promised, is about to be miraculously restored, the notion that she would bear her first child to the adulterous king of Gerar would be intolerable (and if she consented to sex, she would be guilty of adultery as well). Besides, in an age when paternity tests did not exist, how would we know that the child whom Sarah later bears by dint of miracle was Abraham's and not Abimelech's?

Like its much shorter and less complex parallel in Genesis 12:10–20, chapter 20 raises the question of religious quietism: Should Abraham have relied for protection on the God who had issued the as-yet-unfulfilled promises, or was he right in lying about his wife to save his own life? Ought the patriarch to have anticipated God's preemptive action to protect Sarah's virtue and his own marriage and told the truth, or under the circumstances, now portrayed as general throughout their travels (v. 13), was he justified in resorting to his fib? In this regard, we must also ask about the excuse he offers to the indignant Abimelech, that Sarah really is his sister, on his father's but not his mother's side (v. 12). The Jewish tradition, reluctant to ascribe even a white lie to the revered patriarch, thus generally identifies Sarah with the otherwise unknown Iscah, daughter of Abraham's brother Nahor.[37] But even if we accept this tradition as the plain sense (for which Genesis presents no evidence whatsoever), we still must confront Ramban's astute observation: whether she was a full or a half sister, Abraham committed a sin in omitting the all-important point—she was his wife![38]

The story of Abraham and Sarah in Gerar, like the preceding narrative of the destruction of Sodom, serves to retard the action, as the frustrations confronting the patriarch distract him from the key fact that the promise of Isaac's birth has yet to find its miraculous fulfillment. Here again, we find a pattern in which formidable challenges lie between God's pledged word and its realization and severely test the faith of those who receive the promise. But in Genesis 21, the frustrations fall away and the astonishing fulfillment comes about:

> ¹The LORD took note of Sarah as He had promised, and the LORD did for Sarah as He had spoken. ²Sarah conceived and bore a son to Abraham in his old age, at the set time of which God had spoken. ³Abraham gave his newborn son, whom Sarah had borne to him, the name of Isaac. (Gen 21:1–3)

The slow, stately, and rhythmic cadence of these verses, more suggestive of biblical poetry than of prose, adds immense solemnity to the report of the joyous event. At last the long wait is over. Yet it will not be long until Abraham faces new challenges—and his greatest test.

## CHAPTER THREE

## The Test

His eyes shed tears that fell into Isaac's eyes because of his fa-
therly compassion; nonetheless, his heart rejoiced to do the will
of his Creator.

—Midrash[1]

KNOWN IN THE Jewish tradition as the "Binding (or, *Aqedah*) of Isaac"
and in Christianity as the "Sacrifice of Isaac," the episode narrated
in Genesis 22:1–19 has been of enormous significance in both traditions; it has indirectly generated an important parallel in Islam as
well. In the case of Judaism, the Aqedah has played a central role in
two of its most defining sacred occasions, Passover and Rosh Hashanah (New Year's), and to this day it reverberates revealingly in the
liturgy not only of the latter holiday but also of much other Jewish
prayer. In the case of Christianity, the Sacrifice of Isaac served as a
key resource by which the early church developed its understanding
of the role of Jesus, and especially his death, in the history of salvation; it also led to a subtle but momentous redescription of the narrative compared to its shape in Genesis.

The parallels between the two traditions as they have interpreted
this central text are so striking that to speak of the Aqedah in late
Second Temple and rabbinic Judaism (that is, Judaism between about
200 B.C.E. and 500 C.E.) without reference to the parallel interpretations in early Christianity, or vice versa, is myopic and misleading.
In late antiquity, the Aqedah served as the most powerful biblical
revelation of the greatness of Abraham for both Jews and Christians.
For them, as later for Muslims, the story showed him to be a paragon
of obedience to God, faith in God, and love of God.

This understanding of the narrative continues today, alive and
well among many Jews, Christians, and Muslims. But alongside it, and

directly challenging it, is another understanding, one rooted not in ancient theology but in Enlightenment philosophy. This reading inverts the traditional ones and finds in Abraham a paragon of unethical behavior, moral failure, religious fanaticism, and much else, all of it very bad. The Enlightenment understanding, too, needs to be understood, and the deeper sources of its differences from the classical interpretations probed and interrogated.

Our first task, however, is to give Genesis 22 itself a careful reading.

[1]Some time afterward, God put Abraham to the test. He said to him, "Abraham," and he answered, "Here I am."[2]

In biblical usage, "some time afterward" announces the onset of a new narrative, temporally disconnected from one that directly precedes it. The story thus begins abruptly, and one can only speculate as to what provoked the test. Abraham, of course, does not know it is a test, and to the extent that we identify with his situation, we too should not think of the Aqedah as "only" a test. The spareness of the quoted speech—"Abraham" and "Here I am" are each only one word in Hebrew—adds to the eeriness but also the gravity of the episode. "Here I am" is probably as good an English rendering of *hinneni* as there is, but we should remember that the expression connotes readiness, attentiveness, responsiveness; Abraham is telling God about something far more momentous than his location.

[2]And He said, "Take your son, your only/favored one, the one whom you love, Isaac, and go forth to the land of Moriah, and offer him there as a burnt offering on one of the heights that I will point out to you."

The wording closely parallels God's first address to Abraham: "Go forth from your native land, from your kin-group, and from your father's house to the land that I will show you" (Gen 12:1).[3] The expression rendered here as "go forth" (*lekh-lekha*) occurs in these two verses alone in the entire Hebrew Bible. The threefold specification of what he was to leave and to give up—native land, kin-group, and father's house—is reflected in the three designations of his sacrificial offering: son, only/favored one, the one whom Abraham loves. As in the case of the three terms in Genesis 12:1, so here the triad shows a progressive zeroing-in and an intensification of emotion. As the native land is larger and presumably less beloved than the kin-group, and the kin-group than the father's house (a smaller familial unit), so is "son" a more general category than "only/favored one," and "only/favored one" less intense than "the one whom you love."

Key to interpreting the text is that Abraham is to give up somebody he *loves*. There is, of course, no reason to deny that the term refers to the affection the father feels for the son he must give up. It is important to know, however, that in biblical Hebrew "love" can also refer to something more social and legal in character. It can refer to the loved one's relative status as the lover's favorite. Thus, Genesis will later report that "Isaac favored Esau," whereas "Rebekah favored Jacob" (25:28); in each case, the verb for "favored" is the one usually translated "loved" ('ahev or 'ahav), the same word we find here in Genesis 22:2. Similarly, Deuteronomy can speak of a man's favored wife as "loved" and her less favored co-wife as "unloved" (literally but inaccurately, "hated," śenu'ah, 21:15–17).

And so, alongside the obvious affective resonance of Abraham's love for Isaac, we must also consider Isaac's special status now that Ishmael has been expelled. Isaac is not merely the son born to the preferred wife, the free woman Sarah, in her old age and after a lifetime of infertility, and he is not merely the only son who will inherit the Abrahamic covenant, as we saw in chapter 2. He is also the son whom Abraham, in obedience to Sarah's wishes and God's explicit instruction, has favored over Isaac's older half brother Ishmael, now removed from the household. From the standpoint of inheritance and covenant, Isaac is Abraham's only son, his favored son, the one whom, after an initial reluctance, he has promoted over his older son. Everything has now come down to Isaac. Abraham's other possible heirs—Lot, Eliezer, and now even his biological son Ishmael—have all fallen away. The great name, the great nation, the blessing, the land of Canaan—all that Abraham has been promised from his call and commission in Genesis 12—now rests upon Isaac. But it is Isaac he must offer up.

Abraham's own destiny is so entwined with that of Isaac, and the "great nation" that is eventually to descend from him, that the demand is even harder than the demand upon any other loving father to offer up his beloved son. Psychologically, what is asked is not only an inexpressibly painful act of sacrifice; it is also an act of *self*-sacrifice. As the medieval Provençal commentator Rabbi David Qimchi put it, Abraham "loved [Isaac] more than he loved himself" (Radaq on Gen 22:1). Rabbi Bachya ben Asher, a fourteenth-century Spanish scholar, puts it more strongly: "If Abraham had had a hundred bodies, it would have been suitable to give them all up for the sake of Isaac, but this act was not like any other, this trial was not like any other, and nature cannot bear it, nor the imagination conceive it" (Rabbeinu Bachya on the same verse).

For that reason, when Genesis 22:2, unlike the close parallel in Genesis 12:1 with its three terms (native land, kin-group, and father's house), displays a fourth term, the person's name, "Isaac," the word comes with a truly crushing force. It is Abraham's very future, the very promise that issued from the mouth of God, with which he must part.

The striking parallel between those two verses—one from the start of Abraham's call and commission, the other from the start of his great test—suggests that in the Aqedah God has in a sense made Abraham revert to the state in which he stood when he began his journey—alone with God, attentive to an unexpected and mysterious divine command, and prepared to leave home even for a destination that is as yet unspecified ("the land that I will show you" / "one of the heights that I will point out to you"). The man who gave up his father's house must now give up the son on whom he has staked his life.

The "burnt offering" into which he is commanded to make his beloved son is well known from the biblical laws of sacrifice.[4] It is a type of offering in which neither the offerer nor the priest consumes any of the meat; all of it is thus presented to God, rendering this type of sacrifice, as Baruch J. Schwartz puts it, "the gift-offering par excellence." In the modern world, in which such rites are little understood and easily despised, sacrifice is too often seen as having been intended to expiate guilt. Some forms of sacrifice do have that function, but this one does not. "Gift offerings," Schwartz observes, rather, "express the worshipper's desire to present something to the LORD as a token of love and reverence."[5]

In particular, the gift that God enjoins upon Abraham belongs to the category of the first fruits offering, which includes not only the

products of the field, vineyard, orchard, herd, and flock, but, significantly, also the firstborn son.[6] Biblical tradition, like continuing Jewish practice, abundantly testifies to the notion that the firstborn male
belongs to God and must be offered back to his rightful owner, an
idea that, interestingly, long survives not only the abolition of child
sacrifice but also the loss of the Temple and thus of all categories
of sacrifice. Perhaps the most familiar example is the explanation of
the paschal lamb as a remembrance of the redemption of the Israelite
firstborn at the first Passover (Exod 13:1–16). Another example is the
practice of *pidyon habben*, the redemption of the firstborn, in which
the Jewish father to this day buys his firstborn son back from the
priest (*kohen*) for five pieces of silver (see Num 3:44–51). In biblical
times, another substitution ritual for the gift of the son existed: the
donation of the boy to a sanctuary, in which he would serve as a kind
of priest.[7]

But, alas, when Abraham obediently sets out on his journey, none
of these substitutions is in evidence.

> [3]So early next morning, Abraham saddled his ass and took with
> him two of his servants and his son Isaac. He split the wood for
> the burnt offering, and he set out for the place of which God had
> told him.

"Early next morning" suggests that God's command may have come
to Abraham in a dream vision of the sort we see, for example, in the
case of King Abimelech two chapters earlier (20:3). If so, this phrase,
like "Here I am," suggests Abraham's unhesitating obedience; he does
not lose a moment in carrying out the deed that has been enjoined
upon him. The painfulness of that deed is underscored by the identification of Isaac as Abraham's "son"—surely, we already know who
he is—and by the placement of the powerful phrase "his son Isaac"
at the end of this, the second threefold ascending sequence in the
chapter (ass, servants, son).

> [4]On the third day Abraham looked up and saw the place from afar.
> [5]Then Abraham said to his servants, "You stay here with the ass.
> The boy and I will go up there; we will prostrate ourselves and we
> will return to you."

"Seeing" is a theme that reverberates throughout this little narrative. Here, Abraham sees the place for the sacrifice. Soon, he will tell Isaac that "God will see to the sheep for His burnt offering" (v. 8), a clause that will be interpreted as the origin of the name of the place, Adonai-yireh, "the LORD sees/will see," memorialized in a saying apparently common at the time, "On the mount of the LORD there is vision/he is seen/he will be seen" (v. 14). And in verse 13, we shall again hear the language of verse 4, but with a different object of the seeing: "Abraham looked up and saw a ram, caught in the thicket by its horns." The name of the land where all this takes place, Moriah, may be a further play on the root of all these verbs of seeing (*ra'ah*).

Whatever all this means, it is surely significant that Abraham goes forth to a place that he has not seen and whose name has yet to be assigned. The patriarch, in other words, acts in obedience to the divine word that he has heard and not to any vision that he has been given. But, as his journey progresses, as the episode in which it culminates unfolds, and as his own determination to obey the unspeakably difficult command becomes undeniable, he is increasingly granted vision, and the sanctuary that he will found on that site commemorates and perpetuates, even into the narrator's lifetime, the vision of God's redemption, the confidence in God's pro-vision of the means of redemption, that Abraham experienced in his great test.

Abraham's leaving the two servants at the foot of the mountain adds to the tension; now it is a matter of Abraham and Isaac alone, just as, after Lot, Eliezer, and Ishmael had gone their separate ways, the question of the covenant had become a matter of Abraham and Isaac. More difficult are the words "we will prostrate ourselves and we will return to you." There is a long tradition of interpretation, especially prominent in Christianity, that sees in this clause an expression of Abraham's exemplary faith. The New Testament Letter to the Hebrews puts it memorably:

[17]By faith Abraham, when put to the test, offered up Isaac. He who had received the promises was ready to offer up his only son,[18] of whom he had been told, "It is through Isaac that descendants shall be named for you." [19]He considered the fact that God is able even

> to raise someone from the dead—and figuratively speaking, he did receive him back. (Heb 11:17–19, quoting Gen 21:12)[8]

This makes the Aqedah a test of Abraham's trust in God's promise that he will have descendants from Isaac, who is unmarried at the time: a test, in other words, of Abraham's faith that the promised nation Israel will come into existence. As the New Testament writer sees the matter, the patriarch had faith that even were he to slaughter his beloved son, God would still restore him from the dead, just as the writer believed God had done with his own beloved son, resurrecting the executed Jesus. And so, at the end of the Aqedah, when the sacrifice is suddenly called off, Abraham's faith that he would receive his son anew is validated, even if in this instance a literal resurrection has not yet taken place. The patriarch has passed his great test of faith.

In the Jewish tradition, too, the Aqedah is frequently seen as a test of Abraham's faith in God's promise. In our last chapter, we spoke of the key verse, "And because he put his faith in the Lord, He reckoned it to his merit" (Gen 15:6),[9] which in context speaks of Abraham's faith in God's promise that he will father a highly populous nation. Late in Second Temple Judaism, however, the verse had come to be understood as applying not to its immediate context in Genesis 15 but to the Aqedah instead. A case in point is found in the work of Joshua ben Sira, a sage of the early second century B.C.E. who authored a highly important book that, although not part of the rabbinic canon of scripture, remains well known in the Jewish tradition.[10] Here is ben Sira's allusion to the Aqedah:

> He kept the law of the Most High,
> and entered into a covenant with him;
> he certified the covenant in his flesh,
> and when he was tested he proved faithful. (Sir 44:20)

The only time in Genesis that Abraham is ever said to have been tested is in the Aqedah (Gen 22:1), while the only verse that speaks of his faith appears seven chapters earlier in Genesis 15:6.

The same relocation, this time in language even closer to that of the key verse, can be found in 1 Maccabees, a book written about a century later than ben Sira:

Was not Abraham found faithful when tested, and it was reckoned to him as righteousness? (1 Mac 2:52)[11]

In chapter 2, we observed that in the Talmud, the Jewish people are called "people of faith who are descendants of people of faith" and with explicit reference to Genesis 15:6.[12] If we remember that the verse had already been applied to the climactic event of Abraham's life centuries earlier, we will not find this surprising. Indeed, Abraham is a paradigm of faith in Judaism, Christianity, and Islam alike, and in all three traditions the Aqedah serves as the parade example of the extraordinary depth of his faith.

All this can easily make us forget, as over the centuries it has caused many theologians and biblical scholars to forget, that faith is nowhere mentioned in Genesis 22. It may be reasonable to infer that Abraham goes forth to sacrifice his son with a heart and a mind full of confidence that God will fulfill the promise he made in Genesis 21:12, despite all appearances and rational calculations to the contrary. But nothing in the text of Genesis 22 requires this inference, and others can be imagined. The key to one of them can be found in Abraham's words to his servants, "we will prostrate ourselves and we will return to you" (Gen 22:4). Prostration may have been a common accompaniment to sacrifice,[13] and perhaps that is the role it plays here. But it is more often seen in connection with supplication.[14] If that is the connotation here, then we had best translate the end of verse 4 as, "we will prostrate ourselves in order that we may return to you," and the implication may be that Abraham, lacking confidence that he will not have to slay Isaac, in the end plans instead to petition God to call off the sacrifice he had ordered and instead to allow the boy to survive.

If Abraham did harbor such a plan, however, he seems to have given it up by the time he and Isaac finally ascend the mountain, for there is no indication that they engaged in any prostration or petition there. Could it be that Abraham's words to his servants express neither faith in God's promise concerning Isaac nor his own intention to supplicate God to save his son from the slaughterer's knife? Could it be, rather, that Abraham is simply misleading his servants, throwing them off his trail, as it were?

If so, it is not hard to imagine why. Although child sacrifice is known to have been practiced in the ancient Near East, including in ancient Israel—one prophet even said the sacrifice of the firstborn had originally been in accordance with the LORD's will[15]—in none of those societies was it the norm. Surely (the servants might have reasoned), a man who had waited a quarter century for his promised son to be born, a son on whom he had staked his life and his whole hope for the future, should not be allowed to slay him! Better, Abraham might consequently have reasoned, they should think he and Isaac are only going off to prostrate themselves in some sort of religious ceremony and then return to them than that they should feel compelled to prevent the sacrifice.

Or could it be that Abraham's deception (if it be deception) is directed not at the servants but at Isaac? Although Jewish tradition will later interpret Isaac as an adult at the time of the Aqedah and so a knowing and willing participant in what would thus become his own self-sacrifice, Genesis 22 gives scant indication of his age. The medieval commentator Rabbi Abraham ibn Ezra, who assigns Isaac a lower age, argues that Abraham "hid the secret from him" because if he had told him the truth, "he probably would have fled" (comment to v. 4). If so, then better Isaac, too, should think that he and his father will ascend the mountain only for the purpose of prostrating themselves, returning uneventfully soon afterward. If his son is too young to understand, such a disguise would not only ensure the sacrifice would take place as required; under the circumstances, it would also be the kindest thing the father could say to the unknowing and perhaps unwilling child.

Could it be, finally, that Abraham was attempting to deceive neither the servants nor Isaac but himself? Could he have suspected that were he to utter directly the full truth about what he planned, his own resolve would break, and he would no longer be able to proceed in obedience to God's excruciating command? For polite speech is full of euphemisms by which we ward off the full ghastliness of the actual event—"I lost my mother," "I terminated the pregnancy,"

"there was collateral damage." Perhaps Abraham is resorting to a euphemism ("we will prostrate ourselves") and an overstatement ("we
will return to you") to protect both himself and the fact of his compliance with God's will, more precious to him even than Isaac and all
he represents.

> ⁶Abraham took the wood for the burnt offering and put it on his
> son Isaac. He himself took the firestone and the knife; and the two
> walked along together.¹⁶

Abraham's placing the wood that will incinerate Isaac on the pro-
spective victim himself makes for an enormously powerful image.
One reason is that, like other details of wording in the Aqedah, it
recalls the expulsion of Hagar and Ishmael in the previous chapter:
"Early next morning Abraham took some bread and a skin of water,
and gave them to Hagar. He placed them over her shoulder, together
with the child, and sent her away" (Gen 21:14). Hagar carries on her
own shoulder the skin of water that symbolizes (we soon find out)
her son's death by dehydration; arguably, she also carries on her own
shoulder the little boy himself, the victim of Abraham and Sarah's
plan—and God's plan, too. The echo of this scene in the Aqedah,
though, is freighted with an even higher element of suspense, even
greater tension, for however unlikely it is that one skin of water will
suffice a young woman and her child lost in the desert, it is all too
likely that the obedient Abraham will sacrifice the son he loves when
they reach the specified site. The echo thus evinces an illuminating
contrast: whereas Ishmael's ostensibly impending death would be
from natural causes (whatever culpability one might wish to assign
to Sarah, Abraham—the only one of the three with reservations—
and God), Isaac's death will be at his own father's hand and the direct
command of God.

Does Isaac's carrying the fuel for his own incineration make him
a willing participant in the event, as later Jewish tradition generally
insisted he was? Perhaps, but one can also imagine a boy of three or
four carrying, without a second thought, enough fagots to consume
his slain body. Here again, the austerity of the narrative leaves us uncertain, even as it prompts us to fill in the gaps. And so, when the
narrator adds "and the two walked along together," we cannot be sure

this indicates commonality of intent between the offerer and the offering, as the Jewish tradition generally has it, or the innocent child's instinctive trust in his daddy.

> [7]Then Isaac said to Abraham his father, "My father!" And he answered, "Here I am." And he said, "Here are the firestone and the wood; but where is the sheep for the burnt offering?" [8]And Abraham said, "God will see to the sheep for His burnt offering, my son." And the two of them walked along together.

The tension only increases when Abraham must face and address the very person he is about to sacrifice. It is one thing to obey the voice of an unseen God; it is quite another to have to confront the victim of the deed God commands. The repetition of the word "father" in verse 7 and the reiteration of "son" in verse 8 (this is the fourth time the word has appeared in the little narrative) underscore the closeness and specialness of the relationship. "My father!" is a single word in Hebrew ('avi) and, especially if the speaker is a small child, might be better rendered "Daddy." The exchange recalls the opening of the story, in which God said but one word, "Abraham," and Abraham responded with just one *hinneni*, "Here I am" (Gen 22:1). Now Abraham responds to the victim of his intended sacrifice with the identical word, *hinnenni*.[17] But this time there is a second word, *beni*, "my son" (the fifth occurrence of "son"), which not only reinforces the relationship of the two individuals but responds to the narrator's identification of Abraham as "his father" in verse 7 as well. Abraham is as ready, as attentive, as responsive to his beloved son as he is to God. He is as ready, as attentive, as responsive to the one who must be offered back to God as he is to the God who promised Isaac and gave him to Abraham in the first place.

Isaac's question in Genesis 22:7 omits mention of the knife. Whether this is significant or not, the boy clearly knows a sacrifice is about to be performed. If he is a small child, then his question is unbearably poignant. How can his daddy explain to him that the little boy must himself take the place of the sheep for the sacred slaughter? Surely, a father can face no greater test of his stamina than this. If, on the other hand, Isaac is old enough and wise enough to understand— for Abraham would not have brought the wood and the fire but overlooked the offering itself—then why the indirection? Why not tell his father straight-out that he is prepared to play the role that God or Abraham (for we cannot be sure Abraham has told Isaac of the divine speech in verse 2) has assigned him? Here, as in the case of Abraham's words to his two servants at the end of verse 5, we can suspect that Isaac dare not express the gruesome endpoint of the journey on which the two are embarked. If the suspicion is valid—and we have no way of knowing whether it is—then Isaac may be resorting to indirection to spare his father the pain of hearing plainly what he knows inwardly awaits the two of them at the end. Or Isaac may be speaking this way in order to protect his own resolve from the corrosive effects of that very pain.

Abraham's reply in Genesis 22:8, "God will see to the sheep for His burnt offering, my son," anticipates both the outcome of the story (if we assume the appearance of the sheep in verse 13 is owing to God's intervention) and the name given in verse 14 to the otherwise unknown site, Adonai-yireh, "The LORD will see." And so, it would seem that Abraham here speaks the truth.

But does he know it is the truth? Certainly, if we mean that he holds this outcome as an object of secure cognitive possession, the way we know that $2 + 2 = 4$, the answer must be, no, he certainly does not know. But there is another way of knowing, less secure, less objective, but more existential, more personal—knowing through faith, knowing as an act of trust, the way we know a good friend will pay back the money we have loaned him. This kind of knowing engages more than merely the mind; it engages the whole person. If this is the kind of knowing we mean, then it is quite plausible that Abraham does indeed know that "God will see to the sheep for His burnt offering," since, as we have seen, God has already specified that it is from Isaac that the covenanted people will descend. On this reading, the Aqedah is a test of Abraham's faith, and with his words to Isaac in verse 8, he shows his faith in God's promise to be unshakable.

As we have seen, the interpretation of the Aqedah as the great test of Abraham's faith is an ancient one, and can already be detected in the application to this event of Genesis 15:6 ("And because he put his trust in the LORD, He reckoned it to his merit") in the second century B.C.E. If this interpretation is correct, then in his answer to Isaac in

Genesis 22:8, Abraham does not simply articulate his faith; he also "throws the ball back into God's court."[18] Now God must prove faithful in turn, showing that Abraham's faith in him has not been in vain. He must do what Abraham has all along trusted he would do.

There is, however, a problem with the claim that Abraham's answer to Isaac expresses his deep faith. For, again, the text is utterly silent about Abraham's thoughts, and we can easily imagine, as we did in connection with his words to the servants in Genesis 22:5, that he is, instead, simply protecting Isaac from the full emotional impact of what will happen or protecting his own resolve from the same threat. Perhaps Abraham has no expectation, whether through faith or otherwise, that God will countermand his order to sacrifice Isaac. Perhaps he fully expects to make a real sacrifice of his beloved son without any expectation that in the end he will get back what he will donate at the altar. Perhaps it is the ideal of radical obedience, obedience that rises above all calculations of self-interest, and not the power of faith, that the Aqedah has actually come to teach. The narrative is too austere, too cryptic, and too rich in interpretive possibilities for us to say for sure.

It is striking that verse 8, after Abraham and Isaac's exchange, concludes with the identical words as verse 6, which directly precedes it: "and the two of them walked along together." That last word (*yachdav*) recalls not only the term for "only/favored one" (*yachid*) in verse 2 but also the cognate "one" (*'echad*), and thus might well be translated "as one." Whatever Isaac's question to his father and Abraham's answer in verses 7–8 mean, the mysterious exchange has not broken the unanimity of the two. In the words of a midrash, they walked along together, "one to bind and the other to be bound, one to slay and the other to be slain" (*Gen. Rab.* 56:4).

> [9]They arrived at the place of which God had told him. Abraham built an altar there; he laid out the wood; he bound Isaac his son; he laid him on the altar, on top of the wood. [10]And Abraham stretched out his arm and took the knife to slay his son.

Now the pace picks up, with six verbs in one short compound sentence (v. 9); things are rapidly coming to a head. Verse 10, conversely, slows the action down again, as we see Abraham, as if in slow motion, stretching out his arm before he takes the slaughterer's knife in hand. The unusual order of the procedure further heightens the almost unbearable drama of the description. The procedures for a burnt offering in Leviticus ordain that the slaughter occur *before* the placement of the wood (Lev 1:3–13). In this case, however, the narrative foregrounds the father's willingness to proceed with the gift God has commanded.

Why does Abraham bind Isaac? Perhaps this shows that the son was not a knowing and willing participant in the sacrifice. Or perhaps this was standard procedure in the sacrificial slaughter of human offerings. The midrash, committed to the idea that Isaac was at least as much the hero of the Aqedah as his father, proposes that Isaac volunteered to be tied up: "Father, I am a young man, and I am worried that my body may flinch because of the fear of the knife and I will cause you distress, lest the slaughter become invalid and not be accredited to you as a sacrifice. So tie me up very securely" (*Gen. Rab.* 56:8).

> [11]Then an angel of the LORD called to him from the heavens: "Abraham! Abraham!" And he answered, "Here I am." [12]And he said, "Do not raise your hand against the boy, or do anything to him. For now I know that you fear God, since you have not withheld your son, your only/favored one, from Me."

In the Hebrew Bible, an "angel" (the word also means "messenger") generally appears on earth, not in the heavens. This makes it all the more striking that the beginning of verse 11 is almost identical to that of Genesis 21:17, in which the angel announces to Hagar from the heavens that having heard Ishmael's cry, God will rescue her dying son. But here again, the similarity prompts a contrast. In the Aqedah, the angel, before announcing that the order has been countermanded, hurriedly calls Abraham (hence the doubling of his name), who then responds with the identical word with which he responded to God in verse 2 and to Isaac in verse 7. "Here I am" (*hinneni*) once again shows Abraham as one who is ready, attentive, and responsive to the divine will—even before he learns in the next verse that the divine will now is that, having passed his great test, he need not lose his beloved son after all.

The reason for the rescission of the command to sacrifice Isaac is that God has now learned that Abraham "fears" him. That God can learn anything is, of course, antithetical to the Aristotelian notion that the deity must be unchanging, and many Jewish exegetes over the centuries have felt compelled to interpret "I know" (*yada'ti*) in verse 12 as if it were a different word, "I have made known" (*hoda'ti/ yidda'ti*).[19] But this is not the only place where the description of the personal, interacting, dynamic, and feeling God of Israel is not easily reconciled with the perfect, static, and perfectly static God of the philosophers. However the formidable conundrum of divine learning is to be understood philosophically (if at all), the end of our narrative leaves no doubt that God has acquired knowledge he did not have at its outset.

The words "you fear (*yere'*) God" echo the multiple appearances of the root of the verb "to see" (*ra'ah*) that, as we have noted, reverberate throughout the Aqedah, the difference between the two nearly homophonous roots being immaterial to the ancient author.[20] The "fear of God" has many nuances in different collections of biblical literature, and we should be wise to recognize that "fear" in this context does not mean fright.[21] Rather, the use of the expression here, as often, expresses the idea of covenantal service. The suzerain issues a command, and the loyal vassal enacts his commitment to his lord's will through his obedience. Consider this example: "Therefore keep the commandments of the LORD your God: walk in His ways and revere (*leyir'ah*) Him" (Deut 8:6). In the case of the obedient servant Abraham, having set out on the harrowing journey that his lord had enjoined upon him and fully obeyed God's command—a command vastly more difficult, infinitely more painful than most of the stipulations of covenant—the father has amply demonstrated his fear of God and rendered the actual sacrifice of his son pointless.

This covenantal reading does not, of course, invalidate the traditional interpretations that stress Abraham's love of God or faith in him. Indeed, since both "fear" and "love" are part of the standard vocabulary of covenantal service, it is artificial to make a sharp distinction between them.[22] Deuteronomy, to cite that great exemplar of covenant theology again, gives this as the reason God might allow a prophet or dream-interpreter with a false message to perform real miracles:

> ⁴For the LORD your God is testing you to see whether you really love the LORD your God with all your heart and soul. ⁵Follow none but the LORD your God, and fear (*tira'u*) none but Him; observe His commands alone, and obey only His orders; worship none but Him, and hold fast to Him. (Deut 13:4–5)²³

In this passage, we find three terms resonant of the Aqedah in close proximity: "test," "fear," and "obey [His/My] order" (the last appears in Gen 22:18). To be sure, unlike the community addressed in Deuteronomy, in the case of Abraham what is being put to the test is not his exclusive loyalty to the God of Israel as opposed to other deities; as we shall see in chapter 4, the conception of Abraham as an exponent of monotheism and opponent of idolatry, so well known in Jewish and Muslim tradition, is nowhere to be detected in Genesis. Rather, here the alternative to obedience—and what makes the obedience spiritually heroic—is Abraham's paternal affection for the son he loves (v. 2). His fear of God entails the unimaginably painful choice to elevate his love of God over even his love of Isaac and all that Isaac signifies for his own life. In the Aqedah, the alternative is indeed apostasy—in the form, however, not of defection to another god but of withholding the beloved son from the God who gave him, thus elevating the father's personal self-interest over obedience to the God to whom he owes not only Isaac but all his good fortune. That Abraham became a paradigm of the love of God in both Judaism and Christianity, as we shall soon see, is in no way inconsonant with the celebration of him for his fear of God in Genesis 22. But there is a subtle change of emphasis in that shift.

And what exactly is "faith" within this covenantal framework? Here, faith would consist not so much of trusting in a promise as in proving faithful to the lord in covenant by obeying his command, however difficult. As we saw earlier, if we think of Abraham as having unwavering trust in the promise that centers on Isaac, then his obedience is less difficult, for he knows—the way one "knows" through faith rather than through ordinary cognition—that he will not in the end have to sacrifice his beloved son, and the test does not prove that he "fear[s] God" but rather that his faith in God is unshakable. This understanding of the Aqedah, too, yields a profound theology, as the subsequent histories of Judaism, Christianity, and Islam richly demonstrate, but it does not cohere well with the plain sense of Genesis 22. Whether Abraham in that chapter feels toward God the affect that we normally call "love," or the trust and confidence in God that we usually mean by "faith," is unknown. What is known is that when tested, he proves his fear of God by obeying God's order.

> <sup>13</sup>Abraham looked up and saw a ram, caught in the thicket by its horns. So Abraham went and took the ram and offered it up as a burnt offering in place of his son. <sup>14</sup>And Abraham named that site Adonai-yireh, whence the present saying, "On the mount of the LORD he is seen/appears."

Verse 13 recalls the climactic point in the ordeal of Hagar and Ishmael in the previous chapter when, the angel having just allayed the desperate mother's fears, "God opened her eyes and she saw a well of water. She went and filled the skin with water, and let the boy drink" (Gen 21:19). In each case, a sudden vision reinforces the heavenly message of redemption and serves to dissipate the unbearable tension of the preceding narrative. As we have noted, the sudden appearance of the ram—like Hagar's well, perhaps it was there all along, perhaps it wasn't—recalls verse 4, when "Abraham looked up and saw the place from afar," the place, that is, where he would have to say his final good-bye to Isaac. Now, having obeyed God's command nonetheless, he sees a new reality in which he will not lose his beloved son after all. The rapidity with which he sacrifices the ram reinforces our sense of the depth of Abraham's commitment to God. Rather than simply stopping when the sacrifice that God had commanded is called off, he immediately makes use of his knife, altar, wood, and fire to make an offering on his own.

One sometimes hears that the purpose of the Aqedah was to replace children with animals as the proper victims of sacrifice.<sup>24</sup> But in Genesis 22, God neither commands nor commends the offering of the ram, and in the narrator's view, the continuing significance of the event lies not in the sacrificial victim but in the site on which it is said to have been offered and in a saying associated with that location (v. 14). Unfortunately, no place with the name Adonai-yireh is otherwise known, though as we shall soon observe, Jewish tradition quickly filled the gap by identifying it with the site of the Temple in Jerusalem, which at a certain point became the sole legitimate place for sacrifice. Whether "the mount of the LORD" here also refers to the Temple Mount, as it does elsewhere in the Hebrew Bible, is also unknown. It is possible that the end of verse 14 was appended to the story after the site of the Aqedah had been identified with the Jerusalem Temple.

> [15]The angel of the LORD called to Abraham a second time from heaven, [16]and said, "By Myself I swear, the LORD declares: Because you have done this and have not withheld your son, your only/favored one, [17]I will bestow My blessing upon you and make your descendants as numerous as the stars of heaven and the sands on the seashore; and your descendants shall seize the gates of their foes. [18]All the nations of the earth shall bless themselves by your descendants, because you have obeyed My command."

That the angel should speak a second time is odd and suggests his speech here is a supplementation, one that has been aptly characterized as the earliest commentary on the Aqedah.[25] Its prime function is to connect the event more explicitly with Abraham's life theretofore. The language of blessing and plenteous progeny recalls, of course, his initial call and commission (Gen 12:1–3), and the words "as numerous as the stars of heaven" echo the promise made to him just before God sealed his promise in covenant: "Look toward heaven and count the stars, if you are able to count them. . . . So shall your offspring be" (Gen 15:5). Though less exactly, "the sands on the seashore" resonates with the LORD's promise in Genesis 13:16: "I will make your offspring as the dust of the earth, so that if one can count the dust of the earth, then your offspring too can be counted." Finally, the promise that "your descendants shall seize the gates of their foes" reiterates the long-standing promise, given in various forms several times, that Abraham or his offspring will take over the land of Canaan.[26]

What all this shows is that the second angelic address relates the Aqedah back to the beginning of Abraham's journey, when he had yet no son but only the promise of one and of the great nation that would descend from him. But at that time, as we saw in chapter 2, God's amazing promise came as a kind of bolt out of the blue; there was nothing Abram (as he was then called) had done to merit it. The positive term for this situation in which undeserving people benefit is "grace"; the negative term is "arbitrariness." What Genesis 22:15–18 does is to reinterpret those old promises of blessing, descendants, and land so that they, though gracious, are no longer arbitrary; they have now become consequences of the Aqedah. No longer are they totally undeserved; now they are, in part, the condign fruits of Abraham's heroic act of obedience.

And no longer is God's election of Abraham a matter of grace alone, which is to say, an act of sheer arbitrariness. For now Abraham has vindicated God's faith in him. In the end, Abraham has proven worthy of the promises God graciously extended to him in the beginning. It is "because you have done this" that God takes a solemn oath—his first in the entire Bible—to fulfill his outstanding promises to Abraham. If we remember that oath-taking and covenant-making overlap, and that "oath" itself can be a term for covenant, we will see that the Aqedah has now become the basis for the Abrahamic covenant, or, to state the reverse, the Abrahamic covenant has now become a consequence of the Aqedah. Abraham's great act of obedience stands to the benefit of the nation that derives from him for all time.

Were the purpose of the Aqedah to prohibit child sacrifice and to replace it with animal offerings, would it not be passing strange that God so richly rewards Abraham for his willingness to do precisely what the text has come to forbid? Rather, in both angelic addresses, the operative dichotomy is not between human and animal but between giving and withholding (Gen 22:12, 16). Abraham passes his great test only because he refuses to hold back his beloved son, only because he is willing to make even that donation, painful beyond words. The great paradox is that because he proves willing to donate Isaac, he not only retains him but to some degree merits the extraordinary promises that rest on his only/favored son.

Here an analogy from the story of King Solomon suggests itself. When God appears to Solomon in a dream and announces, "Ask, what shall I grant you?" and the king asks for "an understanding mind to judge Your people," God responds with a double gift:

> [11]Because you asked for this—you did not ask for long life, you did not ask for riches, you did not ask for the life of your enemies, but you asked for discernment in dispensing justice—[12]I now do as you have spoken. I grant you a wise and discerning mind . . . [13]And I also grant you what you did not ask for—both riches and glory all your life—the like of which no king has ever had. (1 Kgs 3:5, 9, 11–13)

By preferring discernment to riches and glory, Solomon receives all three. By preferring the fear of God to Isaac and all that his beloved son signifies for his relationship with God (and otherwise), Abraham retains the son he did not withhold and receives anew all the promises that have so long stood at the heart of his relationship with God. In the paradoxical, sacrificial logic of which this text is the outstanding Jewish example, it is our ungrudging willingness to give that leads to gaining and retaining that which is most precious. It is in rising above self-interest that we secure that which a calculus of self-interest can never yield—or understand.

> [19]Abraham then returned to his servants, and they departed together for Beer-sheba; and Abraham stayed in Beer-sheba.

The word for "together" (*yachdav*) again recalls not only the key term "only/favored one" (*yachid*) that we have now seen three times (vv. 2, 12, 16) but also the clause "and the two walked along together" that brackets the poignant exchange between father and son (*yachdav*, vv. 6, 8). This makes Isaac's absence here all the more conspicuous. An ancient midrash memorably solves the problem by imagining that Abraham had sent his son off to study Torah. "Everything I have has come to me only because I have involved myself with the Torah and commandments," the biblical patriarch reasons with impeccable rabbinic theology; "therefore I do not want it ever to depart from my progeny" (*Gen. Rab.* 56:11).

In our time, however, people often give a less idealistic interpretation by imagining that Isaac was traumatized by the Aqedah and ran off or refused to return with his father. In support of this, one often hears that Abraham and Isaac never again spoke with each other. One slight problem: they never spoke before the Aqedah either. One could just as well argue that they were never so close, never so united in spirit and purpose, as they were in that great test.

Historical criticism of the Bible suggests another way to account for the anomaly of Isaac's apparent failure to return, though it is not a solution that most historical critics have embraced. Note that most of Genesis 22 uses the E-name for the Deity (*'elohim*, translated "God"), whereas the two angelic addresses and the verse about Abraham's naming the site use the J-name (YHVH, translated "the LORD"). This may suggest a difference in authorship. If, in fact, we excise the two angelic speeches as interpolations from a different source, we have every reason to think that Abraham did indeed sacrifice Isaac, and his return with only the two servants in verse 19 makes perfect sense. Less drastically, if we excise the first angelic address and the verse about the ram (vv. 11–15), along with the words "the LORD declares" in verse 16, then we are left with a text—the more original version, according to one theory—in which Abraham took the knife to slay his son and then heard the voice of God commending him for having performed the sacrifice, "By Myself I swear: Because you have done this and have not withheld your son." And after that, Abraham returns to his two servants and goes home, Isaac having been immolated on the altar in Moriah, just as God had commanded. Once child sacrifice had come to be seen as an abomination, so the theory goes, a later redactor inserted the idea that an angel had called off the sacrifice in the nick of time and the obedient Abraham had substituted a ram instead, as biblical law later required. That Isaac appears alive and well afterward is no counterargument to this theory, which points out that none of those texts come from the E source. No surviving text, in fact, enables us to know what parentage E assigned to Jacob, whom the other sources see as Isaac's son.[27]

Those committed to the traditional doctrine of the unitary (Mosaic) composition of the Torah can easily dismiss such reconstructions, and indeed they have no choice, since the very idea of the interpolation of later passages into earlier ones contradicts their commitment. But this does not mean that they adhere strictly to the text of the Torah, either, for faced with the absence of Isaac in Genesis

22:19, these traditionalists not infrequently answer with their own interpolation, such as the one mentioned above, that has Abraham sending Isaac off to study Torah. Even without the traditional doctrine of unitary composition, however, there are reasons to suspect the claim that the sparing of Isaac is a later insertion, for that claim is speculative in the extreme and depends on an assignment of sources that, in the nature of things, is less than ideally secure. What is worse, it depends on an argument from silence, for the key verse that reports that Abraham actually went through with the sacrifice is still missing even after the proposed excisions. In sum, the speculation that in an earlier version of the Aqedah, Abraham did indeed sacrifice his beloved son remains exactly that—an intriguing speculation, but one necessarily less than convincing on the basis of the extant evidence. It also creates, or at best reconstructs, a text different from the one that has scriptural authority in Judaism and Christianity, and that underlies the one with comparable scriptural authority in Islam as well. Whatever its value as history, that hypothetical text is not Torah.

Apart from the very different answers of midrash and historical critical reconstruction, another explanation for the absence of Isaac in Genesis 22:19 must be considered. This explanation stresses that the Aqedah ends where it begins, with Abraham and not with Isaac. Only the father is mentioned in verse 1; in the biblical version, God puts Abraham to the test, not Abraham and Isaac. And Abraham, having passed the test, returns. The pattern is familiar to folklorists: the hero goes out to face his ordeal; the hero, having triumphed in the ordeal, returns home. However important Isaac's individuality and personality may seem to us today, and to Jewish interpreters even in postbiblical antiquity, in the biblical story he is not the focus, and his return requires no special mention.

The event on the unnamed mountain in the land of Moriah is the summit and climax of the story of Abraham in Genesis. The ensuing genealogy of Abraham's surviving brother in Genesis 22:20–24 helps release the enormous tension that the preceding narrative has built up, but it also subtly picks up themes in the Aqedah itself. Nahor's brood of twelve sons, eight from his primary wife and four from his secondary wife, foreshadows the twelve tribes of Israel, eight of whom descend from Jacob/Israel's primary wives and four from the secondary wives, the slaves who serve as surrogate mothers to their mistresses. More directly, only one female descendant of Nahor is mentioned (v. 23), and it is surely no coincidence that she turns out to be none other than Rebekah, who, two chapters later, becomes Isaac's wife and thus the second matriarch of Israel. And, in fact, the blessing that Rebekah receives just as she is about to leave to meet her fiancé, "May your offspring seize / The gates of their foes" (Gen 24:60), repeats almost exactly the words of the second angelic address at the end of the Aqedah, "and your descendants shall seize the gates of their foes" (22:17).[28] The transition to the second patriarchal generation has begun.

After the Aqedah, as one would expect, the story of Abraham is rapidly winding down. In the next chapter, Sarah dies and her widower must acquire a burial spot. The negotiations with the Hittite natives underscore his tenuous and vulnerable status—"I am a resident alien among you" (Gen 23:4)—yet also result in his first acquisition of real estate in the land promised him, "the cave of the field of Machpelah, facing Mamre—now Hebron—in the land of Canaan" (v. 19). Later, Abraham will himself be buried there, according to Genesis, as will Isaac and Rebekah and Jacob and Leah (Gen 25:9; 49:29–32). The site where the cave is thought to be has become sacred to practitioners of all three religious traditions that are called Abrahamic— Jews, Christians, and Muslims alike. In Jewish tradition, it comes to be seen as the burial place even of Adam and Eve. In Muslim tradition, Hebron, the city in which the cave is located, acquires its Arabic name, al-Khalīl ("the friend"), from the Qur'anic report that "Allah has taken Abraham for a friend" (4:125; see Isa 41:8).

The post-Aqedah passing of the patriarchal mantle to Isaac continues in the last full chapter about Abraham, in which the patriarch arranges for Isaac to marry an ethnically suitable wife, someone, that is, from his extended family and not from the Canaanites. But the LORD and Abraham's unnamed majordomo ensure that the girl that is found is also ethically suitable to marry into the family of the generous and hospitable patriarch:

[13]Here I stand by the spring as the daughters of the townsmen come out to draw water; [14]let the maiden to whom I say, "Please,

lower your jar that I may drink," and who replies, "Drink, and I will also water your camels"—let her be the one whom You have decreed for Your servant Isaac. Thereby shall I know that You have dealt graciously with my master. (Gen 24:13–14)

Rebekah passes her own test with flying colors (Gen 24:18–19), proving that she is Isaac's *basherte*, his "destined mate," to use the Yiddish term—destined in this case, however, by nothing less than divine providence working to fulfill the promise that Abraham won anew through his great test.

Although the Hebrew Bible almost never refers to the Aqedah outside of Genesis 22 itself, the significance of the event grows exponentially over the course of Second Temple and rabbinic Judaism.[29] The name Moriah is an early example, for the only other appearance of that word in the Hebrew Bible occurs in Chronicles, a late book, where it is the name of the mountain on which King Solomon builds his temple in Jerusalem.[30] The implication is clear: the Aqedah has become a foundation legend for the Jerusalem Temple.

Targum Onqelos, an Aramaic translation of the Torah from the rabbinic period, makes the point well. Whereas Genesis 22:14 reads, "And Abraham named that site Adonai-yireh, whence the present saying, 'On the mount of the LORD he is seen/appears,'" Onqelos renders, "And Abraham performed an act of service and prayed there, in that place, and said before the LORD, 'Here will be the service of the generations'; therefore it is said today, 'On this mountain Abraham performed an act of service for the LORD.'" The unnamed mountain in the land of Moriah in Genesis 22 has become the Temple Mount in Jerusalem, the sole locus for legitimate sacrifice among the Jews, and, conversely, the Temple Mount has acquired another name, "Mount Moriah." Abraham's obscure reference to vision just after he offers the ram has been transformed into a vision of the people Israel's worship of God in Jerusalem throughout the generations.

That Targum Onqelos, unlike Genesis, depicts Abraham in prayer after the Aqedah is a point not to be underestimated. For the rooting of Jewish worship in the Aqedah did not end with the loss of sacrifice after the Romans destroyed the Temple in 70 C.E. Instead, as is well known, the Talmudic rabbis see prayer, "the service of the heart," as one of the appropriate substitutes for sacrifice now that the Temple has become unavailable, and thus the Aqedah comes to underlie prayer as well. That very movement from sacrifice to prayer can be detected, in fact, in a midrash in the name of Rabbi Yochanan, a Talmudic sage who lived in the Land of Israel in the third century C.E.[31] According to this reading, after the angel of the LORD has called off the sacrifice of Isaac, Abraham points out that all along he had solid theological grounds for refusing to obey the command. After all, God had already promised him that his chosen line would come through Isaac (Gen 21:12). But did he refuse?

> Heaven forbid! I did not do this, but suppressed my feelings of compassion in order to do Your will. Just so, may it be Your will, O LORD our God, that, when Isaac's descendants come into trouble, You remember that Binding and be filled with compassion for them! (*Gen. Rab.* 56:10)

Here, Abraham prays that his subordination of paternal compassion in order to do God's will may become the ground for a reverse movement on the part of God: God should subordinate his own will, in turn, to compassion for the Jewish people in its affliction. The sacrifice having been called off, the positive results of sacrificial action thus paradoxically remain a real possibility.

Indeed, behind Rabbi Yochanan's midrash about the Aqedah we can detect the momentous change that has happened to Judaism and the Jews with the destruction of the Temple. In a sense, God's calling off the sacrifice of Isaac here foreshadows the loss of sacrifice, just as Abraham's prayer foreshadows the evocation of the Aqedah in the continuing Jewish liturgy, where it comes to play a prominent role. Suddenly finding himself unable to sacrifice, the obedient patriarch turns instead to prayer, but prayer that invokes the Aqedah in order to elicit compassion for the beleaguered Jewish people. The beneficial effects of Abraham's willingness to offer up his beloved son long survive the loss not only of child sacrifice (forbidden already in the Torah) but of animal and vegetal sacrifice as well. It is often said that in Judaism prayer replaced sacrifice, but in the theology underlying this text, prayer, instead, *re-presents* and *reactivates* sacrifice, and the paradigmatic sacrifice, the one that lies at the foundation of the Temple service and the service of the heart alike, is the Aqedah.[32] The first person to invoke it in prayer is, appropriately enough, Abraham himself.

In the Middle Ages, in some regions the idea emerged that it is commendable to recite the Aqedah every day, and eventually Genesis 22:1–19 made its way into many Jewish prayer books, where it now appears early in the morning service.[33] The prayer that follows it closely resembles Abraham's prayer in Rabbi Yochanan's midrash. The Jewish community petitions that just as Abraham suppressed his compassion to do God's will wholeheartedly, so God should now suppress his own anger and instead activate his mercy so as to fulfill his covenantal promise to the Jewish people. Abraham's prayer has become the prayer of the whole Jewish community and a basis for the continued existence of the oft-beleaguered people who still call him their father.

A different appropriation of the Aqedah into the continuing Jewish tradition appears first in the book of Jubilees, a retelling of Genesis and part of Exodus that dates to the second century B.C.E. Although Jubilees is not part of the Jewish canon of scripture that has come down over the centuries, it is a precious resource for anyone who wants to understand the history of Jewish biblical interpretation; indeed, some rabbinic interpretations are first attested in this pre-rabbinic book.

In the case of the Aqedah, Jubilees prefaces a debate in the heavenly cabinet, as it were, in which Prince Mastema (a diabolic adversary whose name means "Hostility") questions Abraham's faithfulness. "Behold, Abraham loves Isaac, his son," Prince Mastema observes to the LORD. "And he is more pleased with him than everything. Tell him to offer him [as] a burnt offering upon the altar. And you will see whether he will do this thing. And you will know whether he is faithful in everything in which you test him" (Jub 17:16). The narrator goes on to observe in his own voice that the LORD knew that "Abraham was faithful in all his afflictions because he tested him," and then lists seven such tests.[34] But Prince Mastema's accusation, though obviously modeled on Satan's challenge to God in the first two chapters of the biblical book of Job, cannot be dismissed out of hand, for if Abraham loves Isaac and is more pleased with him than with anything or anybody else, then the previous tests have been too limited to serve as true indications of the depth of the patriarch's faithfulness to God in affliction.

In Genesis, only the Aqedah is described in the language of testing; it is in Jubilees that we first meet the notion, so familiar to modern Jews from rabbinic tradition, that Abraham's life was punctuated by a set of ten tests. But whereas the rabbis saw the Binding as the grand finale, Jubilees, oddly, sees it as only the eighth, followed by Abraham's demonstration of self-control in negotiating with the Hittites for a grave site for Sarah and, last, by his refusal to accept the cave of Machpelah as a gift. Lest this be seen as an indication that Jubilees attributes little importance to the Aqedah, however, we must consider the date on which that book maintains it took place.

Prince Mastema renders his charge against Abraham on the twelfth day of the first month of the year. If we remember that it takes Abraham's party three days to arrive at the site of the sacrifice, we can reasonably infer that they did so toward the end of the fourteenth of the month. The late afternoon of the fourteenth of the first month is exactly the time when the Torah specifies that the Passover sacrifice must be offered.[35] Were there any suspicion that this is but coincidence, it would disappear with the notice in Jubilees that upon his return to Beer-sheba, Abraham instituted a seven-day festival to commemorate his journey. "And thus," Jubilees concludes its retelling of the Aqedah, "it is ordained and written in the heavenly tablets concerning Israel and his seed to observe the festival seven days with festal joy" (Jub 18:19). The only seven-day feast in the first month is, needless to say, Passover.

Abraham's instituting of Passover in Jubilees represents an early example in a pattern of things about him that will become familiar in later Jewish tradition. There is, for instance, his observance of laws (in this case the laws of the holiday) that, as the Torah would have it, would not be publicly revealed until the time of Moses.[36] Giving Passover an Abrahamic origin also establishes a tighter bond between the experience of the patriarch and that of his descendants than one would ever suspect on the basis of Genesis. When Passover is rooted in the Aqedah, Israel's slavery in Egypt becomes in turn a trial on the order of Abraham's great test. Indeed, in Jubilees the diabolic Prince Mastema plays a prominent role in the story of the Exodus, just as he did in the Aqedah. It is he who tries to kill Moses as the latter is returning to Egypt to confront Pharaoh; he who tries to aid Pharaoh's magicians as they attempt to counter Moses's miracles; and he who instigates the Egyptian pursuit of the emancipated Israelites. Only because the LORD at last binds and shuts away their diabolic accuser can the people Israel succeed in escaping from the House of Bondage.[37] Jubilees thus makes both the Aqedah and the Exodus testify to the existence of malicious and groundless accusations against the Jewish people and the intense suffering this might cause, yet also to God's gracious rescue of them after adversity.

The interlacing of Aqedah and Passover that we first find in Jubilees was perhaps inevitable, for both the stories of Abraham's near-sacrifice of Isaac and that of the Israelite redemption from Egypt reflect a ritual, known also outside of Israel, in which a sheep was substituted for the firstborn son who would otherwise be sacrificed.[38] As we have seen, the tension that energizes the Aqedah would be dissipated if we assumed that God always prefers the substitution, so that the sacrifice demanded of Abraham would never come about. Indeed, no such principled preference appears in Genesis 22, and Abraham's sacrifice of the ram in place of Isaac comes after a gracious, and startling, reprieve and with no indication that Israelite fathers over the generations are to imitate the practice. By contrast, the tenth plague in the story of the Exodus serves explicitly as the source of the substitution: "When Pharaoh stubbornly refused to let us go," the Israelite father is to tell his inquisitive son, "the LORD slew every first-born in the land of Egypt, the first-born of both man and beast. Therefore I sacrifice to the LORD every first male issue of the womb, but redeem every first-born among my sons" (Exod 13:15). In both the Aqedah and the story of the first Passover, the sheep substitutes for the son. The ram Abraham offers has become, as it were, the first paschal lamb.

Although the connections of the Aqedah with Passover will become highly important for understanding early Christianity, as we shall soon see, they have largely disappeared from Judaism. But some remnants of the earlier association may still be found in rabbinic Judaism, such as this text:

> "When I see the blood [I will pass over you]" (Exod 12:13). I see the blood of the Binding of Isaac. For it is said, "And Abraham named that site Adonai-Yireh ['the LORD will see']," etc. (Gen 22:14). Further on it says, "[God sent an angel to Jerusalem to destroy it,] but as he was about to wreak destruction, the LORD saw and renounced further punishment," etc. (1 Chr 21:25). What did he see? He saw the blood of the Binding of Isaac, as it is written, "God will see to the sheep," etc. (Gen 22:8). (*Mekhilta de-Rabbi Ishmael, pischa'* 7)

The verse cited from Exodus speaks of the blood of the paschal lamb, offered in protection of the Israelite firstborn in Egypt. To the rabbinic interpreter, however, that blood is only a cipher for the real blood of redemption—the blood of the Aqedah.

Since no blood is drawn from Isaac in Genesis 22, the question arises as to just what is meant here. Perhaps the comment reflects the rabbinic tradition that Abraham wanted to draw a token amount of blood from Isaac or, alternatively, the one in which he asked God to regard the sacrificial portions of the ram as if they were those of Isaac.[39] Or perhaps the comment assumes that God accounted Abraham's willingness to shed Isaac's blood as if the sacrifice had actually taken place, the intention being the equivalent of the deed. In any event, the point of this midrash is clear. It is to interpret the name that Abraham gives the place, "the LORD will see," as an indication that God will look upon the Aqedah when Israel is in dire straits in the future. God will not lose sight of the Binding of Isaac: it will stand to the benefit of the Jewish people in all their generations.

The notion that both the Aqedah and the Exodus involve the active opposition of a diabolic adversary fits well with the worldview of Jubilees in general, one in which God's struggle with demonic forces is central, as it is in much Second Temple Judaism. In rabbinic Judaism, too, the idea that the Jewish people are threatened by a demonic adversary who must be silenced and overcome remains alive and well.

In the rabbinic case, however, the theme comes to the fore not on Passover (which has a very different character) but on Rosh Hashanah, or, more broadly, on the ten days of repentance that extend from Rosh Hashanah through Yom Kippur, the Day of Atonement. In the liturgy that develops around those Days of Awe (as they are known), one of the most prominent images is forensic. The Jewish people stand accused of all manner of wrongdoing; they are on trial for their very lives. The difference from Passover in Jubilees is as simple as it is frightening: this time they are guilty and, to receive the acquittal they seek, they cannot possibly depend on their own moral record. They have no choice but to throw themselves upon the mercy of God and confess their manifold sins, resolve to do better, and suppliantly remind God of his irrevocable commitments to their ancestors (especially Abraham, Isaac, and Jacob) and the merit that those exemplary forebears, so unlike their sinning descendants, accrued. "Confound the Accuser and encourage the Defenders," reads one of the great liturgical poems of Rosh Hashanah, referring respectively to the diabolical adversary of the Jewish people and their angelic advocates.[40] And, as in the case of Prince Mastema in Jubilees, what could confound and silence the Accuser more effectively than the Aqedah? Where did God ever state his irrevocable commitment to the ancestors of the Jews more directly than in the second angelic address of Genesis 22:15–18? And, finally, where do we see his gracious intervention to convert a sentence of death into a gift of life more powerfully than in the story of the near-sacrifice of Isaac?

And so the idea emerged that the Aqedah took place not in the first month, Nisan, when Passover occurs, but in Tishri, the seventh month, in which the Days of Awe occur. One midrash connects the word for "seventh" (*shevi'i*) with that for "oath" (Aramaic, *shevu'ata*), for it was in that month, it is now said, that God swore the oath to Abraham after the patriarch had passed his great test (Gen 22:16). The midrash following this one represents a telling variant of Rabbi Yochanan's prayer that "when Isaac's descendants come into trouble, You remember that Binding and be filled with compassion for them!" This time the prayer has acquired a ritual occasion:

Thus, when the descendants of Isaac become involved in transgressions and bad deeds, may You remember for their benefit the Binding of Isaac and leave the Throne of Judgment for the Throne of Mercy, and, filled with compassion for them, may You have mercy upon them and change the Attribute of Justice into the Attribute of Mercy for their benefit. When? "In the seventh month." (*Leviticus Rabbah* 29:9, quoting Lev 23:24).

The dynamic of condemnation and reprieve, justice and mercy, gradually eclipsed the affinity of the Aqedah with the tenth plague and the paschal lamb, and the rabbinic tradition replaced Passover with the Days of Awe as the season to which the Aqedah was deemed most pertinent. Thus, the shofar, the ram's horn sounded on Rosh Hashanah, came to be associated with the ram "caught in the thicket by its horns" (Gen 22:13), which Abraham was graciously allowed to offer in place of his son. "Blow the horn of a ram before Me," a Talmudic sage presents God as commanding, "so that I may remember for your benefit the Binding of Isaac" (*b. Rosh Hashanah* [*Rosh. Hash.*] 16a). The "sacred occasion commemorated with loud blasts" of which the Torah speaks (Lev 23:24) is now an occasion for the Jews not only to commemorate Abraham's unflinching obedience and God's merciful intervention on Mount Moriah; it is also an occasion for them to remind God of the implications of that event for Abraham's unworthy descendants ever after.

Eventually, perhaps because the rabbis thought it was on Rosh Hashanah that "The LORD took note of Sarah as He had promised" (Gen 21:1),[41] Genesis 21 and Genesis 22 became the readings for the first and second days of Rosh Hashanah, respectively. It is on those days that Abraham's great test, always at the heart of religious Jews' relationship to God, becomes central to their worship as well—a recurring and unforgettable note in the rhythm of Jewish life.

We have noted that, whereas the biblical text leaves Isaac's age at the time of the Binding unclear, later Jewish sources are eager to make him an adult and thus a knowing and willing participant in what thereby becomes an act of self-sacrifice. The Jewish historian Flavius Josephus, for example, writing at the end of the first century C.E., tells us Isaac was twenty-five; a bit later, rabbinic tradition ascribes an age of twenty-six or thirty-seven.[42] One reason for the change is not hard to imagine—the desire to exonerate Abraham of the charge of child sacrifice. For, notwithstanding the sloppy use by many today of the term "paganism," the sacrifice of a child had never been the norm in the ancient Near East, and in Greco-Roman culture it was generally abhorred. Even for those lacking an apologetic motive like that of Josephus, who wrote in Greek for a Gentile audience, the implication that the revered first patriarch of the Jews was guilty of filicide was abhorrent. And since the Torah itself forbids child sacrifice and prophets roundly denounce it,[43] it is an implication that traditional Jews could not allow to stand unchallenged. If child sacrifice had ever been understood to be a principal theme of the Aqedah, that moment had long since vanished from memory.

A related reason for seeing Isaac as an adult—and indeed for shifting a major part of the focus to him—has to do with the profound effect of persecution and martyrdom on the evolution of Judaism. The English term "martyr" comes from a Greek word that signifies a "witness"; a martyr is at base a person who refuses to falsify his or her testimony about God even at the point of death. The sacrifice made by martyrs is not of property or even of loved ones; it is of themselves, of their very lives. That Abraham, in Qimchi's words, "loved [Isaac] more than he loved himself" may well be true of the narrative in Genesis 22, but it is no derogation of the father to point out that this says nothing about Isaac's understanding of the event. And it is in the position of Isaac, not as the agent but as the intended victim of the sacrifice, that martyrs find themselves.

Thus, after the bloody persecution of the Jews by the Seleucids, a Syrian dynasty of Greek origin in 167–164 B.C.E. (the holiday of Chanukkah commemorates the Jewish victory over the Seleucids), the Aqedah assumed new importance, but this time with Isaac as a major focus. Fourth Maccabees, a Jewish treatise written perhaps two hundred years later and not part of the Jewish canon of scripture, is a particularly moving example. It enlarges upon a well-known incident, already reported in 2 Maccabees 6–7, in which the aged priest Eleazar and a Jewish woman and all seven of her sons choose death over obedience to the tyrant Antiochus's decree that all Jews must "eat pork and food sacrificed to idols" (4 Mac 5:2), that is, violate the commandment of the Torah in public.[44] The stout refusal of the Jewish traditionalists to renounce their Torah and the God who commands it serves as exceptionally powerful evidence for the central argument of this very philosophical, very Greek, yet very traditionally Jewish work—that reason can be sovereign over the emotions and provide equanimity even in the face of death.

Note especially the scriptural reference in the description of Eleazar as the fire was consuming him:

> [13]Most amazing, indeed, though he was an old man, his body no longer tense and firm, his muscles flabby, his sinews feeble, he became young again [14]in spirit through reason; and by reason like that of Isaac he rendered the many-headed rack ineffective. [15]O man of blessed age and of venerable gray hair and of law-abiding life, whom the faithful seal of death has perfected! (4 Mac 7:13–15)

The aged priest triumphs over his torturers—and over the physical and mental pain in which he found himself—"by reason like that of Isaac." This is not an Isaac who knows not what awaits him or objects to it or cowers before it. This, rather, is the Isaac who is the prototypical Jewish martyr—faithful and unafraid to the end, master of his destiny because it is the destiny God has decreed and to which he has submitted, thereby making God's will his will.

Isaac's name appears again in a speech of the mother to her children after they have seen Eleazar's physical demise but spiritual victory:

> [16]"My sons, noble is the contest to which you are called to bear witness for the nation. Fight zealously for our ancestral law. [17]For it would be shameful if, while an aged man endures such agonies for the sake of religion, you young men were to be terrified by tortures. [18]Remember that it is through God that you have had a share in the world and have enjoyed life, [19]and therefore you ought to endure any suffering for the sake of God. [20]For his sake also our father Abraham was zealous to sacrifice his son Isaac, the ancestor of our nation; and when Isaac saw his father's hand wielding a knife and descending upon him, he did not cower. (4 Mac 16:16–20)

Here, the mother takes the role of "father Abraham," urging her children to sacrifice themselves rather than to shame the Torah and the nation that has so long kept it. As the narrator in his own voice puts it, "Sympathy for her children did not sway the mother of the young men; she was of the same mind as Abraham" (4 Mac 14:20). And, for their part, they are to be of the same mind as Isaac, who, in this interpretation of the Aqedah, actually "saw his father's hand wielding a knife and descending upon him [but] did not cower."

This new image of Isaac at the Aqedah has reverberated throughout the long history of Jewish martyrdom. More generally, it has brought about a refocusing in which he as much as his father becomes the hero of the story. To Jews not facing martyrdom—for in Judaism martyrdom is something that happens, not something to seek or provoke—Isaac is still a model: he is a model of the wholehearted surrender to the will of God that is expected of every Jew and available any time a mitsvah (commandment) comes to hand. Earlier, we excerpted a Talmudic statement that shows how the shofar came to be associated with the Aqedah. The full statement shows in striking fashion the transformation that we have been tracing:

> Rabbi Abbahu said: Why do we blow the horn of a ram? The Holy One, blessed be He, said: "Blow the horn of a ram before Me so that I may remember for your benefit the Binding of Isaac, and I will account it to you as if you had bound yourselves before Me." (b. Rosh. Hash. 16a)

Through the shofar sounded on Rosh Hashanah, the Jews keep the Aqedah alive in circumstances in which its literal enactment has become quite impossible. They cannot commit themselves to God's will and providence in quite the way Isaac did, but through the shofar ritual they can demonstrate their willingness to do so and, in the process, benefit from the grace of God that continues to flow from the memory of Abraham's—and Isaac's—test. The intention is, again, the equivalent of the deed.

Turning now to Christian interpretation of Abraham's great test and its connection to the Jewish one, we recall first of all that in Jubilees and the Jewish traditions it reflects, the Aqedah is the origin of Passover; but for the LORD's sudden intervention, Isaac would thus have been the first paschal lamb.[45] Paschal associations are likewise of paramount importance in the reports of Jesus's death in the New Testament.

The first three gospels, in fact, present the trial and execution of Jesus as taking place on the first day of Passover, a Friday; John, by contrast, reflects a year in which Passover began not on a Thursday evening but on a Friday evening, so that the Sabbath and the onset of Passover coincided. In John's telling, Jesus thus dies just as the sacrificial slaughter of the paschal lambs is about to be performed in the Jerusalem Temple. But John goes even further: in this account, the Roman soldiers, seeing that Jesus, unlike the two criminals crucified with him, is already dead, decline to break his legs "so that the scripture might be fulfilled, 'None of his bones shall be broken'" (John 19:36, quoting Exod 12:46).[46] The scriptural verse in Exodus actually speaks not about a person but about the paschal lamb. Its application to the Crucifixion indicates beyond doubt that the evangelist conceives of Jesus's death just before Passover as itself paschal and sacrificial.

In early Christian literature, in one way or another, the identification of Jesus with the Passover sacrifice is in plentiful evidence. Paul, for example, is more explicit than John. "For our paschal lamb, Christ," he writes, "has been sacrificed" (1 Cor 5:7). But we should not be surprised by this. In light of the tight connection between the first paschal lamb and Isaac in Jubilees as well as the ubiquitous "son" language applied to Jesus throughout the New Testament, we have here, in the identification of Jesus with Isaac, a triangle completed.

Consider this text from one of Paul's early letters:

> Now the promises were made to Abraham and to his offspring; it does not say, "And to offsprings," as of many; but it says, "And to your offspring," that is, to one person, who is Christ. (Gal 3:16)

Here, Paul spins his own midrash on the word *sperma*, which is used in the Jewish translation of the Torah into Greek to render the Hebrew word *zera'*, meaning "seed" but also "offspring, progeny, descendants." Both terms are singular in form but collective in meaning: they refer to a group of people—in the case at hand, to Abraham's offspring who inherit the promise made to him.[47] Paul, however, takes the fact that the word is singular in form to indicate that it does not, after all, refer to the Jewish people, but to just one descendant of Abraham.

Were Jews to do likewise, they would say that in Genesis the one descendant is Abraham's promised son, the only one who inherits the covenant and to whom God specifically applies the promises, namely, Isaac. But Paul has another descendant of Abraham in mind; in his mind, Jesus is the real beneficiary of the promises to Abraham.

It is not wrong to say that Isaac here serves as a typological foreshadowing of the Christ, in a way that recalls the use of the Aqedah as a foreshadowing of the death and resurrection of Jesus in the Letter to the Hebrews, as we have seen. That, however, is to miss a key fact: Isaac's name is missing from this passage in Galatians. Isaac does not foreshadow Jesus so much as Jesus *supersedes* Isaac. The Crucifixion, then, comes about "in order that in Christ Jesus the blessing of Abraham might come to the Gentiles" (Gal 3:14).[48] As in the case of the Aqedah, so in that of the Crucifixion, in the end all the nations of the world are, at least potentially, affected for the better. Where this new Aqedah leaves the Jews, however, is at best ambiguous and at worst ominous.

If Jesus is a realization of Isaac, who then is the realization of Abraham? Given Jesus's identification as the "Son of God," the answer is obvious. As Jesus becomes the new Isaac, so God becomes the new Abraham. Consider this famous verse from the Gospel of John: "For God so loved the world that he gave his only Son, so that everyone who believes in him may not perish but may have eternal life" (John 3:16). In context, the "giving" in question can refer only to Jesus's sacrificial death. The verse may, in fact, reflect Exodus 22:28—"You shall give Me the first-born among your sons"—where "give" must refer to an act of sacrifice or a ritual substitution for it. In John, though, it is not a case of people giving God their sons, but of God giving people his son, and doing it, significantly, from the motive that in some Jewish interpretations underlies Abraham's obedience in the Aqedah: the motive of love.

It is in Paul, though, that the precedent of the Aqedah becomes explicit:

[28]We know that all things work together for good for those who love God, who are called according to his purpose. [29]For those whom he foreknew he also predestined to be conformed to the

image of his Son, in order that he might be the firstborn within a large family. [30]And those whom he predestined he also called; and those whom he called he also justified; and those whom he justified he also glorified.

[31]What then are we to say about these things? If God is for us, who is against us? [32]He who did not withhold his own Son, but gave him up for all of us, will he not with him also give us everything else? (Rom 8:28–32)

Here, too, we see the theme of love and the language of giving, but in verse 32 the opposite of giving is, tellingly, cast in the language of "not withhold[ing]" so familiar from the two angelic addresses in the Aqedah (Gen 22:12, 16). God, like Abraham, has passed his great test, and having not withheld his son, he will surely give every other good thing to those who, proving themselves also to be like Abraham, love God. God and the Christians have both, as it were, been reenvisioned in the image of Abraham, just as Jesus and the Christians (again) have been reenvisioned in the image of Isaac.

Reverberating throughout Christian tradition, this interpretation of the Aqedah as an adumbration of the Crucifixion and the Resurrection becomes more explicit and more detailed—in the same centuries, and often in the same lands, in which the rabbis were filling in the gaps with their own midrashim. That the commonality can be misleading, however, is evident from this representative fragment from Melito of Sardis, a bishop in Asia Minor (now Turkey) in the late second century C.E.:

As a ram he was bound,
he says concerning our Lord Jesus Christ,
and as a lamb he was shorn,
and as a sheep he was led to slaughter,
and as a lamb he was crucified.
And he bore the wood on his shoulders,
going up to slaughter like Isaac at the hand of his father.
But Christ suffered.
Isaac did not suffer,
for he was a type of the passion of Christ which was to come.[49]

Melito shatters the convenient sense of concord between the narratives—and thus between Judaism and Christianity in general—with that one brief but enormously significant contrast: "But Christ suffered. / Isaac did not suffer." Isaac is the type, the sketch, the symbol. But Christ is the reality, and the reality always surpasses the symbol. Indeed, like most Christians until modern times and some even now, Melito finds indefensible the continued Jewish adherence to what now, in his mind, has become only an "Old Testament":

37) When the thing comes about of which the sketch was a type,
that which was to be, of which the type bore the likeness,
then the type is destroyed, it has become useless,
it yields up the image to what is truly real.
What was once valuable becomes worthless,
when what is of true value appears.

40) Thus the people was a type, like a preliminary sketch,
and the law was the writing of an analogy.
The Gospel is the narrative and the fulfillment of the law,
And the church is the repository of reality.

41) So the type was valuable in advance of the reality,
and the illustration was wonderful before its elucidation.
So the people were valuable before the church arose,
And the law was wonderful before the illumination of the Gospel.

42) But when the church arose and the Gospel came to be,
the type, depleted, gave up meaning to the truth:
and the law, fulfilled, gave up meaning to the Gospel.
    (*On Pascha*, 37, 40–42)[50]

A modern critical historian would say that the Aqedah, as filtered through centuries of Jewish teaching, has colored the interpretation of the very end of Jesus's life in the New Testament—more, that it has had an important role in shaping key Christological concepts. To an early churchman like Melito, however, the direction is the reverse:

Christology unlocks the meaning of the Aqedah, just as it unlocks the meaning of everything else in the Old Testament. Once that meaning has become known, the preliminaries stand voided of their meaning; the Jewish people and their Torah have been replaced by the Church and its Gospel, to which they always pointed.

That the Jews would continue to exist as a distinct community and devote themselves to their Torah was no less significant to the rabbis than to Melito. But what was extremely positive to them was equally negative to him. And this is not just a matter of the past. Still today, the fact that Judaism and Christianity share scriptures in general and revere the narratives about the patriarchs in particular constitutes a historical bond, and even a theological bond of sorts; but it also constitutes a formidable barrier. All the talk in the world about the common scriptures of Judaism and Christianity, their common rooting in Father Abraham, and the similarity of their interpretive techniques and moral and theological claims cannot paper over the great question that the survival of the Jews and Judaism after the rise of Christianity poses for Christian theology and for Jewish-Christian relations.

If, in the New Testament, the Aqedah makes itself felt only through citation and echo, in the Muslim scripture, the Qur'an, it appears as a narrative in its own right, though a very short and cryptic one.[51] It begins with Abraham's announcing to his son that while sleeping,[52] he has seen himself slaughtering him. "My father, do what you are commanded," the son replies, "you will find me, Allah willing, one of the steadfast" (37:102). But after they have both submitted, God calls out to Abraham to tell him that it is but a test and provides a large sacrifice by way of ransom. And with that the story is over.

In the Qur'an, the son's urging his father to obey the command and proving to be "one of the steadfast" reflects the long-standing Jewish tradition in which Isaac is a fully witting adult, a prototype, in fact, of the martyr. It is possible that Christian traditions about Isaac's Christlike submission to the cross also play a role here. There is, however, an enormous difference between the biblical and the Qur'anic accounts, and it involves the identity of the son brought for sacrifice.

In Genesis 22, the one bound is Isaac, who is named four times. In the Qur'anic account, the son is unnamed throughout. Early Muslim exegetes engaged in a vigorous debate over his identity, dividing about equally between proponents of Isaac and proponents of Ishmael.[53] Having surveyed the relevant material from the first two Muslim centuries, Reuven Firestone concludes that the identification of the unnamed son with Isaac was the older tradition.[54] But subsequent centuries have seen such a massive shift toward Ishmael that it is not unusual for contemporary Muslims to be surprised to learn that respected figures in their tradition ever thought otherwise. Already in the eleventh century C.E., an important Muslim commentator wrote, "The Jews claim that it was Isaac, but the Jews lie."[55]

The Qur'anic silence about the identity of the son reflects a much larger and more portentous difference between the understandings of the Aqedah in Judaism and Christianity, on the one hand, and in Islam, on the other. Recall that in Genesis 22, Abraham's refusal to withhold his son results in God's reiteration, this time under oath, of his promise to Abraham of blessing and national greatness. Within Genesis, the promise can be realized only through Isaac, who alone is the heir to the covenant (Ishmael is explicitly barred from that status in Gen 17:21); by the time of the Aqedah, Ishmael has been removed from the Abrahamic household and has anyway been reported to have married an Egyptian woman. In leaving the identity of the son open, the Qur'an indicates that the question of the chosen nation is of no import to the story—which is quite the opposite of the biblical narrative.

Another way of putting this is to say that the Qur'anic Abraham is not the father of the Jewish people or the Christian Church at all: he is, rather, a faithful, obedient, and monotheistic prophet, a member of a chain of prophets that begins with Adam, includes men like Moses and Jesus, and culminates in Muhammad, "the seal of the Prophets" (33:40). Here Abraham is best seen as a prefiguration of Muhammad, and his obedience in what Jews call the Aqedah is one example among several of his "submission" to God (the meaning of Arabic *islām*, which names a spiritual act and not merely a religion). In the Qur'an, he is not, as for the Jews, "Our Father Abraham." He is a Muslim prophet, and, as the Qur'an puts it, "the people who are worthiest of Abraham are those who followed him, together with this Prophet and the believers" (3:68)—"this Prophet" being, of course, Muhammad.

Whereas Jews and Christians argue about the interpretation of their common text, often augmenting and thus altering it in the process, Muslims begin with a different text, a different story—and, as a result, arguably a very different Abraham.

In 1798, near the end of his life, the great German philosopher Immanuel Kant published a short volume entitled *The Conflict of the Faculties*. Dealing with the relationships among different disciplines in the university, the book argues vigorously in favor of the Enlightenment ideal of academic freedom and, more specifically, against the notion that philosophy must defer to theology. In particular, philosophical thinking precludes a rational person from accepting the claim that any given text represents the word of God:

> For if God should really speak to a human being, the latter could still never *know* that it was God speaking. It is quite impossible for a human being to apprehend the infinite by his senses, distinguish it from sensible beings, and *be acquainted with* it as such. —But in some cases the human being can be sure that the voice he hears is *not* God's; for if the voice commands him to do something that is contrary to the moral law, then no matter how majestic the apparition may be, and no matter how it may seem to surpass the whole of nature, he must consider it an illusion. (emphasis in the original)

What is clear for Kant, then, is the moral law; what can never be clear is that the commanding voice one hears, or imagines one hears, is God's. If that voice commands something immoral, however, we can be quite sure it is not God's. In a footnote, Kant then provides a familiar illustration:

> We can use, as an example, the myth of the sacrifice that Abraham was going to make by butchering and burning his only son at God's command (the poor child, without knowing it, even brought the

wood for the fire). Abraham should have replied to this supposedly divine voice: "That I ought not to kill my good son is quite
certain. But that you, this apparition, are God—of that I am not
certain, and never can be, not even if this voice rings down to me
from (visible) heaven."[56]

If in Genesis 22 and its Jewish, Christian, and Muslim interpretations Abraham passed his great test, in Kant's thinking he failed it
miserably. He proved willing to kill an innocent person in response
to a voice whose very command proves beyond doubt that it cannot
be of God.

There are, in fact, serious problems of interpretation concealed
in Kant's brief and ostensibly commonsensical handling of the Aqedah.[57] For one thing, one would never guess from it that the biblical story derives from a tradition in which child sacrifice had been
strictly forbidden and even, as we have seen, branded as emblematic
of idolatry at its worst. That, from an early period and perhaps from
the beginning, the story must have served as a paradigm of something other than the forbidden practice may seem obvious to us, but
it quite escaped Immanuel Kant. It is fascinating to speculate why.

One reason is that Kant abstracted the story not only from the
larger web of biblical law and theology but also from the story of
Abraham in Genesis. His Abraham is not a unique personage, the
bearer of a divine promise and of a special, unparalleled destiny.
And his Isaac is not the long-awaited son, born of a unique promise
and in defiance of nature, the person on whom Abraham's promise depends. Rather, Kant's Abraham is Everyman, Isaac is simply
Everyman's "good son," and Everyman should surely know to avoid
"butchering and burning" his good son. That the phrase "butchering
and burning" may not do justice to the complex, if mystifying, dynamics of sacrifice in biblical Israel is another thought that Kant does
not entertain. For him, sacrifice is simply killing. The all-important
difference between the two acts in Israelite culture (and biblical terminology) quite eluded him.[58]

The effect of Kant's thinking is to remove the Aqedah from the
realm of narrative and theology and to relocate it foursquare within
the domain of ethics. Once the story is analyzed as an ethical parable,

Abraham, of course, can be only a negative model.[59] How could it ever be ethical to kill an innocent boy in cold blood?

In locating the story exclusively within the domain of ethics, Kant proved to be a forerunner of much with which we are familiar today, when in some circles the negative interpretation of the Binding of Isaac has become a staple and Abraham is seen as a model of the abusive father, the violent male, the man pathologically anxious about the paternity of his offspring, the hideousness of "patriarchy" in general, and much else along the same thoroughly repellent lines.[60] The man the Jews have for millennia called "Our Father Abraham" has now become the parade example of a horrible father, indeed even of everything that is wrong with fatherhood in general. The great patriarch of the Bible and Qur'an has become the great object lesson in the evils of patriarchy. And as if that were not enough to invert the traditional evaluation, an effort has now been made to associate our narrative with the motives underlying the September 11, 2001, terrorist attacks on the United States. One biblical scholar, for example, focuses on two letters by the Muslim hijackers that were found in the Boston airport. Such elements as references to God and use of the Arabic word for a sacred slaughter—a sacrifice, in other words—suggest to her that "the two al-Qaeda documents more than hint at an allusion to the Abrahamic sacrifice in the Qur'an."[61]

Efforts to cast Abraham's behavior in the Aqedah as villainous rather than heroic are rather obviously indebted to Kant's uncompromising and enormously influential subordination of religion to ethics. As such, they draw attention to the huge gulf between the religious traditions in their premodern form, on the one hand, and contemporary thinking, on the other. In so doing, though, they also raise the question of why the stigmatized behaviors in question are not more widespread among practitioners of the traditions that revere Abraham. In other words, why are Jews, Christians, and Muslims *not* sacrificing their beloved sons? Why are so few Muslims engaged in mass murder à la the 9/11 suicide bombers? Let us turn first to the cases of Judaism and Christianity.

From contemporary arguments about Abraham the villainous child abuser, one might miss just how rare such behavior is in Western societies—all the more striking in light of the frequency of the preaching, studying, and reading of the Bible, especially in American culture. One book roundly indicting Abraham and the Aqedah, for example, centers on the case of a man in California who, some time after Genesis 22 had been studied in his church (it is not clear he was there), murdered his daughter in response to what he took to be the voice of God. It turns out, however, that the man had suffered head injuries, had a long history of alcoholism, hallucinated about a variety of voices, and was diagnosed as mentally ill by the professionals who examined him. If the problem is so common, why did the author not pick a stronger example?[62] And is there any reason to think that an individual so deeply impaired really needed Genesis 22 to perpetrate his gruesome crime?

Leaving aside the mentally ill, let us ask about the necessary assumptions that sane Christian or Jewish adults today would have to make in order to imagine that Genesis 22 authorizes the murder of their children. Our answer will be critical to determining the religious identity of such persons—and why they are so very rare.[63]

One obvious assumption would have to be that the Torah's prohibitions on human sacrifice in general, and child sacrifice in particular, do not apply. For with those prohibitions, the Torah criminalizes the imagined act. Similarly but more generally, the Torah's absolute restriction of sacrifice exclusively to the Temple in Jerusalem prevents all sacrifice today. Indeed, the Torah explicitly draws an uncompromising distinction between what was permitted in this regard before Sinai and what is permitted ever after.[64] Since the Temple was destroyed by the Romans in 70 C.E. and has never been rebuilt, Judaism quite forbids the act that some imagine Genesis 22 legitimates.

These points may seem rather technical, but they are very prominent in the Torah and Jewish tradition more broadly. They are also very well known among people with even a minimal Jewish education. Clearly, then, the fathers who would seek to sacrifice their sons because Abraham did so would not be practitioners of traditional Judaism. For, to use the rabbinic idiom, they would have thrown off the yoke of the Torah. They would be acting in violation, not fulfillment, of their religion.

Might they then be Christians? After all, Christianity has long taught that the law and the commandments have been entirely or mostly nullified or superseded but that the nonlegal sections of the

Pentateuch should be revered nonetheless. To put the issue again in rabbinic terminology, some Christians, having *aggadah* (story) but not *halakhah* (law), might theoretically try to use a Pentateuchal narrative, in violation of the explicit norm, as the basis for practical action, something the rabbinic tradition cannot countenance. Another assumption of such people would presumably be that an individual can determine moral action by scrutiny of the Bible alone, without deference to any continuing authority. In Roman Catholic terms, for example, they would not acknowledge the teaching authority of the bishops. So, we would be dealing not with Christians in general or people who think like Christians but specifically with Protestant Christians or people who, on this issue, think like Protestants—or, to be more precise, Protestants of the particular sort that acknowledge no authority other than their personal interpretation of the Bible. (Not surprisingly, Kant's own background was Protestant, though he would probably not have been too happy to find out how much it had biased and narrowed his understanding of the Bible and religion in general.)

A third assumption that any who would imitate Abraham's deed must make is that prophecy not only exists today but also has authority— so much authority, in fact, that it can override the explicit norms of scripture, not to mention other sources of authority to which the vast majority even of Protestants defer. This last assumption is critical because without it, those who think they hear the voice of God would have to concede Kant's point that, since we cannot be sure the voice really *is* God's, we must not act on the basis of its directive alone. But that assumption, in turn, baldly contradicts the major lines of thinking in both Judaism and Christianity. In a society that does not generally regard prophecy as alive and authoritative (unlike ancient Israel), it is also a notion that is likely to cast a reasonable suspicion of mental illness upon the person who holds it.

As for Islam, here the issue is more complex. The accusation that the Qur'anic version of the Aqedah lies in the background of the mass murders and suicides of September 11, 2001, and kindred atrocities underestimates the ostensible theological basis for the crimes in the minds of the perpetrators themselves—namely, the

Muslim institution of jihad.[65] But jihad is a matter of law, and as such has long constituted a highly complex issue and been the subject of much disagreement among Muslim authorities. In particular, we must not miss the constraints that some authorities have historically placed on the practice—constraints upon the conditions that render jihad either legitimate or illicit, upon who may be targeted, and upon what sort of force may be used—as well as the willingness of some Muslims in our time to act in violation of traditional restrictions and their justifications for so doing.

Now if this is true for jihad, the immediate theological basis for 9/11 in the minds of its perpetrators, it is all the more true for the Muslim story of Abraham's near-sacrifice of his unnamed son. As in the cases of traditional Judaism and Christianity, there would be profound theological and legal problems with a devout Muslim who, on the basis of that story, tried to kill people, whether office workers in an American skyscraper, Israelis on a bus, or his own son. Here again, the attempt to make the Aqedah the parade example of religiously inspired violence is forced. The violence is surely a problem; the connection to the Aqedah is, at best, weak.

The extreme rarity of attempts to imitate the Aqedah turns out, then, to be no coincidence. The three religious traditions through which the Aqedah is handed down have almost always bundled it with prohibitions upon child sacrifice (and murder, of course) that make it quite illicit to duplicate Abraham's deed today. Simply citing the story without concern for these larger traditional structures and their characteristic ethics hardly justifies the idea that it is a source of violence against children among religious people. Before we could accept such a claim, we would need to have a scientific comparison of the rates of such violence among two groups—those who regularly read the Bible (including, of course, Genesis 22) and those who do not—controlling, of course, for other variables, including mental illness. It would also help to have a scientific comparison of the same rates in cultures in which Genesis 22 is known and respected and those in which it is not, such as those in which Christians and Muslims are few and far between. Indeed, we can go further. Since the story told in that text is most important and most frequently cited in Judaism, it would be interesting to see whether the rates of child abuse are, as the hypothesis would predict, higher among Jews than among Christians (or Muslims), for whom it is less central.

Though such studies have not, to my knowledge, been conducted, there is good reason to suspect the results would embarrass those who, to one degree or another, charge the Aqedah with contributing to such societal ills. If so, this would raise other important questions: Why, for example, has the charge become so popular, and why do those who advance it feel so little need for empirical evidence to support it?

We have been arguing that in the three Abrahamic religious traditions Abraham's literal deed is not presented as something to be duplicated by those who revere his memory. This does not, however, render the story obsolete, as many in the modern world have wished to do. Rather, it directs our attention away from child sacrifice (which may never have been its focus) onto Abraham's absolute commitment to God—his obedience to God, his faith in God, his love of God. These, the traditions maintain, are priceless spiritual habits whose relevance, like that of the Aqedah, has not faded.

In the case of Judaism, the Aqedah becomes, as we have mentioned, a paradigm for the Jews' commitment to God's will. Precluded from performing a sacrifice like Abraham's and, most of the time (thankfully), from testifying to their God and his Torah with their very lives like Isaac, Jews can still reenact the profound message of the Aqedah in their self-surrender to the will of God in the form of observance of the mitsvot, the commandments of the Torah. The daily life of the practicing Jew itself can continue to enact the profound spiritual dynamics that are at the heart of the Binding of Isaac.

## CHAPTER FOUR

## The Rediscovery of God

> You are searching for the God of gods, the Creator, in the under-
> standing of your heart. I am he.
>
> —Apocalypse of Abraham[1]

ONE ASPECT OF the Hebrew Bible that immediately draws even a ca-
sual reader's attention is the intense and pervasive rivalry it records
between the God of Israel and the deities of the environing peoples.
The former, most often referred to by the four-letter name "YHVH"
(rendered into English as "the LORD"), is very often depicted as em-
broiled in fierce competition against the other gods for the loyalty of
the people Israel. Although the biblical texts portray these rivals as
foreign, they cannot deny their appeal to the Israelites or disguise the
fact that those loyal to the LORD alone found themselves at times a
pronounced and vulnerable minority. "How long will you keep hop-
ping between the two boughs?" the ninth-century prophet Elijah, no
friend of interfaith services, thunders on Mount Carmel. "If the LORD
is God, follow Him; and if Baal, follow him!" (1 Kgs 18:21).[2] Offering abundant evidence for the ferocity of the struggle for YHVHistic
purism, biblical law proscribes anyone who sacrifices to another
god, demands that the Canaanite altars and icons be smashed to
pieces, and specifies capital punishment for any Israelite, prophet or
layman, who counsels that those gods be worshipped.[3] "For he urged
disloyalty to the LORD your God . . ." Deuteronomy explains. "Thus
you will sweep out evil from your midst" (13:6).

The issue in these texts is not ontological but political or, better,
theopolitical; that is, the question is not whether these other gods
exist but whether Israel may serve them, and to that question the
answer is, of course, a resounding "no!" As the loyal servant of their

lord in covenant, Israel must demonstrate exclusive fealty to YHVH; anything else is treason—a betrayal of God's own love and a misdirection of the love he expects in return. No wonder that prophets invoke a wife's adultery as a metaphor for Israel's apostasy. And no wonder that some biblical texts, especially from or about an early period, assume the existence of other deities, the other gods that Israel is not to have above or besides the LORD.[4]

In such texts, that outsiders may worship the other gods with impunity is either assumed or simply unaddressed. As time went on, however, in their eagerness to dissuade Israelites from defecting to these gods or including them in their worship, biblical texts began to identify each god with his or her physical icon. The message is loud and clear: Only the LORD is a transcendent personal being, whereas his longtime rivals are but wood and stone, "the work of men's hands" (Ps 115:4; 135:15), and their worshippers the worst of fools, unable to understand that material objects cannot save them.[5]

It need not concern us here that this reductive conception of icons did not correspond well to the ways those who used them understood their relationship to the divine person they represented or manifested. Such satires were for internal consumption, directed not at the Gentiles but at the Israelites themselves. Within that audience—though there was always unevenness and backsliding—they eventually had a powerful effect.

One other development is worthy of attention here. With the increasing Mesopotamian influence in Israelite culture in the eighth and seventh centuries B.C.E. (when Assyria was the dominant power, and Israel and Judah were sometimes its vassal), the worship of heavenly bodies as manifestations of deities and as portents became prominent. Thus, at the beginning of a polemical oracle cautioning the House of Israel against icons, seen again as only "the work of a craftsman's hands" unable "to do any good" (Jer 10:1–5), the prophet Jeremiah sounds a new note:

Thus said the LORD:
Do not learn to go the way of the nations,
And do not be dismayed by portents in the sky. (Jer 10:2)

The heavenly bodies are no more divine, no more in control of history, and no more worthy of worship than the hunks of wood and stone out of which the craftsman produces his scandalous icon.

The message is clear once more: Those who lift their eyes to the heavens may be just as idolatrous as those who fabricate or adore graven images. What is more, the gods they worship have no right to exist. As an Aramaic gloss in the same chapter of Jeremiah (which is otherwise altogether in Hebrew) puts it, "Thus shall you say to them: Let the gods, who did not make heaven and earth, perish from the earth and from under these heavens" (Jer 10:11). There is only one creator, and he is the master of all that is in the heavens above and on the earth beneath. And that is very bad news for his rivals.

When we turn to the story of Abraham in Genesis, we cannot but be struck by the absence of any hint of this familiar interreligious rivalry. At no point there does Abraham utter even a word of testimony to the uniqueness, incomparability, or exclusive claim of his God, and at no point does he direct even a word of criticism at the gods of those with whom he interacts or the ways they are worshipped. When "the LORD afflicted Pharaoh and his household with mighty plagues on account of Sarai" in Genesis 12:17, neither the narrator nor Abram (who says nothing at all) gives any indication that Pharaoh was an idolater who failed to understand the source of his adversity. This, needless to say, stands in striking contrast to the account of Pharaoh in the Exodus narrative.[6]

Similarly, when Abraham passes his wife off as his sister a second time (Gen 20), on this occasion with King Abimelech of Gerar, and God appears to the latter in a monitory dream, there is no sense that the foreign monarch worships another god or shamelessly identifies the Deity with an icon. In fact, it is Abraham who mistakenly thinks, "surely there is no fear of God in this place," and the foreign king who berates the Israelite prophet for his ethical lapse (vv. 9–11): a man-bites-dog story if ever there was one. In his encounter with Melchizedek, priest-king of Salem, Abram receives without protest the latter's blessing in the name of "God Most High (*'El 'Elyon*), / Creator of heaven and earth." Far from rejecting this God as an intolerable rival to his own, Abram soon thereafter swears in the name of "the LORD, God Most High," thus identifying the two (Gen 14:17–24).

It bears mention that in the expression rendered as "God Most High," both terms (*'El* and *'Elyon*) are known as names of deities in the ancient Near East apart from Israel. One scholar makes a good case that the second word here "serves as a proper epithet of [the Canaanite god] 'Ēl and is not an intrusive element in the formula."[7] This alone would strongly argue against seeing Abraham as standing in opposition to the gods of the surrounding peoples in Genesis.

Even when Abraham does act in opposition to others, as in his campaign in the same chapter against the four Mesopotamian kings, there is no sense that he is motivated by any religious difference. The same goes for his pleading on behalf of a hypothetical righteous minority in Sodom in chapter 18, with its implication that the city could plausibly be other than a den of benighted idolaters. Indeed, nothing in that episode suggests that the Sodomites' theology or their modes of worship had anything to do with their wickedness. Finally, when Abraham instructs his steward to avoid "the daughters of the Canaanites" (Gen 24:3) in his search for a wife for Isaac, the reason commonly given elsewhere for avoiding intermarriage—that "their daughters will lust after their gods and will cause your sons to lust after their gods" (Exod 34:16)—is conspicuous for its absence.

Historians offer a variety of explanations for this distinctive pattern. Some see it as reflecting a very ancient situation in which the interreligious rivalry dominant in most of the Hebrew Bible had not yet emerged. Other scholars move in exactly the opposite direction, interpreting the Abraham narrative as reflecting the Persian period (538–332 B.C.E.), when the Jewish community, some of its members only recently returned from exile in Babylonia, was a vulnerable sector of a religiously plural province governed by the Persians and thus in no position to attack anybody else's religion. Still others see the difference as social rather than chronological and believe the patriarchal narratives reflect the religion of the family, with its focus on land, lineage, and inheritance, rather than that of the royal city and its Temple, so concerned with priesthood, liturgy, and power relations.[8] Although religious traditionalists might at first be inclined to advocate the first option, since it presupposes the historical accuracy of the biblical narrative, in the case of the thoughtful Jewish traditionalist the matter is more complicated still. For the Jewish tradition over the centuries develops an Abraham who, it turns out, is every bit as involved in interreligious polemic as Elijah or Jeremiah.

If Genesis offers no direct support for the transformation of Abraham into a monotheistic purist, a better prospect is the farewell address of Joshua, Moses's successor:

> ²Then Joshua said to all the people, "Thus said the LORD, the God of Israel: 'In olden times, your forefathers—Terah, father of Abraham and father of Nahor—lived beyond the Euphrates and worshiped other gods. ³But I took your father Abraham from beyond the Euphrates and led him through the whole land of Canaan and multiplied his offspring. I gave him Isaac, ⁴and to Isaac I gave Jacob and Esau. I gave Esau the hill country of Seir as his possession, while Jacob and his children went down to Egypt.'" (Josh 24:2–4)

This makes Abraham's exodus from Mesopotamia a change not only of location but also of gods, unless, of course, Abram worshipped the LORD while still in his father's idolatrous household. That he did just that, breaking with his father even before his call and commission in Genesis 12, is the claim in Jubilees, an important but noncanonical Jewish book from the second century B.C.E. that we mentioned in chapter 3. "The lad began understanding the straying of the land, that everyone went astray after graven images and after pollution," Jubilees reports, so that when he was fourteen, Abram "separated from his father so that he might not worship the idols with him" (Jub 11:16). More than that, Abram confronts his father. "What help or advantage do we have from these idols before which you worship and bow down?" he demands to know. "Do not worship them. / Worship the God of heaven" (Jub 12:2–4). Terah acknowledges the truth of his son's argument, but professes himself afraid of the violent reaction of the townsmen, should he renounce their idols for the true God. And so Abram takes matters into his own hands, burning down the temple that housed the idols. This, it would seem, is what precipitates Terah and Abram's departure from Ur of the Chaldeans (that *'ur* in Hebrew means "fire" may have catalyzed the connection). It was the first leg of a journey from the world of idolatry to the world of service to the true God of the universe. Having rediscovered God, Abram had to move away from his townsmen and kinsmen who were still in bondage to their misconceptions.

A similar point, though with an interesting twist, appears in the *Apocalypse of Abraham*, a Jewish book of uncertain date (but certainly written after the destruction of the Temple in 70 C.E.) that appears in no scriptural canon. In this case, Abraham's father is an idol-maker by trade. One day, the story goes, Abraham sees one of his father's gods fallen to the ground, and when he and his father lift it back up, its head falls off. So the father simply carves a new head and smashes the old (Apo Abr 1). On another occasion, Terah sends his son to sell his gods, three of which fall off the donkey. So Abraham throws those three into the river Gur. "And," this interesting text tells us, "they sank into the depths of the river Gur and were no more" (2:9).

These testimonies to the impotence of the idol lead young Abraham to ask, "Is it not [my father] who is god for his gods, because they come into being from his sculpting, his planing, and his skill? They ought to honor my father because they are his work" (Apo Abr 1 3:3–4). As in Jubilees, he then raises the question with his father directly. "Listen, my father Terah . . . They did not help themselves; how then can they help you or bless me?" (4:3–4). But his father refuses the lesson (here, unlike Jubilees, there is no indication that Terah does not believe in his own idols).

In one version of Abraham's confrontation with his father in this text, the monotheistic son, having reasoned his way to the view that all natural phenomena are subordinate to God, closes with the wish, "If [only] God will reveal himself by himself to us!" (Apo Abr 7:12),[9] and no sooner does he say this than it happens: "You are searching for the God of gods, the Creator, in the understanding of your heart. I am he. Go out from Terah, your father, and go out of the house, that you too may not be slain in the sins of your father's house" (8:3–4). Abraham begins in philosophy, as it were, reasoning logically to the insight that his father's idols cannot be God. But then revelation crowns philosophy, as the true God whom he has been approaching intellectually reveals himself to him personally. Young Abraham's search points him toward God, and God rewards him with a personal relationship and with deliverance from the idolatry he saw through.

As the story goes on, it becomes clear that Abraham's search for and discovery of God and God's self-revelation to him actually save his life. "And I went out. And it came to pass as I went out—I was not yet outside the entrance of the court—that the sound of a great thunder came and burned him and his house and everything in his house, down to the ground, forty cubits" (Apo Abr 8:5–6).

On this reading, God's command in Genesis, "go forth . . . from your father's house" (Gen 12:1) is actually an act of deliverance on God's part. It saves Abraham from the idolatry of his father's house (here taken to be not a kin-group but a building) and the death that idolatry brings. To recognize the identity and character of God is not an optional or neutral act: it is indispensable to human survival. The alternative is lethal.

The story of Abraham and his idol-maker father is also found in rabbinic tradition, where it has become a staple of Jewish folklore and elementary education. In the best-known version, Terah leaves on a trip and puts his son in charge of the shop. A woman comes in with a plate of fine flour and leaves it with the request that Abram offer it to the gods. Instead, he takes a club and smashes all the idols but the largest, in the hand of which he then leaves the club:

> When his father came back, he said, "What have you done to them!" He replied, "Why should I hide it from you? A woman came with a plate of fine flour and asked me to offer it to them. One said, 'I'm eating it first!' and another one said, 'I'm eating it first!' The biggest one then took the club and smashed them." He said, "Why are you deceiving me? Do they know anything?" He answered, "Do your ears not hear what is coming out of your mouth?" (*Gen. Rab.* 38:11)

Unable to refute his son's argument, Terah turns Abram over to the idolatrous King Nimrod, and Nimrod, a fire-worshipper, consigns him to the flames (*'ur*). Yet Abram emerges unscathed.

The same, alas, cannot be said for his indecisive brother Haran, who makes a kind of Pascalian wager. "If Abram wins, I will say, 'I am of Abram's party.' If Nimrod wins, I will say, 'I am of Nimrod's party,' " he reasons here. But when Abram is saved from the fiery furnace and Haran, too clever by half, sides with what he takes to be the winning party, Nimrod throws him in anyway; that is why "Haran died in the lifetime of his father Terah, in his native land, Ur of the Chaldeans" (Gen 11:28). The confession of the true God must be based on conviction, not self-interested calculation. Not only must the ears hear what the mouth is saying; the mouth must say what the mind is thinking. And the mind must think about something far larger than self-preservation.

This tale of Abraham's conflict with King Nimrod has obviously been influenced deeply by Daniel 3, the biblical story of Shadrach, Meshach, and Abed-nego, the three Jews who refuse to bow down to the Babylonian king Nebuchadnezzar's golden statue and yet, with an angel's help, survive the fiery furnace into which he has them thrown. In our previous chapter, we saw that Second Temple and rabbinic tradition reinterprets the Aqedah so as to make Isaac a kind of martyr, testifying to what he holds highest—higher than his own life. In this tale of Abraham and Nimrod, we find a parallel development for Abraham himself. The patriarch discovers more than the God whom his father has forgotten; he discovers that the public profession of that God comes at an enormous cost, for something in human nature prevents the worshippers of the false gods from seeing the limitations of what they serve, the limitedness of what they imagine to be absolute.

Abraham's preference for giving up his life over accepting the false gods testifies graphically to the absoluteness of the God he professes. He, like Isaac, survives his brush with death, but, lest the underlying theology degenerate into pious Pollyannaishness, we must acknowledge forthwith that others in his situation did not. The high priest Eleazar and the mother and her seven sons in 4 Maccabees (whose story we examined in chapter 3) immediately come to mind. It is precisely the possibility that the martyrs may have to lose their lives that makes their testimony to the true God courageous. And that is the same possibility that the three Jews in Babylonia recognize in their own stout refusal to engage in idolatry:

[16]Shadrach, Meshach, and Abed-nego said in reply to the king, "O Nebuchadnezzar, we have no need to answer you in this matter,

¹⁷for if so it must be, our God whom we serve is able to save us from the burning fiery furnace, and He will save us from your power, O king. ¹⁸But even if He does not, be it known to you, O king, that we will not serve your god or worship the statue of gold that you have set up." (Dan 3:16–18)

In early Christianity, this Jewish conception of Abraham as the redis-coverer of the God whom his father has forgotten and as the icono-clast, the icon-smasher, who refuses to offer service to the false gods, is not developed.[10] In Islam, however, it becomes prominent and, in fact, holds scriptural status. Thus the Qur'an:

51. And We gave Abraham his right judgement formerly; for We knew him well.
52. When he said to his father and his people: "What are those statues to which you are devoted?"
53. They said: "We found our fathers worshipping them."
54. He said: "Indeed, you and your fathers have been in manifest error."
55. They said: "Have you brought us the truth, or are you one of those who jest?"
56. He said: "No, your Lord is the Lord of the heavens and the earth, Who created them both; and I bear witness to that.
57. "And by Allah, I will show your idols my guile, after you turn your backs."
58. Then he reduced them to pieces except for their chief, so that they might turn to him. (Qur'an 21:51–58)

When the people then ask Abraham whether he committed the crime, he has his answer ready: "No, but their chief did this; so ask them if they can speak" (v. 63). In the end, the idolaters "were utterly confounded" (v. 65), and the iconoclast draws the familiar conclusion:

66. He [Abraham] said: "Do you, then, worship, besides Allah, what does not profit or harm you a whit?

67. "Fie on you and on what you worship besides Allah. Do you not understand?" (Qur'an 21:66–67)

Their reaction is also familiar, though Nimrod's name does not appear, as it did in the midrash:

68. They said: "Burn him and support your gods, if you are going to do anything."
69. We [Allah] said: "O fire, be coolness and peace upon Abraham." (Qur'an 21:68–69)

One reason that this ancient Jewish conception of Abraham as iconoclast is so prominent in the Qur'an, and thence in the larger Muslim tradition, is that Muhammad, too, faced intense opposition from the practitioners of traditional Arabian religion who were highly resistant to his message of the one, incorporeal God.[11] Consider this verse from the Qur'an:

And [remember] when the unbelievers plotted against you, so as to confine you, kill you or expel you. They schemed and Allah schemed, but Allah is the Best of schemers. (8:30)

And so, Abraham's townsmen scheme, and his father does as well—at one point he even threatens to stone his son (19:46)—but Allah stands by his prophet in each case, outscheming the opposition. In the case of both prophets, Abraham and Muhammad, the murderous forces of idolatry prove unable to stop the spread of the proper worship of the one God. So much of the Jewish story of Abraham, beginning with Genesis itself, focuses on the emergence of the chosen family that it was of no use to the seventh-century Arabian prophet of the one and invisible God. (Soon after his death, though, biographers of Muhammad would record his own descent, but not that of all Muslims, from Abraham through Ishmael.) But the Second Temple and rabbinic legends of Abraham the iconoclast and restorer of true worship were another matter altogether, and the conception of Abraham that resulted from them has been central to the Muslim tradition ever after. Obviously, this idea of Abraham correlates with the strict prohibition on the portrayal of the Deity in painting or sculpture characteristic of both Judaism and Islam. The iconoclastic Abraham and the aniconic worship of the God he rediscovered constitute an important bond between those two religions.

It is, moreover, a bond that is not altogether shared by the third Abrahamic religion. For the Christian attitude toward icons has, in various centuries and among various communions, ranged from devout veneration to total rejection. The visual descriptions of the biblical God that one often hears—an old man with a long white beard is the most familiar—are more peculiarly Christian than those who repeat them usually recognize. For the most part, the Jewish and Muslim traditions are more circumspect than Christianity about describing the appearance of the Deity, and this surely correlates to a substantial degree with the rejection of iconography that they attribute to Abraham.

Contemporary readers may be forgiven if they find all these discussions of religious iconography rather quaint and wonder why so much is made of them. For surely if any ancient worshippers ever exhaustively identified their gods with their statues in the manner of the rank idolaters of the prophetic tirades (and it is not clear any did),[12] this is no threat today. It would, however, be a capital error to limit the issue at stake in these texts to technical matters of liturgical paraphernalia alone. The stories may seem childlike, and, to be sure, their vividness has undoubtedly helped Jewish and Muslim children absorb the message of the one God of Abraham over the centuries. But it would be a mistake to allow the narrative simplicity of the tales to distract us from the deeper dimension within them. For there are profound philosophical issues lurking behind these seemingly naive stories, and they, too, like the accounts of Abraham's iconoclasm, reverberate through the conception of our patriarch over the centuries.

One such philosophical issue is the relationship of God to matter. These stories go out of their way to strike against the notion that God is limited, like the wood and stone out of which a statue of him or his rivals is carved. When the icon is broken, loses its head, or sinks into the river, we are made painfully aware of its limitedness, its materiality, and thus, most important, its vulnerability. It is but an object in the world, and like all objects it cannot save itself or, ultimately, those who put their faith in it. The living God, by contrast, is not an object. He is not spatially limited (the powerful scriptural language of divine presence, absence, and embodiment must therefore be taken in some measure as metaphorical) and does not pass into and out of existence like Abraham's father's graven images. And for that reason, Jewish, Christian, and Muslim philosophers in the Middle Ages, reformulating the Hellenic heritage in similar ways, would all argue that God's existence is of a different order from the existence of the things that we encounter in the world. It does no good, then, to argue for or against the existence of God in the way some people argue about the existence of Big Foot, the Loch Ness Monster, or aliens from outer space. Whatever the term "existence" means when it is predicated of such things, it refers to something different when predicated of God.

In these philosophical discussions, as in the childlike stories of Abraham's confrontations with his father from an earlier time that are ostensibly so unphilosophical, the underlying claim is the same: God radically transcends the world. This is the same claim that underlies the doctrine that God created the word ex nihilo, out of nothing.

Over the centuries, this question of creation has often been taken, as most people still take it today, as asking about origins: How did the universe, with all its physical laws, begin? This, to put it differently, is a question of time: What was there before the world came to be? (The word "before" in that sentence is, of course, immensely problematic, as any student of the theory of relativity knows.) The deeper, and enduring, philosophical question is different. It asks about the nature of the existence of the universe: Is it necessary, so that the universe must exist and it cannot *not* exist? Or is the existence of the universe contingent, so that in principle there might always have been nothing all along? If the latter is the case—if the universe does not exist by its own intrinsic necessity—then we are within our rights to ask about what brought into existence our world, which did not necessarily have to exist at all. The classical Jewish, Christian, and Muslim answer is that God not only brought it into existence but continues to sustain it. For his existence is necessary, whereas the existence of the world is contingent on him. To fail to see this is to step onto the path that leads to idolatry.

The cultural situation in which the Jews found themselves after Alexander of Macedon (or, the Great) brought down the Persian Empire (333 B.C.E.) must have played a role in creating both this reconception of Abraham as the iconoclast and the self-consciously philosophical presentations of the underlying idea of God that came to be associated with him. For two centuries or so before Alexander, Greek thought had been developing a critique of the anthropomorphism of the traditional mythology, that is, the tendency to think of the gods in human form. Most memorable in this regard are the fragments of Xenophanes of Colophon (born about 570 B.C.E.), who makes biting observations on the foolishness of predicating human characteristics of the deities:

> But mortals suppose that gods are born,
> wear their own clothes and have a voice and a body. (Fragment 14)
> But if horses or oxen or lions had hands
> or could draw with their hands and accomplish such works as men,
> horses would draw the figurines of gods as similar to horses, and
>                                 the oxen as similar to oxen,
> and they would make the bodies
> of the sort which each of them had. (Fragment 15)
> Ethiopians say that their gods are snub-nosed and black;
> Thracians that theirs are blue-eyed and red-haired. (Fragment 16)[13]

Given this long-standing philosophical critique of the traditional theology, the Jews, now finding themselves within the cultural world of the Greeks, must have seemed woefully backward to many (including to many Jews). For the Hebrew Bible often speaks of the LORD as having clothes, a voice, hands, wings, eyes, ears, a mouth, and a sword. To be sure, the fact that he can make himself invisible is evidence that he transcends his physical manifestations, but the images that pervade the descriptions of him in the Hebrew Bible surely qualified him for the critique of the gods and of vulgar religion that some sophisticated Greek intellectuals had been making.

Against these Jewish vulnerabilities, though, one can cite certain not inconsiderable strengths. The belief in the singularity of God might suggest that the Jews subscribed to something more majestic than a crude mythology, and the fact that their God was never to be represented in statuary could be taken to mean that he transcended the anthropomorphism of unphilosophical worshippers. That this train of thought, or something approximating it, is more than a speculation can be seen from the ways some Greek thinkers describe the Jewish people.

Clearchus of Soli, for example, a philosopher in the fourth and third century B.C.E. and a student of Aristotle's (as was Alexander), describes the Jews as descended from a caste of Indian philosophers and describes an encounter of one of them with Aristotle, in which it is the Jew, and not the Greek, who imparts wisdom to the other man.[14] Theophrastus, who lived about the same time, gives evidence of the same sort of understanding of the Jews by some early philosophers. "Their religious feeling," one scholar writes, "expressed by the observation of the order and movement of the stars (clearly interpreted as the demonstration of the existence of God who is in a way sought for in the heavens), appeared to Theophrastus as being very close to Greek philosophical thinking and the Jews were without hesitation called by him philosophers." In fact, Theophrastus explicitly calls the Jews a "race of philosophers."[15]

That in such a cultural situation the father of this philosophical people should have been reconceived as a philosopher is thus no cause for wonderment. Here is how Josephus, the Jewish historian writing in Greek at the end of the first century C.E., characterizes Abraham:

> He was a man of ready intelligence on all matters, persuasive with his hearers, and not mistaken in his inferences. Hence he began to have more lofty conceptions of virtue than the rest of mankind, and determined to reform and change the ideas universally current concerning God. He was thus the first boldly to declare that God, the creator of the universe, is one, and that, if any other being contributed aught to man's welfare, each did so by His command and not in virtue of its own inherent power. (*Jewish Antiquities* [*JA*] 1:154–55)

And note the additional motivation that Josephus ascribes to Abram's visiting Egypt in Genesis 12:10–20:

> Some time later, Canaan being in the grip of a famine, Abraham, hearing of the prosperity of the Egyptians, was of a mind to visit them, alike to profit by their abundance and to hear what their priests said about the gods; intending, if he found their doctrine more excellent than his own, to conform to it, or else to convert them to a better mind should his own beliefs prove superior. (*JA* 1:161)[16]

In sum, Abraham is not simply a migrant, even a migrant chosen by the LORD to father the special people whom he has graciously singled out to bear witness to him. He is also a teacher of philosophy, open-minded and eager to hear what his foreign colleagues think, on the one hand, but committed, on the other, to convincing people everywhere of the truth of monotheism—that there is but one God, the creator of the universe, and all other beings, however benevolent, are subordinate to him. "The first boldly to declare that God, the creator of the universe, is one," Abraham has become the founder of a school of thought. And the people whom he fathered have become more than another nationality: they have become a "race of philosophers," upholding their forefather's revolutionary insight in word and deed.

How did Abraham come to deduce that great theological principle? Josephus makes it clear that this was, in the first instance, an empirical deduction rather than the result of divine revelation. "This he inferred from the changes to which land and sea are subject," Josephus observes, "from the course of sun and moon, and from all the celestial phenomena; for, he argued, were these bodies endowed with power, they would have provided for their own regularity."[17] In other words, the imperfections in the courses of the stars and planets attest to something higher than those bodies themselves: an invisible hand, as it were, whose very shaping of their movements shows it to be superior to its handiwork and to have imparted to them an imperfection that they, were they perfect, would never have imparted to themselves. Not the heavens, but God alone is divine. He is their creator, and they, for all their majesty, are but his creation.

It is important to underscore that this is not the argument from design, or, as it is sometimes known, the teleological argument, which infers God from the intelligence observable in nature—Intelligent

Design, so to speak.[18] Such reasoning was well known in Josephus's world (it would also carry over into later Jewish, Christian, and Muslim philosophy). A century and a half before he wrote, for example, the Roman statesman and philosopher Cicero had put the argument in the mouth of his spokesman for Stoicism: "The most potent cause of the belief [in the existence of God] he said was the uniform motion and revolution of the heavens, and the varied groupings and ordered beauty of the sun, moon and stars, the very sight of which was in itself enough to prove that these things are not the mere effect of chance . . . [One is] compelled to infer that these mighty world-motions are regulated by some Mind (*mente*)."[19] Note, however, that where Cicero's Stoic speaks of "Mind," Josephus speaks of "God," who, as "the creator of the universe," transcends his handiwork. The mind of God can, to some degree, be inferred from the natural order; it is not internal to the natural order. Nature is not ultimate. At best, it points to what is beyond itself. At worst, the unwary do not allow it to do so and thus become ensnared in idolatry.

How did Abraham come to be weaned away from the idolatrous involvement in astrology or astronomy (the two are essentially the same in this period) that, as these Second Temple sources have it, dominated the spiritual environment of his youth? The book of Jubilees seems again to be our earliest example of an attempt to answer the question:

> Abram sat up during the night on the first of the seventh month [Rosh Hashanah in rabbinic law] so that he might see what the nature of the year would be with respect to rain. And he was sitting alone and making observations; and a word came into his heart, saying, "All the signs of the stars and the signs of the sun and the moon are in the hand of the LORD. Why am I seeking?
> > If he desires, he will make it rain morning and evening,
> > and if he desires he will not send (it) down;
> > and everything is in his hand." (Jub 12:16–18)

Unlike Josephus, the author of Jubilees does not present Abram as reasoning his way to the recognition that there is a higher power than the movements of the heavenly bodies. The actual process, rather, was more akin to prophetic revelation; "a word came into [his] heart" that pointed out to him that astral phenomena are not independent and ultimate but strictly under God's control. What we might call the signs of the zodiac do not determine destiny, and one's relationship with the LORD is a better indication of one's future than, to use a modern example, reading one's horoscope.

The demotion of astrology in Jubilees is of a piece with Abram's rejection of his father's idols in the same book. Indeed, in the deeper cultural background of this text is the sentiment we have already seen in a polemic against idolatry in Jeremiah—"do not be dismayed by portents in the sky" (Jer 10:2). Just as the sovereignty, freedom, and personality of God transcend material objects, so do they transcend even the majestic and luminescent bodies in the heavens and the enormously complex courses that they traverse. The alternative view is not just false; it is a rejection of God and a replacement of him with his own creation—a deadly danger from which the word that came into Abram's heart that night graciously saved him.

Using an allegorical method well known in his culture, Philo of Alexandria, a Jewish philosopher writing in the first half of the first century C.E., decodes the deeper, and ongoing, spiritual meaning of Abraham's journey from Ur to Haran:

> The migrations as set forth by the literal text of the scriptures are made by a man of wisdom, but according to the laws of allegory by a virtue-loving soul in its search for the true God. For the Chaldeans were especially active in the elaboration of astrology (*astronomian*) and ascribed everything to the movements of the stars. They supposed that the course of the phenomena of the world is guided by influences contained in numbers and numerical proportions. Thus they glorified visible existence, leaving out of consideration the intelligible and the invisible . . . [T]hey concluded that the world itself was God, thus profanely likening the created to the Creator. In this creed Abraham had been reared, and for a long time remained a Chaldean. Then opening the soul's eye as though after a profound sleep, and beginning to see the pure beam instead of the deep darkness, he followed the ray and discerned what he had not beheld before, a charioteer and pilot presiding

over the world . . . And so to establish more firmly in his understanding the sight which had been revealed to him the Holy Word
follows it up by saying to him, "Friend, the great is often known
by its outlines as shown in the smaller, and by looking at them the
observer finds the scope of his vision infinitely enlarged. Dismiss,
then, the rangers of the heavens [that is, the planets] and the science of Chaldea, and depart for a short time from the greatest of
cities, this world, to the lesser, and thus you will be better able to
apprehend the overseer of the All." (Philo, *On Abraham*, 68–71)[20]

Philo here plays on the identification of Chaldea with astronomy.
As one scholar puts it, "So great was the association between Chaldea and the study of the stars that the very word 'Chaldean' came to
mean 'astronomer' in both Aramaic and Greek."[21] In Philo's interpretation, then, Abraham's journey from his birthplace in Ur of the
Chaldeans to Haran is a change of location only at the literal—and
the lower—level of interpretation. At the higher level disclosed by
allegorical reading, the first leg of Abraham's physical journey derives from an infinitely more profound spiritual, intellectual, and
moral journey. In this journey, he moved away from the world of
regular, predictable phenomena, familiar to any scientist of Philo's
days or ours, because of his recognition that the world was not God
and that God was not contained in or limited by those phenomena.
Rather, he transcended them. They were but his creation, and he was
their creator. The course of human events is not determined by the
mathematical relationships that underlie astronomy but by the sovereign will of God, who governs the world through his providence.
Philo's opponents here are not simpleminded pagans who mistake
their icons for gods or goddesses. They are sophisticated intellectuals
who think that what we call "science" represents the final and highest truth. They, too, "glorified visible existence," missing the invisible
intelligence and moral order behind and above it.

We have now examined two variant accounts from Second Temple
Judaism of Abram's learning to see beyond astronomy or astrology,
one in Jubilees and one in Philo. Over against the text from Josephus
that we examined, the theological claim made by these two accounts
appears in fuller boldness.[22] For Josephus, as for Cicero's Stoic (and
many other thinkers) beforehand, Abraham "inferred" that "God,

the creator of the universe, is one . . . from the changes to which land and sea are subject, from the course of sun and moon, and from all the celestial phenomena." Although Josephus speaks of a "creator" (*demiourgos*) whereas the Stoic speaks of a "mind" (*mens*), both of them base the recognition of the higher reality on an examination of nature.

In the case of Jubilees and Philo, however, the higher reality—God—revealed himself to Abram, when "a word came into his heart" (Jubilees) or "opening the soul's eye as though after a profound sleep," he "discerned what he had not beheld before" and a "Holy Word" then explained its implications (Philo). And what that word points out to Abram is the error of thinking that an empirical examination of the celestial phenomena will give a good and full accounting of the higher reality: "Dismiss, then, the rangers of the heavens and the science of Chaldea." One might say that whereas the Stoic and Josephus reason like contemporary advocates of Intelligent Design, inferring a supranatural power from the symmetries (or, in Josephus's case, the asymmetries) in nature, Jubilees and Philo speak of a self-revealing God who controls nature but is not readily or fully inferable from nature alone. If nothing else, this issues a caution about scientific arguments developed for or against the existence of God. For the God therewith affirmed or denied may not be the God of Abraham.

Unlike the texts that we have been examining in one respect but like them in others, a midrash in the Talmud presents Abram as resistant to giving up his reliance on astrology. It augments the narrative in Genesis 15:1–6, in which Abram first despairs that he will ever have a child but then shows faith after the LORD "took him outside and said, 'Look toward heaven and count the stars, if you are able to count them.'"

> Rav Judah said in Rav's name: How do we know that Israel is not subject to the stars? Because it is said, "He took him (*vayyotse'*) outside." Abraham said to the Holy One, blessed be He: Master of the Universe, "My steward will be my heir."
> Not so, He replied, "none but your very own issue shall be your heir." Master of the Universe, he answered, I have looked at my horoscope and I am not fated to beget a child.
> Go forth (*tse'*) from your horoscope, for Israel is not subject to the stars! (*b. Shab.* 156a)[23]

Here, as in Jubilees and Philo, Abram begins as one who believes and practices astrology until God intervenes to bring him into a larger vision of destiny. And here, too, we can detect a spiritual journey in Abram's life that does not appear in the plain sense of Genesis. When God "took (*vayyotse'*) him outside" to view the stars, he was thus really telling him to step outside of the astrological framework he had inherited and uncritically continued. For that framework, whatever else it may govern and however accurate it may prove in other contexts, does not apply to Israel, the special people that will descend miraculously from Abram. After this exchange, the text implies, Abram saw the stars differently.

Finally, we must note that just as the postbiblical Jewish legends of Abram's conflict with his father appear (with variations, of course) in the Qur'an, so does the account of his coming to see through astrology. In fact, the two themes can appear together:

74. And when Abraham said to his father Azar, "Do you take idols for gods? I see you and your people are in manifest error."
75. Thus We show Abraham the kingdom of the heavens and the earth, that he might be one of those possessed of certainty.
76. And when night fell, he saw a star; so he said: "This is my Lord," but when it set, he said: "I do not like those that set."
77. Then, when he saw the moon rising, he said: "This is my Lord," but when it set, he said: "If my Lord does not guide me rightly, I will be one of the erring people."
78. Then, when he saw the sun rising, he said: "This is my Lord; this is larger," but when it set, he said: "O, my people, I am innocent of what you associate [with God].
79. "I turn my face towards Him Who fashioned the heavens and the earth, as an upright man, and I am not one of the polytheists." (6:74–79)

Here, the observation that the celestial bodies all eventually set is what causes Abraham to conclude that they are finite and limited and cannot really be his lord. Only the one who created the heavens and the earth can truly and rightly be their—and our—master.

As in the case of Abraham's rejection of iconography, so in the case of his rejection of astrology, contemporary readers inclined to dismiss this as quaint would be well advised to have another look. It is certainly true that astrology has generally declined in prestige over the last four centuries or so, although it remains alive in popular culture, as a glance at the horoscopes in newspapers, magazines, and Web sites easily demonstrates. Commanding much more prestige, however, is the underlying philosophy that these Jewish and Muslim texts about Abraham are opposing, and the issue they address is very much alive. For the relationship of the material world to its lord and creator—together with the prior question of whether it even has a lord or creator—shows no sign of vanishing. To be sure, no serious philosopher or scientist would believe that the celestial bodies govern human destiny. But many would believe that other material factors—genes or other biological structures, economic factors, or social forces—give a complete and completely satisfactory account of human life and destiny and falsify all claims that there is something higher than material things.

The enemy in these Jewish and Muslim texts is not science; there is no reason to think their authors would have opposed an astronomy shorn of its astrological purposes. Their enemy, rather, is what some have called *scientism*, the philosophical (not scientific) claim that science provides the final and truest description of all reality and thus discloses the exhaustive and insurpassable truth. It is hard to see how anyone committed to one of the Abrahamic religions could fail to detect, in that claim, a whiff of idolatry.

In Josephus's description of Abraham the philosopher, we heard a note that now deserves more attention, for it foreshadows momentous developments in the subsequent histories of the Abrahamic religions. Josephus's patriarch, recall, "began to have more lofty conceptions of virtue than the rest of mankind, and determined to reform and change the ideas universally current concerning God. He was thus the first boldly to declare that God, the creator of the universe, is one." Now, the obvious question is: Whose conceptions of virtue was he trying to elevate and whose idea of God was he trying to reform with his bold declaration?

Read according to its plain sense, Genesis gives no answer; worse, it gives no reason to think that Abraham engaged in any public teaching or preaching at all. But if he really was not only the father that he is in Genesis but also the philosopher that Josephus and other Jews (and perhaps non-Jews) in the Greco-Roman world saw in him, then he must have sought to influence the morals and theology of people outside his own family. For in that world philosophy was, to quote the title of a famous study, "a way of life," and philosophical schools in many ways more closely resembled religious sects than the academic departments to which philosophy is usually relegated today.[24] And if that is the case, then Abraham should be not only a father and a philosopher; he should also be a missionary.

Rabbinic tradition makes this connection explicit. A case in point is a midrash on Genesis 21:33: "[Abraham] planted a tamarisk at Beer-sheba, and invoked there the name of the LORD, the Everlasting God." The likelihood is that in the biblical context the tree mentioned here had sacral connotations and the verse originally recorded Abraham's founding a particular shrine in whose liturgy the name 'El 'Olam ("Everlasting God," or, more literally, "the God of Eternity") figured prominently. But this would have been very much in the past by the time of the Talmudic rabbis and very foreign to their understanding of religion. To make matters worse, the term for that tree ('eshel), translated as "tamarisk," is rare in the Hebrew Bible, and to the rabbis the connection between planting a tree and calling upon the name of the LORD with a particular epithet ("the Everlasting God") had become obscure in any case.

Fortunately, though, the words in the verse could easily have suggested something else in their cultural context. In rabbinic Hebrew 'olam could mean "world," whereas in the biblical phase of the language the word had referred only to time. Add all this together, and it is not hard to come up with an interpretation in which 'eshel designates not some obscure tree but the locus at which Abraham proclaimed that the LORD is the God of the world. This seems to be the logic underlying an interpretation given by a rabbi of the second century C.E.:

According to Rabbi Nehemiah's opinion, [that 'eshel denotes] an inn, Abraham used to welcome travelers, and when they had eaten and drunk, he would say to them, "Make a blessing," and they would say to him, "What should we say?" He said to them, " 'Blessed be the Everlasting God / God of the World of whose bounty we have eaten.' " (*Gen. Rab.* 54:6)

To be sure, Abraham here does not convert people in the sense of having them undergo certain rites, such as circumcision, that redefine their communal identity. He does, however, introduce them to the Everlasting God/God of the World and to the grateful recognition of him that eating and drinking impose.

In other midrashim, Abraham is seen as producing actual converts to Judaism. One such text centers on the verse that mentions "the persons (*nephesh*) that they had acquired (*'aśu*) in Haran" (Gen 12:5). Here, too, a change between biblical and rabbinic Hebrew facilitated the new role for Abraham. In the older phase of the language, "persons" would be a good translation of *nephesh* and *'aśu* could simply mean "they acquired" and did not have to mean "they made." In its original context, the verse simply refers to the slaves that Abram and Sarai obtained. In the culture of the Talmudic rabbis, however, man was seen not as a psychophysical unity but as an amalgam of body and soul, and *nephesh* could be seen as one of the words for the latter:

Rabbi Leazar said in the name of Rabbi Yosé ben Zimra: If all the nations were to come together to create one gnat, they could not inject a soul into it. Yet you say, "the souls that they had made"? Rather, it refers to the converts.

Then let it say, "that they had *converted*"! Why "that they had *made*"? Rather, it is to teach you that anyone who brings a Gentile near is as though he had created him.

Then let it say, "that *he* made"! Why "that *they* had made"?

Rabbi Chunia said: Abraham would convert the men, and Sarah would convert the women. (*Gen. Rab.* 39:14)

The convert, to Judaize a well-known Christian phrase, is born again, given a new soul, a new spiritual identity, and Abraham and Sarah were embarked on this process of building up the people Israel by their preaching even before they had brought forth the promised son Isaac.

Another midrash, one of the rare rabbinic texts critical of Abraham, plays on the same word, *nephesh*:

> Rabbi Abbahu reported that Rabbi Eleazar had said: Why was Our Father Abraham punished and his descendants enslaved to Egypt for 210 years? . . . Rabbi Yochanan said: Because he prevented people from coming under the wings of the Shekhinah, as it is said, "[Then the king of Sodom said to Abram,] 'Give me the persons (*nephesh*), and take the possessions for yourself'" (Gen 14:21). (*b. Nedarim* 32a)

The Shekhinah is the indwelling presence of God; "coming under the wings of the Shekhinah" is a rabbinic expression for conversion to Judaism. In this interpretation, Abram's relinquishing the persons he had captured to the pagan king was the equivalent of consigning their souls to separation from God. Presented with a prime opportunity to attract proselytes, Abram failed to perform. For that, the midrash claims, his descendants were themselves consigned to nothing less than servitude in Egypt.

The implications of this image of Abraham and Sarah as missionaries reverberate throughout history. In the case of Judaism, in which converts change not only their religion but their familial and ethnic identity as well, Abraham and Sarah become their new parents. Maimonides, the great Jewish philosopher and legal authority of the twelfth century, made the point nicely. A convert to Judaism asked whether he was permitted to use the traditional liturgical formulation, "God of our fathers," since he was not biologically descended from Jews. Maimonides replied affirmatively and in no uncertain terms:

> The reason is this, that Abraham our Father taught the people, opened their minds, and revealed to them the true faith and the unity of God; he rejected the idols and abolished their adoration; he brought many children under the wings of the Divine Presence; he gave them counsel and advice, and ordered his sons and the members of his household after him to keep the ways of the Lord forever, as it is written, "For I have known him to the end that he may command his children and his household after him, that they may keep the way of the Lord, to do righteousness and

justice" (Gen. 18:19). Ever since then whoever adopts Judaism and confesses the unity of the Divine Name, as it is prescribed in the Torah, is counted among the disciples of Abraham our Father, peace be with him. These men are Abraham's household, and he it is who converted them to righteousness.[25]

One might have thought that by Maimonides's time, the changes we have been tracing had totally transformed Abraham the father into Abraham the founder, the man who rediscovered and preached the one true God, and that the Jews had become a voluntary association of like-minded individuals united only by their common beliefs. Instead, the fatherhood of Abraham and the identity of the Jewish people as a natural family remained intact, even while the father's teachings provided an opening for outsiders willing to accept them to join the family. And descendants and disciples alike are under an obligation to heed those teachings and "follow in his ways."

Given the importance in Islam of the Jewish legends about Abraham's challenge to idolatry and his declaration of the oneness of God, it is not surprising that Abraham appears there, too, as the model of the religious person and thus an archetype for Muslims even before Muhammad. After speaking of Abraham's obedience, uprightness, and monotheism, the Qur'an gives this injunction: "Follow the religion of Abraham, the upright, for he was not one of the polytheists" (6:123).

That "the religion of Abraham" is Islam itself is clear in the Qur'an. In this case, too, Gentiles can indeed be remade in the image of Abraham, though they are not reborn as members of his family, as they can be in Judaism. Rather, they become Gentiles who practice Abraham's religion of submission to God alone—now known as Islam. They become not Jewish—for they do not practice the Mosaic Torah—but Abrahamic.

The idea of Abraham as a missionary and the father of converts played an important role in early Christianity, too, though in a different way from those of Judaism and Islam. Consider again the apostle Paul's identification of Abraham: "the father of all who have faith without being circumcised and who thus have righteousness reckoned to them, and likewise the father of the circumcised who are not only circumcised but who also follow the example of the faith that our father Abraham had before he was circumcised" (Rom 4:11–12). Here, Abraham's legacy is neither a philosophical teaching nor a practice; it is not belief in the one immaterial God, creator of the universe, or even circumcision that defines the descendants of the patriarch. It is, rather, faith of the sort that comes from the preaching of the Christian gospel, a saving faith already anticipated in God's declaration that Abraham was righteous in Genesis 15:6, well before circumcision was commanded.

In Paul's thinking, Jewish and Gentile Christians are equally the descendants of Abraham, "the father of all who have faith"—the biblical archetype of faith apart from the mitsvot, the commandments of the Mosaic Torah. But in the case of Paul and other early Christians, for whom the Torah was canonical in a way that it is not in Islam, this also raises a large problem: the problem of why, if at all, the Gentile descendants of Abraham should be exempt from the mitsvot that obligate his Jewish descendants. To that problem, and the Jewish interpretations with which it is strikingly associated, we turn in chapter 5.

## CHAPTER FIVE

## Torah or Gospel?

Anyone who accepts a single commandment in faith is worthy to
have the Holy Spirit rest upon him.

—Midrash[1]

IN CHAPTER 4, we traced the process by which Abraham the father of
the Jewish people became Abraham the founder, or rediscoverer, of
belief in the one true God as well. Whereas the chapters about him
in Genesis focus on God's promise of progeny, land, and blessing and
give no indication that Abraham had any teaching at all, by some
point in the second century B.C.E. he has become an active adversary
of idolatry and the materialist presuppositions upon which it rests.
Abraham has, in a word, become a philosopher, and with this came
the notion that his vocation is of great import even to those outside
his own family. The entire world needs to acknowledge and obey its
divine creator and master, it was now taught, and give him the testimony and service that are his due. In testifying to a higher truth, the
philosopher opens a portal through which outsiders can enter and
dwell within that truth.[2]

But there are problems. To say, as Philo does, that Abraham came
to see that there was "a charioteer and pilot presiding over the world"
leaves troublingly vague the question of how one is to enter into relationship with that charioteer and pilot. The same can be said for the
rabbinic legend that Abraham established an inn in which he asked
his guests to make the benediction, "Blessed be the Everlasting God /
God of the World of whose bounty we have eaten."[3] Compared with the
rich texture of the traditional Jewish, Christian, or Muslim life, these
affirmations, however essential they may be, seem too thin to support
a whole identity, too frail a skeleton on which to rest a lasting religious
community or to sustain and nourish a life-changing insight.

It is therefore not surprising to see, as we did in chapter 4, that rabbinic tradition could sometimes conceive of Abraham and Sarah as missionaries, respectively converting men and women not simply to a nondescript monotheism but to Judaism. It will similarly not be surprising to see, as we soon will, that Christianity found in Abraham a foreshadowing of the theological basis for the Christian life and that Islam conceived of itself as the reestablishment of the "religion of Abraham," of which the Jews and Christians had lost sight. In sum, although both Christianity and Islam came to see themselves as the restoration of Abrahamic religion after a long interruption, neither of them represents the pattern of religious practice of the figure in Genesis. And neither does Judaism.

All this points to one of the most peculiar aspects of Abraham in all the Abrahamic religions. On the one hand, all three revere the man and find him paradigmatic for their own communities, each in its own way. On the other hand, in each set of scriptures the central action of God occurs in a much later period than that of Abraham.[4] In Judaism, it lies with God's gift of the Torah in the time of Moses on Mount Sinai. In Christianity, the central event of all human history lies with Jesus, to some degree with his teaching but even more so with his redemptive death and subsequent resurrection and ascension to his divine father (what New Testament scholars sometimes call "the Christ Event"). In Islam, it lies with God's dictation of the Qur'an, his highest and final revelation and the only true guide for human beings, to Muhammad through the medium of the angel Gabriel.

The peculiar thing for Judaism and Christianity is this: Although on the plain sense of Genesis Abraham lives a life without the benefit of Sinaitic revelation or the Christ Event, neither of these two traditions belittles him for the lack or sees him as a benighted pagan devoid of access to the highest truth, righteousness, or salvation. To the contrary, both see him as at least foreshadowing that truth in a major way and sometimes as living it in all its rich detail.

The case of Islam is different—since, as we have noted, Genesis is not in its canon and the Qur'anic Abraham diverges from the biblical figure in ways great and small. Still, in Muslim scripture and tradition Abraham is again a highly positive figure, a faithful and courageous prophet paradigmatically living a life of submission (Arabic, *islām*) to the one true God and at odds with the idolaters—very much like Muhammad, whom he clearly foreshadows there. We shall return to Islam in chapter 6. Here, we shall concentrate on how the two religious traditions that share Genesis manage to find in Abraham a positive model for their own religious traditions, even though he lived long before Sinai or Jesus.

We have said that in Genesis Abraham has no teaching; he is a father, not a founder like the Buddha, Jesus, or Muhammad. That he, like them, nonetheless becomes a paradigm to be imitated is therefore all the more unusual and interesting. One factor facilitating the transition is the presence of a very few verses in the Abraham narrative of Genesis that allude to issues of normative behavior, thus tying the patriarch to the behavior expected of the family he engenders. Our first example is from the monologue in which God divulges his reason for sharing with Abraham the anticipated fate of Sodom:

> [17]Now the LORD had said, "Shall I hide from Abraham what I am about to do, [18]since Abraham is to become a great and populous nation and all the nations of the earth are to bless themselves by him? [19]For I have singled him out, that he may instruct his children and his posterity to keep the way of the LORD by doing what is just and right, in order that the LORD may bring about for Abraham what He has promised him." (Gen 18:17–19)

Here, the LORD regards Abraham as a prophet, a role that he is explicitly said to hold only once, in Genesis 20:7. As in that verse, here too his prophetic office seems to focus on intercession in the face of a calamity induced by the righteous God. In this passage, he cannot discharge his prophetic duty without becoming privy to God's counsel, as one should expect of prophets.[5] What is distinctive here is the correlation of Abraham's prophetic role with the promise that we examined at length in chapter 1, namely, that he is to father a great and numerous nation and become a byword or medium of blessing for all the nations of the earth.

The implication is clear: his destiny as father and, indeed, the originating promise of the whole narrative about him are intrinsically tied to the prophetic role that he and the promised nation are to exercise, a role centered on "doing what is just and right." The word translated "I have singled him out" (*yeda'tiv*) probably denotes covenant-making here,[6] but in this case it adds a note about God's rationale for such covenant-making that we do not hear in the extensive covenantal narratives in Genesis 15 and 17. It is immaterial whether this means, as some argue, that Genesis 18:17–19 is a later insertion made under the transformation of Father Abraham into a religious paradigm in Second Temple Judaism.[7] Either way, on at least this one point, the canonical text now authorizes a normative connection between the father's conduct and that expected of his descendants.

Another example appears in an oracle that Isaac receives after Abraham's death:

> [2]The LORD had appeared to him and said, "Do not go down to Egypt; stay in the land which I point out to you. [3]Reside in this land, and I will be with you and bless you; I will assign all these lands to you and to your heirs, fulfilling the oath that I swore to your father Abraham. [4]I will make your heirs as numerous as the stars of heaven, and assign to your heirs all these lands, so that all the nations of the earth shall bless themselves by your heirs— [5]inasmuch as Abraham obeyed Me and kept My charge: My commandments, My laws, and My teachings." (Gen 26:2–5)

This passage, too, is replete with echoes of the Abrahamic narrative. The instruction to Isaac not to go down to Egypt in a time of famine (as 26:1 specifies) recalls Abraham's less than ideally successful journey there in Genesis 12:10–20. That God should promise the land, innumerable progeny, and blessing to the chosen son, as he had to the faithful father beforehand, stands to reason. What is curious, and highly revealing of future developments in the Jewish conception of Abraham, is the reason these promises remain valid. That reason is specified in the last verse (Gen 26:5): that Abraham had been obedient to various categories of divine norms. The clause "inasmuch as Abraham obeyed Me" unmistakably echoes the conclusion of the second angelic address at the Aqedah, "inasmuch as you have obeyed Me" (Gen 22:18).[8] Indeed, it underscores the point of that address, which is that the Aqedah underlies those promises and Israel's inheritance of them ever after. In fact, Genesis 26:5 is arguably the only direct echo of Genesis 22 in the entire Hebrew Bible.

But what are we to make of the report in the same verse that Abraham kept the LORD's "charge, commandments, laws, and teachings"? If we understand this only within the context of Genesis itself, we can with some difficulty see it as describing Abraham's obedience to the directives God gives him there, beginning with the command to "go forth" from his father's house, continuing through the injunctions about circumcision and the expulsion of Hagar and Ishmael (for example) and culminating in the Binding of Isaac.[9] The difficulty is that the four terms—charge, commandments, laws, and teachings—are rather specialized. In the aggregate, they suggest various categories of law rather than situational instructions given to a character in a story.

In fact, the closest parallel to the list in Genesis 26:5 appears in Deuteronomy, the biblical book that insists most centrally on the importance of keeping the LORD's norms: "Love, therefore, the LORD your God, and always keep His charge, His laws, His rules, and His commandments" (Deut 11:1).[10] If we compare these two lists of four items, we find that three appear in common, with only "rules" (*mishpatav*) in Deuteronomy 11:1 or "teachings" (*torotav*) in Genesis 26:5 preventing a perfect match. The implication of this is that Genesis 26:5 has sought to present Abraham as one who is meticulously observant of Sinaitic revelation, even though Moses and the Torah given through him have yet to be.[11]

The depiction of Abraham as a Torah-observant Jew is one that will reverberate in Jewish biblical interpretation through the centuries, although, as we shall see, not without dissent. One question comes immediately to mind: How could the patriarch have observed norms that were not yet revealed in his lifetime? Here, a variety of answers was proposed. For the book of Jubilees, the Jewish source from the middle of the second century B.C.E. that was mentioned earlier, the answer is that many of those norms were known before the events of Sinai, so that figures in Genesis could adhere to practices otherwise unknown to that book. Thus, for example, the feast of Shavuʿot (also known as Weeks, First Fruits, and Pentecost, among other names) has its origin, according to Jubilees, in the time of Noah, had to be revived by Abraham, and was observed by Isaac and Jacob afterward—even though the first mention of it in the Torah as we have it appears in a law given to Moses generations later.[12]

And how was Abraham able to revive long-neglected practices? Here, Jubilees tells us that after the Angel of the Presence (the narrator of the book) had taught him Hebrew, which had been forgotten, Abraham took his father's books and began studying them.[13] In other words, just as in Jubilees, Abraham revived the true worship of the one God in an age of idolatry (our subject in chapter 4), so did he revive the faithful observance of God's law in an age of widespread deviant or nonexistent practice. He was devoted to the book of God's law, even though in Genesis no such book is so much as mentioned. He was a man of Torah even before the Torah was given.[14]

Philo of Alexandria, the prolific Jewish philosopher from the early first century C.E., had a different view of how it was possible to keep the Torah before it was revealed:

> In these men [that is, all the worthy figures of Genesis] we have laws endowed with life and reason, and Moses extolled them for two reasons. First he wished to shew that the enacted ordinances are not inconsistent with nature; and secondly that those who wish to live in accordance with the laws as they stand have no difficult task, seeing that the first generations before any at all of the particular statutes was set in writing followed the unwritten law with perfect ease, so that one might properly say that the enacted laws are nothing else than memorials of the life of the ancients, preserving to a later generation their actual words and deeds. For they were not scholars or pupils of others, nor did they learn under teachers what was right to say or do: they listened to no voice or instruction but their own: they gladly accepted conformity with nature, holding that nature itself was, as indeed it is, the most venerable of statutes, and thus their whole life was one of happy obedience to law.

Apparently referring to Genesis 26:5, Philo concludes his treatise on Abraham with these words:

> To these praises of the Sage, so many and so great, Moses adds this crowning saying, "that this man did the divine law and the divine

commands." He did them, not taught by written words, but unwritten nature gave him the zeal to follow where wholesome and untainted impulse led him. . . . Such was the life of the first, the founder of the nation, one who obeyed the law, some will say, but rather, as our discourse has shown, himself a law and an unwritten statute. (*On Abraham* 5–6, 275–76)[15]

Unlike the Abraham of Jubilees, then, Philo's did not learn the Torah from a book and, if he had, Judaism would have been the lesser for it. Since no book is accessible to everyone, a law dependent on a book fails to be universal and cannot mediate the will of the creator and governor of the universe. What is universal, though, is "nature" (Greek, *physis*), and it was from nature that Abraham learned the laws of God, as Philo sees it. Anyone who would declare the Jews parochial because of their particular observances (for example, the laws governing diet, circumcision, or the Sabbath) need only consider that the first father of the Jewish people was able to infer those very practices from the "unwritten law," the law of nature, to which all peoples are accountable. What is more, Abraham became "a law and an unwritten statute" himself, not only an exemplification but a personification of the Torah.[16] That we of the later generations are, alas, unable to infer statutes from nature speaks to the necessity of the "enacted laws" of Moses's book. Those laws themselves, however, are but instructions in book form of how to live lives like those of the pre-Mosaic heroes, figures who were veritable "laws endowed with life and reason." They were the Mosaic ideal before Moses. They were the ideal that Moses sought to make available to the world.

The rabbis of the Talmudic period continue this Second Temple tradition of the Torah-observant Abraham. In fact, they sometimes enhance it by stressing the totality of his observance. The best-known example comes from a passage appended to a Mishnaic tractate.[17] The immediate context is the drawbacks of various occupations that a man might teach his son:

Rabbi Nehorai says: I would lay aside all the occupations in the world and teach my son nothing but Torah, for a man enjoys its reward in This World but its principal remains for the World-to-Come. But all the other occupations are not so. When a man falls into illness, old age, or adversity, and cannot engage in his work, what happens? He dies of hunger. But the Torah is not so. Rather, it protects him from all evil in his youth and grants him a future and a hope in his old age. . . . And thus it says about Our Father Abraham (peace be unto him!): "Abraham was now old . . . and the LORD had blessed Abraham in all things" (Gen 24:1). We find that Our Father Abraham practiced the whole Torah in its entirety before it had been given, as it is said, "inasmuch as Abraham obeyed Me and kept My charge: My commandments, My laws, and My teachings" (Gen 26:5). (*m. Qiddushin* 4:14)

There are two key words on which Rabbi Nehorai's midrash turns: "old" and "all." Abraham is the first man in the Bible to be described as "old,"[18] but he seems to endure none of the degradations of old age, "dying at a good ripe age, old and contented" (Gen 25:8). He even takes a new wife, Keturah, with whom this extraordinarily agile senior begets another six sons.[19] With its report that "Abraham was now old . . . and the LORD had blessed Abraham in all things," Genesis 24:1 recapitulates the first leading word of the midrash and introduces the second: "all." Surely, this midrash seems to reason, a man who had no knowledge of Torah could not have been blessed in *all* things! (Another midrash reasons the same way about Abraham's lack of a daughter and, in one variant, concludes that *bakkol*, Hebrew for "in all things," was actually his daughter's name.)[20]

Putting Abraham's vigorous old age together with the report of his complete blessedness, as Genesis 24:1 does, we come to the position that it was Abraham's observance of Torah that brought about his exemplary golden years. And it was not just that he observed some commandments and experienced some blessing. Rather, to have been blessed "in all things" he must have observed "the whole (*kol*) Torah in its entirety (*kullah*)."

Indeed, the midrash purports to find this in the very text of the Torah, which lists several categories of commandments that the patriarch observed: "Abraham obeyed Me and kept My charge: My commandments, My laws, and My teachings" (Gen 26:5). So interpreted, the plain-sense wording of the biblical verse confirms the point of Rabbi Nehorai's midrash—and Abraham's maximal observance.

Rabbinic literature therefore offers more than a few examples of the patriarch's observance of norms that would be revealed only later and, in some instances, would depend on historical events that have not taken place in his lifetime. We find him, for example, making unleavened bread for Passover, being appointed a priest, instituting and reciting the morning prayers, and practicing the laws of ritual purity.[21] The question of how literally the rabbis believed all this is open to dispute. It can be argued that their goal in producing or transmitting such anachronisms was to give the practices in question what the historian of religion Mircea Eliade calls "the prestige of origins."[22] In that case, the goal is not so much to make a point about Abraham; it is to make a point about the importance and precious-ness of the practices of the Torah by associating them with the an-cient and revered first father of the Jewish people. Something similar may already have happened in Genesis itself, where God enjoins the practice of circumcision on Abraham and his offspring (chapter 17). In no other book of the Hebrew Bible is circumcision associated with him.[23] That being so, one can speculate that rabbinic tradition, like Jubilees beforehand, continued a reconception of Abraham as Torah-observant that began in Genesis itself.

How did Abraham come into his knowledge of Torah? This, so far as we can tell, is not a matter of great concern to the rabbis. One pas-sage, however, does propose an answer:

Rabbi Shimon bar Yochai said: No father taught him, nor did he have a teacher (*rav*). From where did he learn the Torah? Actually, the Holy One (blessed be He) appointed his two kidneys to be like two teachers (*rabbanim*), and these would gush forth and teach him wisdom, as it is written, "I bless the LORD who has guided me; / my kidneys admonish me at night" (Ps 16:7). (*Gen. Rab.* 61:1)[24]

In this midrash, Abraham did not receive his knowledge of Torah from a book, as in Jubilees, or from a teacher/rabbi of the previous generation, as the rabbis themselves usually claim to have received their own knowledge. Instead, he acquired it from God, who im-planted it like a microchip in his kidneys (often the seat of thinking in ancient Israel), which would release their precious gift at night. As Philo had written a century or so earlier, Abraham "listened to no voice or instruction but [his] own"—except that in Rabbi Shimon bar Yochai's view Abraham's instruction flows not from any ability to decode nature on his own but from God's implanting within him the equivalent of two rabbinic teachers.

And so we have come full circle. The Second Temple notion that Abraham kept the whole Torah, or major parts of it, before it was revealed to Israel at Sinai may have brought about the insertion of the atypical verse that gives four terms for what he observed ("charge," "commandments," "laws," and "teachings," Gen 26:5), and that verse came to provide a textual basis for the new theology of Abraham the man of Torah. This maximalist interpretation of the set of four terms was given its best-known formulation by Rashi, the great biblical and Talmudic commentator who lived in northern France in the eleventh century C.E.:

> *Inasmuch as Abraham obeyed Me*
> when I tested him.
> *And kept My charge:*
> The decrees for prevention of wrongdoing regarding the
>     warnings which are in the Torah, such as incest of second
>     degree and rabbinical prohibitions regarding Sabbath
>     observance.
> *My commandments,*
> Those matters that even if they were not written, would be wor-
>     thy of being taken as commandments, such as the prohibition
>     on robbery and bloodshed.
> *My laws,*
> Matters that the Evil Inclination seeks to refute, such as the pro-
>     hibition on eating swine's flesh and on the wearing of fabrics
>     of mixed wool and linen, for which there is no reason, but
>     [they are simply] the decree of the King and His law for His
>     servants.
> *And My teachings.*
> This includes the Oral Torah, the laws [given] to Moses on Sinai.
>     (Rashi on Gen 26:5b)

Rashi begins with a point that would seem close to incontestable, that the clause "inasmuch as Abraham obeyed Me" refers to the

Aqedah, where, as we have seen, essentially the identical language appears (Gen 22:18). He goes on, however, to find every category of Jewish law in the list—those that protect other elements of law ("charge"), those that can be rationally defended ("commandments"), those that seem irrational and pointless in themselves but must be observed as acts of obedience to the divine sovereign ("laws"), and even those that have no basis in the Written Torah but stand on the authority of rabbinic tradition alone ("teachings," literally, "Torahs," whose plural form is thus taken to indicate the presence of both the Written and the Oral Torahs). Abraham has become a man of Torah in all its senses.

When we move from this Jewish trajectory to early Christianity, we find that although many of the evocations of Abraham in the early church have no resonance at all with the particular tradition of the Torah-observant patriarch, they reflect well other currents in the Jewish appropriation of Abraham.[25]

In the Letter to the Hebrews, for example, Abraham appears as a paradigmatic man of faith, obeying God's instructions when "he set out, not knowing where he was going," and, by dint of that same faith, enduring in the land, trusting in providence when the promise of progeny seemed absurd, and offering up Isaac in the sure conviction "that God is able even to raise someone from the dead" (Heb 11:8–12, 17–19). In other New Testament texts, to say that someone is with Abraham is the equivalent of saying he or she is in a blessed state after death.[26] Interpretations of this sort cannot be said to fall outside the orbit of Jewish thinking at the time—and this is not surprising, since the Church retained the Hebrew Bible (only later to be reclassified as an "Old Testament") as scripture and thus left itself open to the messages of that collection, quite apart from the distinctive Christian theology that was developing alongside it and increasingly adapting it to its own needs.

In other instances, however, the gospel moves in a direction that, while not necessarily unparalleled in Jewish sources, markedly contradicts the general direction of Jewish theology in the period. One thinks, for example, of words attributed to John the Baptist when some

Pharisees and Sadducees (members of two contemporary Jewish sects), heeding his call for repentance, sought baptism at his hand:

> [7]"You brood of vipers! Who warned you to flee from the wrath to come? [8]Bear fruit worthy of repentance. [9]Do not presume to say to yourselves, 'We have Abraham as our ancestor'; for I tell you, God is able from these stones to raise up children to Abraham. [10]Even now the ax is lying at the root of the trees; every tree therefore that does not bear good fruit is cut down and thrown into the fire." (Matt 3:7–10; cf. Luke 3:7–9)

The notion that descent from Abraham protects an individual from divine judgment is not general in ancient Judaism, although it is not hard to imagine that there were Jews who believed it. What is noteworthy here, however, is the extreme discounting of Abrahamic paternity and the correlative emphasis on good works in determining an individual's fate. Although the passage is less than ideally clear, and it is hard to know how literally its supercharged rhetoric is to be taken, it seems to say this: Only "good fruit" enables escape from the impending day of wrath and the hellfire into which the unworthy shall be thrown. The election of Abraham is irrelevant.

A similar point, but conveyed with even greater rhetorical heat, is made in a dispute of Jesus with "the Jews" that appears in John but not in the other gospels:

> [39]They answered him, "Abraham is our father." Jesus said to them, "If you were Abraham's children, you would be doing what Abraham did, [40]but now you are trying to kill me, a man who has told you the truth that I heard from God. This is not what Abraham did. [41]You are indeed doing what your father does." They said to him, "We are not illegitimate children; we have one father, God himself." [42]Jesus said to them, "If God were your Father, you would love me, for I came from God and now I am here. I did not come on my own, but he sent me. [43]Why do you not understand what I say? It is because you cannot accept my word. [44]You are from your father the devil, and you choose to do your father's desires. He was a murderer from the beginning and does not stand in the truth, because there is no truth in him. When he lies, he speaks accord-

ing to his own nature, for he is a liar and the father of lies." (John 8:39–44)

Here, the key thing about Abraham is not whom he fathered but what he did. To the Jews' claim that their father is Abraham, Jesus points to the discrepancy between their deeds and his. What precisely is meant by "what Abraham did" (Greek, *ta erga tou Abraam*, literally, "the works of Abraham," v. 39) is unclear, but the message is patent: "the Jews" ought to be doing the same thing. Indeed, the underlying notion is that paternity is strictly a matter of behavior, so that those who act like "the Jews" cannot be of Abrahamic or divine descent but must be instead—and this charge has resonated through the centuries, sometimes with murderous consequences—the offspring of the devil.[27] In this passage, only those who heed Jesus and love him can have, like him, a divine paternity. The others fall outside the Abrahamic community and the grace of God alike.

As the angry confrontation goes on, Jesus escalates his rhetoric into an assertion that he has priority over Abraham both in time and in importance:

> [56]"Your ancestor Abraham rejoiced that he would see my day; he saw it and was glad." [57]Then the Jews said to him, "You are not yet fifty years old, and have you seen Abraham?" [58]Jesus said to them, "Very truly, I tell you, before Abraham was, I am." (John 8:56–58)

With the fateful words "I am," John immediately evokes the LORD's revelation of his name to Moses and powerfully underscores his belief that Jesus is divine and primordial.[28] Apart from Jesus, the gospel is telling us, any claim to Abrahamic descent or affinity is meaningless.

John's term "the works of Abraham" could not be further from the characteristic use made of Abraham by the apostle Paul, whose letters predate all the gospels. For, especially in his relatively early Letter to the Galatians, Paul was engaged in a fierce dispute with Christians who believed that being faithful to Jesus meant practicing Jesus's own religion, which was, of course, some variety of Judaism and which certainly entailed the observance of Jewish law (however defined)— "the works of the law," in Paul's parlance.[29] In arguing the contrary position, that Christian identity (the term is admittedly anachronistic) does not require Gentiles to practice the full complement of Mosaic commandments, Paul faced formidable opposition.[30] Among his opponents were Jesus's brother, James, and his key disciple, Peter, both of whom, needless to say, knew Jesus well in the flesh. Paul, by contrast, never knew Jesus before the latter's death, and, by his own admission, in the early days of the new community he "was violently persecuting the church of God and was trying to destroy it" (Gal 1:13).

So, whereas James and Peter could base their apostolate on Jesus's own words and deeds, Paul based his on a claim that, as he put it, "God . . . was pleased to reveal his Son to me, so that I might proclaim him among the Gentiles" (Gal 1:15–16). What irritated Paul's opponents in Galatia (now central Turkey) was his bold claim that Jewish law did not to any degree obligate the Gentiles who came into the new community that was focused on Jesus. That claim seemed outrageous, for it contradicted not only the implications of Jesus's own practice but the Torah itself, most of which, after all, is centered on nothing other than the LORD's revelation to Israel at Sinai.

It is precisely here that Paul found Abraham useful. For by the Torah's own report, Abraham lived several generations before Moses and the revelation at Sinai yet nonetheless found favor with God and had become a revered figure in Judaism. If Abraham did not carry out "the works of the law," then why would anyone think that those who become his descendants should do so? Indeed, as Paul read Genesis, Abraham showed an alternative—and better—way to win favor with God. Paul's key biblical prooftext (Gen 15:6) is the same one we have discussed earlier, in chapters 1 and 3:

> [6]Just as Abraham "had faith in God, and it was reckoned to him as righteousness," [7]so, you see, those who have faith are the descendants of Abraham. [8]And the scripture, foreseeing that God would justify the Gentiles by faith, declared the gospel beforehand to Abraham, saying, "All the Gentiles shall be blessed in you." [9]For this reason, those who have faith are blessed with Abraham who had faith. (Gal 3:6–9)[31]

In our earlier examinations of this prooftext, we have rendered it, "And because he [Abram] put his trust in the LORD, He reckoned it to his merit" (Gen 15:6).[32] The verse, it will be recalled, marks the transition between Abram's doubt about God's promise that he will beget offspring and his mysterious trust in God's prediction that his offspring will, in fact, be innumerable. In chapter 3, though, we also saw that already two and a half centuries before Paul wrote his Letter to the Galatians, some Jewish sources had detached the verse from its immediate context in Genesis 15 and interpreted it as a summary comment about the character of Abraham's relationship to God, pronounced only after he passed his great test, the Binding of Isaac (Gen 22:1–19).

Paul, similarly, detaches the verse from its narrative context, but, breaking with those Jewish precedents, he also finds in it a solution to the question he faced in Galatia, the question of the terms under which Gentiles may legitimately enter the family of Abraham. They do so, he claims, the same way the family of Abraham came into existence in the first place, not through the commandments of the Torah, which had not yet been enjoined, but through faith. Indeed, as Paul reads the verse, it entails the further point that "those who have faith are the descendants of Abraham." Whereas the Gospel of John sees the *works* of Abraham—"what Abraham did" (8:39)—as the identifying mark of the patriarch's genuine descendants, Paul assigns the same role to the *faith* of Abraham.

And this, in turn, enables the Apostle to the Gentiles to discover the mechanism whereby the ancient and momentous promise that other nations will be blessed in Abraham can be fulfilled.[33] The nations—or, as the translation above renders the Greek *ethnē*, the "Gentiles"—are blessed when, having acquired a faith like Abraham's, they also become his descendants. In Paul's theology, it is through such faith that Gentiles become, as it were, Jews.

In the whole history of New Testament interpretation, there is perhaps nothing that has been more misunderstood than the intertwined topics of Paul's relationship to the Torah and his understanding of the promise to Abraham, and the consequences of these misunderstandings for Jewish-Christian relations have been catastrophic. In particular, we must correct two long-standing and still widespread misunderstandings of what Paul is actually saying.

The first misunderstanding results from a conflation of Paul's view of Torah law with the view taken by other New Testament sources. In the gospels, we hear Jesus thundering against the "scribes and Pharisees," who he claims, for example, "tithe mint, dill, and cummin, and have neglected the weightier matters of the law: justice and mercy and faith" (Matt 23:23). Here, the assumption is that the observance of the Torah involves obsessive-compulsive behaviors, indifference to social justice, and hypocrisy, at least in the case of those against whom Jesus is preaching. But this is not at all Paul's view. Paul has no problem writing that "the law is holy, and the commandment is holy and just and good" (Rom 7:12). Indeed, the tendentious idea that, before "God . . . was pleased to reveal his Son to [him]," the future apostle was somehow suffering psychologically under the grievous burden of the law has been quite effectively debunked.[34]

Paul's idea is actually very different. In his theology—unlike that of rabbinic Judaism—the Torah and its commandments render a capital indictment but offer no possibility of acquittal. That is to say, the obligation to perform the commandments does not save humans; it condemns them. But since in Paul's thinking the defendants really are guilty—for such is the fallen human condition—this neither indicates an imperfection in the norms themselves nor reflects negatively on the motivation of those who observe them.[35] As E. P. Sanders puts it, "Paul did not preach about men, but about God."[36] His primary focus is not the human condition but the dramatic new situation that he believes God has just brought about through Jesus.

But does not the Torah promise blessings to those who perform its commandments? Paul's reply to this is, in brief, that the blessings promised in the Torah are conditional; they require one to keep the full range of the commandments. "For all who rely on the works of the law are under a curse," he wrote to the Galatian communities; "for it is written, 'Cursed is everyone who does not observe and obey all the things written in the book of the law'" (Gal 3:10, citing Deut 27:36).

Now, within the framework of rabbinic thinking, too, Jews who fail to observe the commandments are in trouble. But they can and should remedy their failure though genuine repentance and (if available) atonement through sacrifice, especially on Yom Kippur (the Day of Atonement). For whatever reason—and scholars vigorously debate the reason[37]—Paul did not think those methods could work.

Instead, he saw the death of Jesus as a vicarious, sacrificial act that effected the transition from curse to blessing, as the Torah could not. In Paul's mind, moreover, this is closely connected with the blessing upon the Gentiles prominent in the promise to Abraham in Genesis. As he puts it in the same passage in Galatians:

> [13]Christ redeemed us from the curse of the law by becoming a curse for us—for it is written, "Cursed is everyone who hangs on a tree"—[14]in order that in Christ Jesus the blessing of Abraham might come to the Gentiles, so that we might receive the promise of the Spirit through faith. (Gal 3:13–14, citing Deut 21:23)[38]

Here, Paul presents the Christ Event as a restoration of the Abrahamic order of things, after the interruption caused by the revelation of the Torah with all its norms and the curses that come with them. The blessing on the nations that was promised to Abraham finally comes about, and with it a return of the way of life that Abraham exemplified—a way of life based in faith in God but without most of the norms of the Torah. Moses and his laws are, so to speak, a parenthesis between the faith of Abraham in the distant past and its restoration in the early Christian community, only recently formed. By appealing to Abraham, Paul enables Jesus (as he understands him) to trump Moses.

The second misunderstanding maintains that Paul's dissatisfaction with the law had to do with his universalism: that is, his desire to bring all people to God. That the Apostle to the Gentiles harbored such an aspiration is beyond doubt. But why would anyone think that such an aspiration requires jettisoning the commandments of the Torah (or some subset of them)? In our last chapter, we pointed to the evidence that at least in rabbinic Judaism (if not earlier), Abraham had come to be seen as a missionary, converting people to Judaism. Indeed, a Talmudic passage memorably terms Abraham "the first of the converts" (*b. Chagigah* 3a), probably because he is the first to undergo *berit milah* (ritual circumcision), as required of all male converts to Judaism. A Jewish aspiration to universalism, then, does not in the least suggest that some means other than conversion to Judaism must be found to incorporate Gentiles into the Abrahamic family.

Whatever caused Paul's perfervid rejection of circumcision—at one point he expresses the hope that his Galatian opponents, the preachers of circumcision, "would castrate themselves" (Gal 5:12)—it was not his universalistic aspiration to convert the whole world to his religion. Like those opponents in Galatia, he could have preached the necessity of circumcision to the Gentiles. There is, in other words, nothing in universalism that points to Paul's particular concept of the gospel and the obligations of non-Jews in light of it. For that matter, there is nothing in universalism that points to Christianity (with whatever type of gospel) rather than to Judaism itself. Someone who aspires to convert the whole world to his own religion could just as easily try to convert it to either of those two religions.

I have been arguing against the idea that Paul's universalist aspiration motivates his recourse to Abraham and his correlative advocacy that the Gentiles are not obligated by most of the Mosaic commandments. There is, however, a counterargument to this, and to it we must now pay attention. The counterargument centers on the fact that the norms of the Torah at issue for Paul are specifically those that separate Jew from Gentile, those that, in other words, demarcate Jews as a distinctive group: circumcision, dietary laws, and the sacred days (sabbaths and festivals).

In the thinking of one scholar, James D. G. Dunn, "the leading edge of Paul's theological thinking was the conviction that God's purpose embraced Gentiles as well as Jews." Hence, the target of his polemic was "nationalistic presumption" and "ethnic restrictiveness," both of them thought to be characteristic of the Jewish understanding of Torah theretofore.[39] To do justice to God's purpose, those community-defining practices would have to be jettisoned and a new people, neither Jewish nor Gentile, would have to come into existence to testify to the God who transcended the unfortunate and unnecessary boundary between the two groups.

Daniel Boyarin expresses a similar point. To him, Paul is very much a figure of "the world of Hellenistic Judaism of the first century." He "was motivated by a Hellenistic desire for the One, which among other things produced an ideal of a universal human essence, beyond difference and hierarchy."[40] In defining the Mosaic-Sinaitic moment as temporary, and as now superseded in a return to the Abrahamic, Paul swept away all those boundary-defining practices "in order that," in the apostle's own words, "in Christ Jesus the blessing of Abraham might come to the Gentiles, so that we might receive the promise of the Spirit through faith" (Gal 3:14, reusing Gen 28:3–4). And it is faith, it will be recalled, not works or commandments, that in Paul's thinking defined Abraham's righteousness.

The problem with this line of thought, however, is that it dramatically underplays the importance of chosenness or election—both the election of Abraham and the election of the Christian—in Paul's theology. Paul may well have wished to put Jew and Gentile on an even footing before God, as Dunn capably argues (though Paul sometimes wavers on this). But the apostle's appeal to the Abrahamic promise nonetheless suggests something very different from the modern universalist's dislike of nationalism, ethnicity, and boundaries.[41]

Abraham is not an exemplar of "a universal human essence," and Paul does not treat him as if he were. If there is such a person in Paul's thinking, it is Adam, the universal human father, and Adam for Paul is a purely negative figure: he represents disobedience, sin, condemnation, and death, and, as such, is the diametric opposite and foil of Paul's Christ.[42] Abraham, by contrast, is a man mysteriously singled out from universal humanity for a new, unprecedented, and unparalleled destiny shared by no one, until the promise to him comes to apply to those descended from him—just as Jesus (as Paul would put it), exemplifies a new, unprecedented, and unparalleled destiny shared by no one until the promise fulfilled in him comes to benefit those who are in him, which is to say, the Church.

One cannot adequately grasp Paul's theology without reckoning with this simple but momentous fact: for Paul, *the Gentile Christian has abandoned the Adamic identity for the Abrahamic.* He has left the universal identity associated with the sin-infected human essence and been recreated as one who attains righteousness in the sight of God on the basis of his faith, just as Abraham did in the Pauline reading of Genesis 15:6.

Were Paul truly intent on transcending the difference between Jews and Gentiles, would he have so stressed the man known as the father of the Jewish people? And would he have advanced the claim that those who have faith in Jesus had, by that very act, become nothing short of descendants of Abraham? For by claiming that the Gentile converts had become the adoptive children of the first

Jewish patriarch, Paul and similar early Christian figures tied the Church necessarily and irrevocably to the Jewish people and its scriptures, even as they distanced it from some of the Jewish practices that the Greco-Roman world found baffling and sometimes offensive, such as circumcision, the dietary laws, and the Sabbath. But Paul did not distance the Church from one such baffling and offensive Jewish practice: "Flee from the worship of idols," he urges the Corinthian Christians (1 Cor 10:14). In upholding this peculiar Jewish refusal to worship gods other than their own, and in stoutly maintaining the uniqueness and exclusive claim of the God of Israel, Paul again showed that the mixed community of Jews and Gentiles that made up the nascent Christian Church did not correspond to "an ideal of a universal human essence, beyond difference and hierarchy." Rather, it represented the adoption of Gentiles into the Abrahamic family.

Paula Fredriksen puts it well:

> Pagans-in-Christ are also from Abraham's lineage, since Abraham was the father of many nations (Gen 17.4; Rom 4.17); but they descend from Abraham *alone*, not also from Isaac and Jacob. Because of the Spirit, however, these pagans too are now sons, heirs to the "promise" to Abraham: like Israel, they too can now call God "Abba. Father" . . .
>
> But this new kinship is not tantamount to "conversion," because these Gentiles are adopted not into Israel's family, but into God's, made such not *kata sarka* [according to the flesh] but *kata pneuma* [according to the Spirit]. Put differently: redeemed Israel and the pagans-in-Christ together share the same heavenly father *kata pneuma*, but *kata sarka* they remain distinct.[43]

In chapter 4, we saw the emergence of an image of Abraham as a missionary seeking to bring outsiders to the one true God. Within the rabbinic framework, this involves their acceptance of the commandments of the Torah and the rites associated with conversion, which, in the case of males, include ritual circumcision. Converts to Judaism, that is, join both God's family and Israel's. They become Jewish in spirit and in flesh alike.

Whether Paul ever knew of and respected such a process of conversion is unclear. Either way, we now see that what he has done is to open up a different means of incorporating Gentiles into God's family and Abraham's, a process that he thinks is brought about exclusively by the Spirit acting on those with faith in the gospel of Jesus Christ; it cannot, he pointedly and repeatedly insists, be brought about by observance of the laws and commandments of the Torah. In the background of this Pauline theology lies the promise to Abraham that he would be "the father of a multitude of nations" (Gen 17:4), a promise made when the Torah and its norms had not been given. But in its background also lies the already ancient Jewish expectation that at the end-time, the Gentiles, without ceasing to be Gentiles, would renounce their idolatry and embrace the worship of the God of Israel alongside the people Israel.[44] Believing that the end-time had arrived and that the messiah himself had already come, Paul saw in the gospel a way—the *only* way—to bring about that very scenario.

Among the points that are maddeningly unclear in Paul's theology is the relationship between the new community, which is the Church, and the old community, which is the Jewish people apart from the Church.[45] At times, especially in his extended meditation on the subject in Romans 9–11, Paul insists, for example, that to his "kindred according to the flesh . . . belong the adoption, the glory, the covenants, the giving of the law, the [Temple] worship, and the promises . . . [as well as] the patriarchs" (Rom 9:3–5). But just after this ringing affirmation of the continuing election of Israel comes a claim that it is the spirit alone, and not the flesh, that determines who Israel really is:

> [6]It is not as though the word of God had failed. For not all Israelites truly belong to Israel, [7]and not all of Abraham's children are his true descendants; but "It is through Isaac that descendants shall be named for you" [Gen 21:12]. [8]This means that it is not the children of the flesh who are the children of God, but the children of the promise are counted as descendants. (Rom 9:6–8)

However these and similar contradictions in Paul on this subject might be resolved, it seems likely that Paul did not expect the problem to last long. Given his expectation of an imminent return of Jesus and the concomitant end to the current world order, the likelihood is that he thought the widespread failure of the Jews—hard-hearted, disobedient, and unbelieving—to be persuaded by the gospel would soon be reversed, and God would grant Paul's own "prayer . . . that they may be saved" (Rom 10:1). But they would be saved the same way Abraham was pronounced righteous, as Paul would have it—by faith apart from the commandments of the Torah. Without the restoration of that Abrahamic path to righteousness, long eclipsed by the Torah and its commandments, the incorporation of Gentiles into the "blessing of Abraham" would never come to be, and it would be as if the messiah had never come.

Our discussion of the variant relationships of Abraham to the Torah lends itself to a contrast of Judaism and Christianity that among both communities is as familiar as it is convenient. The contrast is between a view of Abraham, on the one hand, as the man who, in the words of a famous text found in the Mishnah, "practiced the whole Torah in its entirety before it had been given" and, on the other hand, the interpretation of him in Paul as the man whose faith "was reckoned to him as righteousness," apart from any commandments of the Torah, even the commandment of ritual circumcision that was enjoined upon him before anyone else. The same contrast easily becomes generalized into a depiction of Judaism as focused on law and ethics—the deed, not the creed, as it is often said—and Christianity as focused on faith, theology, and subjective experience.[46] Whatever limited applicability this handy contrast has, it also recalls H. L. Mencken's quip: "There is always an easy solution to every human problem—neat, plausible, and wrong."[47]

To understand why this is wrong for Christianity, one need only consider the great emphasis that non-Pauline traditions in early Christianity place upon one's deeds and not simply on faith alone.[48] In the Gospel according to Matthew, for example, how one has treated the weak determines whether one's ultimate destiny is "eternal punishment" or "eternal life" (25:46). And, then, of course, there are the famous words ascribed to Jesus in the Gospel according to John: "If you love me, you will keep my commandments" (14:15). Although the commandments in question are not those of the Mosaic Torah (despite some overlaps), these texts and many others like them do speak to the high estimation of commandments, deeds, and obedience in early Christianity in a way that one would not expect from the familiar but overdrawn and self-serving contrast outlined in our previous paragraph. In the New Testament, Christianity does not at all reduce to faith alone or consistently imply that good works are not important for salvation—far from it.

Another New Testament document—the Letter of James—insists explicitly on the importance of good deeds ("works" in the parlance of Christian theology) but this time does so by citing none other than Abraham, and in a way that contrasts strikingly, and surely not coincidentally, with Paul's use of the patriarch:

> [20]Do you want to be shown, you senseless person, that faith apart from works is barren? [21]Was not our ancestor Abraham justified by works when he offered his son Isaac on the altar? [22]You see that faith was active along with works, and faith was brought to completion by the works. [23]Thus the scripture was fulfilled that says, "Abraham had faith in God, and it was reckoned to him as righteousness" [Gen 15:6], and he was called the friend of God. [24]You see that a person is justified by works and not by faith alone. . . . [26]For just as the body without the spirit is dead, so faith without works is also dead. (James 2:20–24, 26)[49]

The contrast with Paul's use of Genesis 15:6 is obvious. What is not so obvious is that the unknown author of the letter depends on a Jewish tradition in which that verse was thought to apply only *after* Abraham had passed his great test, the Binding of Isaac, a tradition we examined in chapter 3.[50] This enables the letter writer to attribute Abraham's being reckoned as righteous to a *deed*, a work, specifically his obedience to the divine command to sacrifice his beloved son. With this, the author seeks to prove that works are essential and faith is flimsy without them. To be sure, the works in question are not the commandments of the Torah, and James is *not* addressing the identical question that exercised Paul—the halakhic question of what norms should apply to a Gentile who comes into the Abrahamic family. Rather, the author of James is addressing an extrapolation of Paul's polemic that included *all* works in the indictment—an extrapolation, by the way, that appears again and again in Christian tradition itself, into our own time.

The interpretation of the Aqedah in James 2 not only draws on an antecedent Jewish understanding of Genesis 15:6 as coming into effect only after Abraham had proven willing to obey the painful divine command to offer up his beloved son; it also draws upon the core Christian story of the passion, crucifixion, and resurrection of Jesus. Consider that last verse: "For just as the body without the spirit is dead, so faith without works is also dead" (James 2:26). Today's reader would be more inclined to liken faith to the spirit and works to the body. After all, is not faith something invisible, found deep within, and are not works physical actions done by embodied persons? Indeed, the notion that works are physical but faith is spiritual correlates nicely with a hoary anti-Jewish polemic, in which the Jewish people and the religion of the Torah are described as carnal but the Church and its gospel as spiritual.

James, however, makes exactly the reverse equation: faith alone is a dead body, and works are the spirit. Those who seek to live their lives by faith alone are spiritually deadened and thus in urgent need of the enlivening force of works, for it is works that provide life to the dead body. Now, given the centrality of the proclamation of Jesus's resurrection in early Christianity, it should be clear that James's invocation of the Aqedah has a close association with his understanding of the Christ Event.[51] The implication is that what enables the Christian to participate in Jesus's resurrection is precisely the powerful, enlivening force unleashed by works. Works not only make faith real and complete; together with faith, they do what faith alone cannot do: they resurrect the dead.

If this Christological thinking indeed underlies our passage, how then does the Aqedah advance its argument? I suspect the author of James understood the Aqedah in a manner like this: Abraham, whose faith never wavered, proceeded to act in a way that would normally have resulted in the death of Isaac. In other words, to all appearances the father was about to transform his beloved son into "a body without the spirit," a corpse. Amazingly, the actions he took, up to and including his reaching for the slaughterer's knife, brought about the reverse transformation, so that the son whom we—and perhaps he as well—had given up for dead lived again. Like Jesus leaving his tomb, Isaac got up from the altar that would have been his funeral pyre, and Abraham's faith, only now rendered complete by works, was at last reckoned to him as righteousness. Only then, only after he had chosen obedience to God's command over the life of the son he loved, did Abraham earn the title "friend [or, lover] of God." His sacrificial act, like sacrifice in general, had proven powerful beyond imagining. It had transformed death into life.

In James 2:20–26, the author of this New Testament letter has propounded an interpretation of Abraham that makes of him a paradigm not only of faith, as Paul did, but, more important, of obedience in works as well. In so doing, he has cast doubt on the very dichotomy of faith and works by holding that someone who has one of these but not the other is incomplete, the way a body or a soul alone is incomplete, less than a full person. And by attaching this theological claim to the Aqedah, with its rich resonance in the foundational story of Christianity, the author of the Letter of James argues forcefully against the attempt to define Christianity as the religion of faith and grace, with deeds as secondary implications only; that definition, he insists, is untrue to the gospel itself.

But is there, on the Jewish side, an equivalent undermining of the familiar, self-serving contrast between the two religions? Is there a Jewish understanding of Abraham that sees him as *not* having "practiced the whole Torah in its entirety before it had been given" but exemplary nonetheless?

We can begin to answer that question by turning to the Talmud. There we discover that the interpretation of Abraham as one who observed the entire Torah is presented, like so many ideas in that great collection, as only one position in an argument and not simply as a final and uncontested truth. Alongside this tradition of the fully observant Abraham, which we can label "maximalist," there was also another tradition that saw him as observing far fewer commandments, a position we can call "minimalist." Thus, whereas the early third-century authority Rav taught that "Our Father Abraham fulfilled the whole Torah," citing the end of Genesis 26:5 ("inasmuch as Abraham obeyed Me and kept My charge: My commandments, My laws, and My teachings") as evidence, his colleague, Shimi bar Chiyya retorts, "I can say it applies only to the seven commandments." Here, the reference is to the seven norms that rabbinic tradition thought applied to universal humanity, Jews and Gentiles alike—the requirement that laws and courts be established and the prohibitions on idolatry, murder, sexual immorality, blasphemy, theft, and eating a limb from an animal that has not been slaughtered.[52] Another voice then enters the Talmudic debate to ask about circumcision, which is not one of these seven universally obligatory norms but is explicitly enjoined upon Abraham, and observed by him, in Genesis 17. To this, Shimi bar Chiyya, or someone taking his position, concedes the addition of this one commandment, but this still leaves Abraham with but eight commandments, far fewer than the 613 that traditionally make up the full complement in the Torah. The exchange ends with a question implying that Shimi bar Chiyya's minimalist position does not do justice to the full list of norms given in Rav's prooftext in Genesis 26:5 (b. Yoma 28b).

Although this Talmudic debate ends with the impression that Rav's maximalist interpretation of Abraham's observance won out, the argument, in fact, reverberates throughout subsequent Jewish tradition. Since we gave Rashi's exegesis of Genesis 26:5b as our exemplar of the maximalist view, it is only fair that we cite his grandson, Rashbam (Rabbi Shmuel ben Meir, northern France, ca. 1085–1174), as the great exponent of the opposing opinion:

*Inasmuch as Abraham obeyed Me*
Concerning the Binding of Isaac, as it is written, "inasmuch as you have obeyed Me" (Gen 22:18)[53]
*and kept My charge:*
Such as circumcision, as it is written about it, "And as for you, you . . . shall keep My covenant" (Gen 17:9)
*My commandments,*
Such as the commandment about the eight days [until the father performs circumcision on the son], as it is written, "As God commanded him" (Gen 21:4)
*My laws, and My teachings.*
According to the essence of its plain sense, [it refers to] all the commandments that are [generally] recognized, such as the laws against robbery, sexual misdeeds, and coveting, and the requirement for legal order, and the laws of hospitality. All of these were in force before the Torah was given, but they were [then] renewed and explicated to Israel, and they made a covenant to practice them. (Rashbam on Gen 26:5b)

To Rashbam, then, the key verse refers not to the totality of Jewish law, but only to those elements in it that Abraham could have intuited on the basis of his natural reason, augmented by the one norm he received through special revelation, the commandment of *berit milah*, or ritual circumcision. That those norms that he knew through natural reason (as any Gentile could and should) later became part of God's revelation to Israel on Sinai does not imply that Abraham already knew or practiced the *whole* Torah before it was given. All it implies is that some of the norms of the Torah are rationally discernible and universal in their application. Having observed those commandments along with circumcision and the special directions that God gave him (especially the commandment to sacrifice Isaac), Abraham abundantly proved his compliance with God's will, so far as he could know it.

At first glance, the minimalist position has an affinity with Paul's notion that Abraham's righteousness was the result of his faith, not his practice of the commandments of the Torah. For Paul and Rashbam would have agreed that the example of Abraham testifies to the theoretical possibility of finding favor in God's eyes without the benefit of the whole corpus of commandments, which rabbinic tradition came to define as 613 in number. This possibility ceases to be theoretical when one considers the crucial fact that in the Hebrew Bible, *God gives the Torah to Israel alone, and not to the Gentiles.* If finding favor in the eyes of God ("having a portion in the World-to-Come," as the rabbis would put it, or "being saved," to use the familiar Christian parlance) required observance of the full complement of the commandments, then no Gentile could ever reach the goal. Neither the rabbinic tradition in its broad outlines nor Paul, obviously, took that extreme position. Thus, while it is not so unusual in Jewish religious circles today to hear the commandments of the Torah praised for their supposedly universal and humanistic character, the classical Jewish tradition does *not* see the vast majority of them as applying to universal humanity at all. The commandments in their totality are God's special gift to the Jewish people, and the Jewish people alone are privileged to have them and obligated to practice them. That Abraham, privileged and obligated in other ways, did not know of the 613 commandments that would later obligate his people in no way undermines the deep structure of rabbinic theology.

A closer look, though, reveals important differences between Paul and the rabbinic position that is exemplified by Rashbam. For Paul, the Abrahamic material becomes important because of his belief that Jesus was the messiah and the concomitant claim that the end of time had just arrived, when the Gentiles would not only be brought to faith in the God of Israel, as the Jewish Bible had envisioned, but even grafted into Abraham's lineage. In Rashbam's case, it is doubtful that he thought of Abraham as a Gentile at all, since the patriarch had become circumcised (a rite of conversion to Judaism) and had broken with idolatry, as we saw in chapter 4. Nor is faith the most important thing in Abraham's example. Rather, Rashbam (and the rabbinic tradition behind his comment) thought that the key to finding favor with God for Jews and Gentiles alike is the commandments. That is why, according to the dominant rabbinic doctrine, the good people of all nations can have a "portion in the World-to-Come." The Gentiles have a few commandments, and the Jews many, but for both groups obedience, and with it salvation, is possible. The exemplary practice to which our key half verse, Genesis 26:5b, refers has to do, then, not with the quantity but with the quality of the patriarch's obedience. Contrary to Rav and Rashi, it does not entail the maximalist view of the ancient patriarch's obedience. In the minimalist reading, it simply tells us that Abraham was scrupulously attentive to the divine commandments as they existed in his time. And in his time, they were limited to the norms that obligated all humanity and to those that God had announced to Abraham alone in special revelations.

Another rabbinic text moves in a rather different direction. It, too, underscores the continuity between Abraham and Sinai, in a way, but—and this we have not seen so far—it also insists on the superiority of the Sinaitic moment over the Abrahamic. The Jewish people are like the man they call "Our Father Abraham," for both observe God's commands. The difference is that the Jews have more opportunity for obedience, since they live on this side of Sinai. Appropriately, the text in question is a midrashic sermon for the occasion of Shavu'ot, for rabbinic tradition associates that holiday with the giving of the Torah (in the Hebrew Bible, it is a first-fruits festival only).

The biblical passage for the sermon is from the tribute to the "capable wife" in Proverbs 31:10–31 (familiar to Jews today from its recitation at the Sabbath table on Friday night), and specifically the verse that quotes her appreciative husband's own words of praise:

> "Many women have done well,
> But you surpass them all." (Prov 31:29)

In its midrashic application, the verse is taken to refer to a succession of generations during which the available commandments gradually grew. Thus, Adam, the first of the "many women" (as it were), had six of those seven universal commandments, to which a seventh, the prohibition on eating a limb from an animal that has not been slaughtered, was given to Noah. The commandment of circumcision gave Abraham eight, and Isaac, as the first person to be circumcised at the ideal time, on his eighth day, thus had nine. The prohibition upon eating "the thigh muscle that is on the socket of the hip" (Gen 32:33) was enjoined upon Jacob, making ten. Finally, Jacob's son Judah recognized an eleventh, the requirement that the surviving brother of a man who dies childless provide him an heir through his widow. All of these individuals "have done well," in the words of the biblical text, "but you," the sermon goes on to say, "at Sinai were commanded 613 commandments, 248 positive ones and 365 negative ones." In other words, the superlative wife addressed in the second half of the verse is Israel standing at Sinai, or, as one version of the midrash reads, "the generation of Moses, which was commanded [the 613 commandments]" (*Pesikta de-Rav Kahana* 12:1). She has been given the totality of which her impressive predecessors, including even Abraham, knew only a part.[54]

In this text, too, universal humanity is in no way faulted; everybody, symbolized by the universal fathers Adam and Noah, has commandments and has therefore "done well." But the Jewish patriarch Abraham has done better, surpassing them with his additional commandment of circumcision, even as Isaac, Jacob, and Judah all surpass the generations before them. The process comes to its climax, though, only at Sinai, when the full complement of commandments is given to the whole Jewish people.

As we have seen, the Jewish tradition that saw Abraham as practicing "the whole Torah in its entirety before it had been given" had already found the ideal in their first patriarch, who anticipated the climactic moment (Sinai) in his own lifetime generations before Moses. Paul, too, had seen Abraham as the ideal, and in his view as proof positive of the irrelevance to salvation of Torah law in all its specifics. By contrast, this text from the *Pesikta de-Rav Kahana* breaks the pattern. Now Abraham no longer stands at the climactic point; he is no longer the apex of the process. The climactic moment, rather, is Sinai, and the ideal is the generation of Moses, who received the reality only partially anticipated in earlier times, including Abraham's. Here Moses, as it were, trumps Abraham—though without any implication that the pre-Mosaic generations were bereft of the knowledge of God and his will or the possibility of salvation. The Gentiles (Adam and Noah) and the pre-Sinaitic Jews performed God's commandments, but God has graciously enabled his people Israel to do better.

We began this part of our discussion by addressing the question of whether rabbinic tradition presents any alternative to the maximalist interpretation in which Abraham "practiced the whole Torah in its entirety before it had been given," and we quickly found that indeed it does. In some rabbinic texts, Abraham is presented as practicing only a few commandments (although those few are defined as the totality of known norms). In this view of the patriarch, what seems to matter most is not the quantity of norms available but the spiritual disposition of those who practice them. As a Talmudic rabbi says in a related context, "It is the same whether one does much or one does little, so long as he directs his heart to Heaven" (*b. Berakhot* 5b).[55] On this principle, people who observe with great devotion the few norms open to them would surely welcome more commandments were they to be made available. In that way, the paucity of commandments that Abraham kept (according to the minimalist interpretation) does not in any way invalidate the likeness between him and Israel at Sinai, when "All the people answered as one, saying, 'All that the LORD has spoken we will do!'" (Exod 19:8). Had Abraham stood at Sinai, he would, on this reading, have been eager to accept all that the LORD spoke there, just as, according to Genesis 26:5, he obeyed the LORD and kept his charge, his commandments, his laws, and his teachings in his own lifetime. Like the maximalist interpretation, the minimalist one thus renders the gap between Abraham's religion and that of his Jewish descendants immaterial.

We found a somewhat different view, however, in the midrash on Proverbs 31:29 ("Many women have done well / But you surpass them all") from the *Pesikta de-Rav Kahana* that we just examined. In that text, quantity does matter. Gentile humanity, represented by Adam with six commandments and Noah with seven, did well, but the fullest revelation comes into being only in the generation of Moses, when the whole Torah is finally given to the Jewish people. Abraham with eight commandments did well, but Israel at Sinai, with all 613, still surpassed him. The question of intention does not arise here; presumably, "direct[ing one's] heart to Heaven" is essential, but the actual deeds—and the number of available opportunities to do them—make an important difference nonetheless. And not only is that the difference between the Gentiles, with their few commandments, and the Jews, with their many; it is also the difference between Abraham and the continuing Jewish people, for whom he was a model in his own time (he did well) but not the ideal model today, when Israel has been charged, and graciously given the wherewithal, to surpass him.

With this last version of the minimalist interpretation of Abraham's Torah observance, the debate with the Pauline current in early Christianity takes another shape. The great contest between Christianity and Judaism about which of them most resembles Abraham—which group is made up of true descendants—has here been derailed, at least on the Jewish side. No longer is Judaism trying to present itself as the more Abrahamic of the two. Whereas for Paul, the Abrahamic model—the model of faith reckoned as righteousness—overrides the Mosaic moment, the rabbinic theology underlying the midrash on Proverbs 31:29 moves in quite the opposite direction. Now, the ideal is the generation of Moses, for which Abraham is but a dim, though commendable, foreshadowing. The paradigm is not Abraham pronounced righteous while still uncircumcised and in that sense more a Gentile than a Jew. It is, rather, the Jewish people encompassed by the full complement of commandments and thus joyfully serving the God who, in his boundless love for them, has given them his Torah.

In a deeper sense, though, Paul and the rabbis are speaking to different situations. (It should not be forgotten that, for the most part, rabbinic Judaism is a later development, and we cannot presuppose that Paul knew of its distinctive contours.) For Paul, the overriding issue is the incorporation of Gentiles into the community worshipping the God of Israel, now that the messianic advent has superseded Sinai as God's consummative revelation. As we have seen, essentially two things motivated Paul: the biblical oracles that predicted a universal turn to that God at the end of time and his conviction, widespread among the first generation of Christians, that the end had indeed arrived and the great things promised were about to come to fruition in his own lifetime. In the situation in which Paul thought he stood, then, to turn to Moses and the commandments of the Torah made little sense. For one thing, even those biblical oracles did not envisage the whole world converting to Judaism. They did not, to give a telling example, imagine that all the men on earth would become circumcised. For another thing, it would not make sense to prefer the distinctly Jewish figure of Moses over the man to whom it had been promised, as Paul understood Genesis, "All the Gentiles shall be blessed in you."[56] Thus did Abraham, the man of faith but few commandments (or none), trump Moses, the man of Sinai.

Earlier, we showed that the convenient contrast between a Christianity focused on faith and a Judaism focused on deeds does not do justice to the diversity and complexity of Christian thought, even in the restricted sample of the New Testament, in which Paul's surviving letters are now found. For early Christian literature, like Christian literature of every generation, does not lack an emphasis on good deeds and a warning about the dire consequences of bad ones. And it was even capable of interpreting Abraham as proof that the deed, and not just faith, was indispensable (James 2:20–26). But what about the other half of that convenient contrast? Was the classical rabbinic tradition capable of emphasizing Abraham's *faith*, or did it only focus on his deeds, however few or many they were thought to be? One early midrash provides a striking answer:

And so you also find that our father Abraham inherited both This World and the World-to-Come only as a reward for the faith (*'amanah*) that he had, as it is said, "And because he put his trust (*he'emin*) in the LORD, He reckoned it to his merit" (Gen 15:6). (*Mekilta de Rabbi Ishmael, beshallach* 7)

This midrash goes so far as to attribute Abraham's high status in this world and the next precisely to his faith, and it does so by citing Paul's favorite prooftext. The difference is that, like the New Testament Letter of James, this text refrains from setting faith and works against each other. And so, we again find the familiar and convenient contrast between Judaism and Christianity overdrawn. Not only can the Christian tradition in the aggregate commend works and see Abraham as justified by his works, but Judaism can commend faith and (at least in this one classic text) see Abraham's inheritance of both worlds as dependent on it.[57] There is, to be sure, a difference of emphasis, at least in the aggregate, but the starkness of the familiar contrast, whether intended to serve Christianity or Judaism, cannot be sustained. What is the major note in each tradition is at the least a minor one in the other.

In modern times, many people have been attracted to Paul's faith-centered rather than law-centered strategy for the incorporation of Gentiles, for it seems inclusive and accepting, unlike the Jewish notion of a chosen people whom God singled out to be his own special possession and to whom he therefore gave special obligations—the 613 commandments. As we have seen, however, this is a dangerous misreading of Paul, for whom descent from Abraham (and not from Adam) is the key point and in whose mind the Gentiles without Christian faith—and thus without Abrahamic lineage—are doomed. Whereas Judaism characteristically speaks of the dichotomy between the Jewish people and the nations, Christianity thus speaks of the dichotomy of the Church and the world. Neither of them, as we have had repeated occasion to note, speaks of a natural, undifferentiated humanity as the ideal—hence, the all-importance in Christianity of being baptized, becoming regenerated in Christ rather than Adam, or, in contemporary evangelical parlance, "being born again."

Historically, the cost of this supposed universalism has been, at the very least, a drastic downgrading by Christians of the status of Judaism, and especially the status of Torah observance. To be sure, Paul's stress on God's reckoning of Abraham as righteous through faith without works (even the single commandment of circumcision) has played a role in the debate between the two religions. But so has the Jewish depiction of an Abraham who "practiced the whole Torah in its entirety before it had been given," as well as the claim that though he (and other pre-Sinaitic figures) did well, the Jews, now with the whole 613 commandments, "surpass them all." Indeed, since Abraham is "Our Father" for Jews and "the father of all who have faith" for Christians (Rom 4:11), it was inevitable that these two Abrahamic communities would divide on what exactly it was that Abraham practiced: Torah or gospel.

## CHAPTER SIX

## One Abraham or Three?

And in point of fact his activity has resulted, as we see today, in
the consensus of the greater part of the population of the earth
in glorifying him and considering themselves as blessed through
his memory, so that even those who do not belong to his progeny
pretend to derive from him.

—Maimonides[1]

SEVERAL YEARS AGO, the Global Negotiation Project at Harvard University
began developing a novel and dramatic initiative in quest
of interreligious and international cooperation and reconciliation.
Known as "Abraham's Path," the project aims to develop a kind of
modern, interfaith, and intercultural pilgrimage following the supposed footsteps of the biblical figure on his route from his Mesopotamian homeland to Canaan, the land that, according to the book of
Genesis, was promised to Abraham and his descendants forever.

That the initiative focuses on the figure of Abraham makes emi-
nent sense. He is, as the various publications of the project are at
pains to point out, hailed by Jews, Christians, and Muslims alike as
their spiritual father and thus serves as an appropriate figure, indeed
perhaps the ideal figure, for efforts to replace animosity among them
with cooperation, and their deadly differences with a healing sense
of their common heritage. In the words of one of the Abraham's Path
documents, "Three and a half billion people—over half the human
family—trace their history or faith back to Abraham, considered the
father of monotheism. The Abraham Path honors this shared cultural
heritage by linking together into a single itinerary of outstanding interest and beauty the ancient sites associated with Abraham and his
family." The text goes on to predict success for the initiative. Abraham's Path, it tells us, "will serve as an intercultural meeting place,

inspiring respect and understanding among people, young and old, around the world."[2]

The term "pilgrimage" is not too strong to describe the experience that the planners of Abraham's Path hope it will foster. Its objective is not simply mutual understanding; it is also the creation of a new reality. "A conversation takes place along the Abraham Path that changes someone's life forever," one of their updates reports. Speaking of a Turkish scholar who has become involved in the project, they tell us, "We hope the Path can help him inspire the curiosity and change the lives of many others from around the world."[3] Abraham's Path aims, in other words, at a kind of conversion experience, a conversion away from the particularity of the old communal loyalties and toward a larger and more universal identity. The distinctive characteristics of the Jewish, Christian, and Muslim traditions will not, of course, disappear—if they did, the starting point for the hoped-for reconciliation would as well—but they will pale in the light of their common father, the father of the monotheism that they all practice and the man they all revere, each tradition in its own way.

Abraham's Path builds upon an understanding of Abraham that is now widespread and can be detected at several levels in contemporary Western culture, from the popular to the scholarly. At the popular level, one thinks of Bruce Feiler's best seller, *Abraham: A Journey to the Heart of Three Faiths*, a book that has generated reading groups that, in turn, have doubtlessly helped diffuse the interpretation of the patriarch the volume expounds. In Feiler's view, whatever disagreements the three Abrahamic faiths may have, "What they do concur in is that Abraham occupies such sacred space because he is the first person to understand that there is only *one* God. This is his greatest contribution to civilization and the shared endowment of the Abrahamic faiths."[4]

This is related to another key point for Feiler, that "Abraham belongs to all humanity," a point that he is at pains to note the Christian apostle Paul saw clearly, although it soon began to fade even in Christianity.[5] As for the Jews, they were actually the first to forget what Abraham was all about, and brought upon themselves untold suffering. "And suddenly the carefully balanced message of the Abraham story—that God cares for all his children—a tradition that existed for hundreds of years before the religions *themselves* existed, was put in jeopardy by the inheritors of that tradition," he writes. "Jews have no one to blame for this process but themselves. They initiated it, and they ultimately would pay a stiff price for it."[6] The same deleterious process repeated itself in Islam as well, for as early as the Qur'an itself, alas, "Abraham is moving from being considered a universal figure open to all religions to being considered a more exclusive figure who favors one faith." Hence, the unqualified but deflating remark of an East Jerusalem imam with whom Bruce Feiler discussed the supposedly common father: "Abraham is the father of one religion, and that religion is Islam."[7]

Although a Jew, with a self-professed and long-standing "strong attachment to Judaism,"[8] Feiler here reasons more like a Protestant. It is hard not to hear in his words an echo of one of the rallying cries of the Protestant Reformation—*sola scriptura*, "by scripture alone," the claim that tradition must be subordinated to the Bible if it is not to pervert the truths of the faith. Note that, according to Feiler, it is scripture—or at least the book of Genesis—that gives us the real Abraham, and it is the postscriptural tradition that introduces the deadly distortion. In Feiler's own words, speaking of Judaism, "The text had been outstripped; the commentaries now reigned."[9]

There is, though, a problem with the application of this Protestant principle to interreligious issues. Since the book of Genesis does not have the status of scripture in Islam (for which the Qur'an alone is scripture), Feiler, perhaps unwittingly, himself "favors one faith," that of the Hebrew Bible, though shorn of its Jewish and Christian interpretations. For at least Jews and Christians have access to the "universal figure open to all religions" through their scriptures, which include Genesis. Not so Islam.

But is it really true that in Genesis Abraham "is the first person to understand that there is only *one* God" and that he "belongs to all humanity"? In chapter 4, we were at pains to note that monotheism is simply not an issue in Genesis. There is no sense that the people with whom Abraham comes in contact—for example, the pharaoh, Melchizedek the priest-king of Salem, the king of Sodom, or Abimelech king of Gerar—worshipped a plurality of gods or were otherwise engaged in what would come to be regarded as idolatry.

Thus Abraham utters nary a peep of protest against the religions of the peoples among whom he travels and betrays no indication that he is the first person to understand that there is but one God.

The idea of Abraham as one who broke with the idolatry of his age is, of course, richly attested in Second Temple Judaism and, later, in Islam, as we have seen at length (though Abraham does not discover, but rather, rediscovers the nature of God). The irony is again obvious: it is only because the tradition has augmented the scripture, or, in Feiler's terms, because the commentaries have outstripped the text, that this image of Abraham as a rigorous monotheist has become part of the legacy of the Abrahamic religions. If all we had were the Hebrew Bible and the New Testament, the idea that Abraham was "the first person to understand that there is only *one* God" would be unknown to Jews and Christians alike. And, historically speaking, had it not been for the postbiblical Jewish traditions of Abraham as the one who saw through idolatry, including the idolatry of his father, the Muslim appropriation of the same traditions centuries later would not have come about.

Another point, finally, must be made about this supposed concurrence of the three traditions on the monotheistic revolution sparked by Abraham. As prominent and familiar as this image of Abraham is in (postbiblical) Judaism and in Islam, it is unattested in ancient Christianity and unfamiliar to this day to most committed and well-informed Christians. In Christian tradition, Abraham is celebrated not for his monotheism or his uncompromising opposition to religious iconography, but, as again we have seen at length, for his *faith*.[10] And so the one thing on which Feiler thinks the three Abrahamic religions concur is not so common to them after all. In this case, it is Judaism and Islam that are favored, and Christianity that is not.

Identifying monotheism as the key marker of membership in the threefold family of Abrahamic religions, moreover, poses problems for Christianity beyond the obvious one that it does not associate Abraham with monotheism, as the other two do. For most forms of Christianity over the centuries have affirmed not simply that God is one, but that he is *triune*, a word that comes from the Latin words for "three" and "one."

The Nicene Creed (325 C.E.), recited in one version or another by the vast majority of professing Christians to this day, begins on a note of oneness: "We believe in one God, the Father Almighty, Maker of all things visible and invisible." But it does not leave the matter there. The same sentence continues, "and in one Lord, Jesus Christ, the Son of God, born of the Father . . . God from God, Light from Light, true God from true God, born, not made, of the same substance as the Father, through Whom all things have come into being." It pronounces a solemn condemnation on anyone who would say that the Son did not exist before Jesus was born.[11] What the Nicene Creed asserts here is that the Son is not constrained by time (the Son is no younger than the Father, nor the Father older than the Son), and shares the essence or "substance" with the Father. It mentions the third member of the Trinity, the Holy Spirit, only briefly, but at the Council of Constantinople (381 C.E.), the assembled bishops and theologians formulated a creed that declared that the Holy Spirit, too, was Lord, shared in the same substance or essence with the Father and Son, and was to be adored and glorified with them.[12] Although the second person of the Trinity, the Son, lived on earth in human form (as Jesus) only briefly, in this theology the Christian God was thus always triune, never other than Father, Son, and Holy Spirit. The Son and the Holy Spirit are not creations of the one God. They are as much the one God as the Father is, and they have been so from all eternity.

Now to call this theology, affirmed by hundreds of millions of Christians—Roman Catholic, Eastern Orthodox, and Protestant—simply "monotheistic," as Judaism and Islam are monotheistic, is, if not wrong, at least seriously misleading. The difference, in fact, is one that those last two traditions have themselves long noted. The Qur'an, for example, says of God, "He did not beget and is not begotten" (112:3)—words that, significantly, appear along with kindred verses on the outer and inner faces of the Dome of the Rock, the great Islamic shrine that has dominated the skyline of the Old City of Jerusalem for more than thirteen hundred years. Sidney H. Griffith, a scholar of Christianity under Islamic dominance, puts it well: "The import of these repeated Qur'anic phrases is crystal clear: Islam has supplanted Christianity even in Jerusalem on the Temple Mount where previously Christians had seen the signs of their own succession to the Jews."[13] Having wrested Jerusalem from the Christians, Islam triumphant corrects what it judges to be the grave theological error central to the defeated religion. The true God is not a father who begets nor is he a son who is begotten. Nor is he in any way three:

> O people of the Book, do not exceed the bounds of your religion, nor say about Allah except the truth. The Messiah, Jesus, son of Mary, is only Allah's Messenger and His Word, which He imparted to Mary, and is a spirit from Him! So believe in Allah and His Messengers and do not say "three" [gods]. Refrain; it is better for you. Allah is truly One God. How—glory be to Him—could He have a son? To Him belongs what is in the heavens and on earth. Allah suffices as a Guardian! (Qur'an 4:171).

The Qur'an, then, will have no truck with the idea that there is plurality within the one God.[14] It is thus not surprising that the orthodox Christian claim that God is and always has been Father, Son, and Holy Spirit so often sounds to Muslim ears as an affirmation of polytheism: Trinity is taken for tritheism. In this light, consider again Feiler's claim that Judaism, Christianity, and Islam all "concur . . . that Abraham occupies such sacred space because he is the first person to understand that there is only *one* God." At best, this posits the correctness of the orthodox Christian self-understanding that the Trinity in no way compromises the oneness of God, that the belief in the triune Deity is no less monotheistic than the Jewish or Muslim belief in the one God of Abraham. But this is a concession to Christian belief that Muslims have not traditionally made, and for good reason: if the Christian belief is valid, then the Muslim understanding of divine unity, as affirmed in the Qur'anic verses that attack the Christian theology, must be in serious error. For, if there is one thing in which Christians and Muslims have not historically concurred, it is the implications of the oneness of God. And if we add to this the fact that Islam, beginning again already with the Qur'an, has historically seen itself as the religion of Abraham, then from a Muslim point of view, the notion that Christianity is somehow as Abrahamic as Islam itself is extremely weak.[15]

Jews have traditionally had problems with the Trinity similar to those of the Muslims. The problems begin in antiquity,[16] but become very explicit in the Middle Ages. Maimonides, for example, characterizes the Trinity accurately when he calls it "what the Christians say: namely, that He is one but also three, and that the three are one." But for him, this is a parade example of the inability to understand "true Oneness" and, accordingly, the nature of the one God (*Guide of the Perplexed* 1:50). Maimonides readily grants that "there are things that are common to all three of us, I mean the Jews, the Christians, and the Moslems: namely, the affirmation of the temporal creation of the world, the validity of which entails the validity of miracles and other things of that kind." But he immediately takes note of "the study of the trinity into which the Christians plunged" as something alien to the Jews (*Guide* 1:71).[17]

Given the fundamental misunderstanding of the nature of God that Maimonides attributes to Christians, it is far from shocking that he classifies Christianity as a form of idolatry, with all the legal implications for Jews that such a classification involves.[18] Although Maimonides had positive things to say about Christianity and its role in bringing pagans to God, the notion that Christianity is as monotheistic as Judaism is not one that he could brook. And since, as we shall soon see, he interpreted Abraham as the man who arrived at a correct understanding of God and, correlatively, of idolatry as well, the notion that Maimonides would have found Christianity as Abrahamic as Judaism is profoundly wrong.

Maimonides's classification of Christianity as idolatry was not, of course, the last Jewish word on the subject. At roughly the same time that he wrote, Talmudic commentators living in Christendom (Maimonides lived in Islamic lands all his life) found ways to mitigate the tradition. A case in point is the question of whether a Jew could accept the validity of an oath that a Christian swears that includes mention of Jesus. The Talmud had established the law that a Jew should avoid partnership with a Gentile, since if a legal dispute arose and the Gentile swore by his god, the Jewish partner would have broken the Torah's commandment against making "mention of the names of other gods" (Exod 23:13). Twelfth-century French rabbis ruled, however, that a Jew could accept the validity of the oath of Christians because even though the latter mention Jesus, this is not the name of an idolatrous god:

> For they mean the Maker of Heaven, and although they associate the Name of Heaven [i.e., God] with something else, we do not find that it is forbidden to cause others [that is, Gentiles] to make such an association. (*Tosaphot b. Sanh.* 63b on *'asur*)[19]

In other words, the Christian oath-taker does not mean to invoke anything or anyone other than the true God. To be sure, his mention of Jesus associates something else with God, but this does not violate any norm obligatory upon Gentiles (were a Jew to take such an oath, however, he would be in grave violation). The great historian Jacob Katz was surely correct when he wrote, "The assertion that the Gentiles are not bound to uphold the strict unity of the Godhead opens up the possibility of condoning the Christian adherence to the doctrine of the Trinity so far as the Gentiles, though not the Jews, are concerned."[20] But this position, and even the farther reaching ones that developed in the ensuing centuries, still fall short of attributing to Christians the monotheism that the Jewish tradition associates with Abraham.

In the world of Jewish-Christian dialogue, it is often said (and almost always assumed) that Jews and Christians agree on God but disagree on Jesus. What this happy formulation misses is that in orthodox Christian theology, as expressed in ancient creeds, in a very real sense Jesus *is* God.

Even before some of those creeds were promulgated, an assumption already existed that Jesus had always been active and involved in the world, as befits God. The Christian apologist Justin, for example, writing about the middle of the second century C.E., claims to prove from Old Testament texts "that it was Jesus who appeared to and talked with Moses, Abraham, and, in short, with all the Patriarchs, doing the will of the Father."[21] In Justin's mind, of course, this in no way compromises monotheism. His self-understanding, like the self-understanding of orthodox Christians to this day, was that of a believer in one God, and not in a set of gods. The question for outsiders, though—Jews, Muslims, and others, including non-Trinitarian Christians—is whether that self-understanding is accurate or misconceived.[22] About one point there can be no doubt, however: in the eyes of Jews and Muslims for whom monotheism is a key legacy of Abraham, the idea that it was "Jesus who appeared to and talked with [him]" has historically been seen as profoundly mistaken, casting some doubt on the monotheism of the Church.

And what of Feiler's other claim, that "the carefully balanced message of the Abraham story [is] that God cares for all his children," so that "Abraham belongs to all humanity"?

The idea that God cares for all humankind is one that can surely be found in all three Abrahamic religions, beginning already in their different scriptures, but is it associated with Abraham? Yes, the patriarch demonstrates generosity and hospitality and pleads to the LORD to spare Sodom on the basis of the righteous minority (who, it turns out, did not exist there). But none of this testifies to the message that God cares for all his children (true though that be), and in the case of Sodom, Abraham is explicit that the issue is one of divine justice; it is hardly one of universal solicitude.[23]

We can go further. If the message is universalism, the Jewish and Christian Bibles have figures on whom to focus—Adam and Noah, the universal fathers of the human race, as the biblical narrative would have it. We have seen that it is to these very figures that rabbinic Judaism appeals when it develops the seven commandments binding on all human beings, Jews and Gentiles alike. The Christian apostle Paul focuses on Adam when he wishes to discuss the natural and universal human condition (one of disobedience, sin, condemnation, and death, reversed only through Jesus).[24] Since Judaism and Christianity both display the message that "God cares for all his children," why do they, unlike Bruce Feiler, not associate that message with their common father Abraham?

The answer is simple. In the Hebrew Bible, Abraham is not the father of all humanity, but only of one subset thereof; not even all his biological descendants, but only a further subset of them, fall heir to all that God has promised him. Thus, as we saw at some length in chapter 2, although God blesses Abraham's elder son Ishmael and promises him fertility and national greatness, it is, rather, with Isaac, born of the aged and long-infertile Sarah, with whom God maintains his covenant. The covenant, in turn, is the basis for God's gift of Canaan.[25] He grants that land to the coming descendants of Isaac, not those of Ishmael or, for that matter, the other six sons of whom we hear ever so briefly at the report of Abraham's death in Genesis 25:1–11. There, significantly, Abraham, having sent his other sons away with gifts while he was still alive, "willed all that he owned to Isaac" (vv. 5–6).[26]

Whatever the biblical basis for Feiler's claim "that God cares for all his children" may be, then, it is anything but the "message of the Abraham story" in the Hebrew Bible. Although elements of universal blessing can be found there, the focus lies instead on the question of chosenness, or in the language of Christian theology, "election." Postbiblical Judaism did not create that focus, and if indeed it has proven negative for the Jews, Feiler is dead wrong that "Jews have no one to blame for the process but themselves." The blame, if there is any, lies not with the victims but with the book of Genesis itself.

And what about Christianity? Surely in the Church, where the proclamation that "God cares for all his children" is so central, the same message must take Abraham as a key focus. In Feiler's thinking, that is how things started out, but soon the same harmful forces of particularism overcame the unqualified universalism that he associates with the biblical Abraham. "The idea that Abraham belongs to all humanity, which appears at least in spirit in the Letters of Paul, began to dissipate rapidly in early Christian writing," he writes.[27] The problem with this is easily stated: in both spirit and letter, Paul did not simply accept but actively stressed the election of Isaac over Ishmael and firmly identified the Christians with the former, and not in the least with universal humanity.[28]

It is not even clear, or consistently so, that the Apostle to the Gentiles considered the Jews to be among the elect descendants of their patriarch. "For not all Israelites truly belong to Israel," he wrote toward the end of his life, "and not all of Abraham's children are his true descendants. . . . It is not the children of the flesh who are the children of God, but the children of the promise are counted as descendants" (Rom 9:6–8).[29] In other words, in Paul's theology to become a descendant of Abraham one must move from the flesh to the promise, and it is no secret how this miraculous transformation is to be brought about. For, in reality, the promised offspring of Abraham are only from "one person, who is Christ" (Gal 3:16). Those who are "in Christ" (to use a Pauline phrase) or united with Christ thus fall heir to the Abrahamic promise, but those who are outside Christ do not.

When Paul, a longer-lived contemporary of Jesus, wrote these letters, those in Christ were a statistically insignificant segment of humanity—not larger but much smaller than the Jewish people. To be sure, like other Christians in his own and every other era, Paul aspired to bring all humanity into union with Christ before the latter returned, which he thought would happen in his own lifetime.[30] But the idea that all mankind urgently needs to become Christian and thus heirs to the promise to Abraham does not equate with the idea that "Abraham belongs to all humanity." Indeed, all humanity has never been Christian, and today Christians constitute only about one-third of the world's population. In some areas, such as China and Africa, Christianity is growing rapidly. In others where it was once dominant, such as North Africa, it is now quite weak, having been displaced by Islam centuries ago. In some places, such as Western Europe and the Middle East, it is currently in steep decline, having been displaced by secularism or Islam or both.

By the time the popular writer Bruce Feiler was arguing that Judaism, Christianity, and Islam are best understood in light of their common father Abraham—and that Abraham is the key to good relations among them—the Catholic theologian Karl-Josef Kuschel had already developed the idea in a more scholarly way.[31] In this case, too, some major logical and historical problems unfortunately confront the advocate of Abrahamic reconciliation.

For starters, Kuschel is keenly aware that the three traditions have separate histories and different authoritative documents that they cannot wish away. "For Judaism, Christianity and Islam are three different religions," he writes, "not simply three different confessions of Abraham."[32] From this Kuschel concludes that "any talk of Abrahamic ecumene [worldwide community] cannot be a suspension which forgets the origins but is rather a concretion of the faith of Abraham which is relevant to the present—in the light of Torah, Gospel, and Qur'an."

The very next sentence, though, undercuts this severely: "Abraham remains a point of reference by which the later traditions of synagogue, church, and Umma, can and must be measured critically." Like Feiler, then, Kuschel subordinates "later traditions" to the figure of Abraham. But where, if not in those very traditions, are we to find him? Here, like the Jew Feiler, the Catholic Kuschel echoes, oddly, the Reformation Protestant principle that scripture must be supreme: "For faithfulness to Abraham is more than a slogan only if people in all three traditions are still ready to listen to the Abraham of scripture as he has been handed down in all his dimensions, neither in the Talmud nor in the New Testament nor in the Qur'an, but in the book of Genesis." And Kuschel even goes further. He insists that the task of Abrahamic reconciliation requires us to excavate within the sources out of which Genesis itself has been composed. "What is really common to all," he writes, "is the patriarch Abraham as he appears in the earliest strata of the traditions of Genesis."[33]

This is a much more sophisticated articulation of the claim of unity through Abraham than one finds in popular statements, but it has not overcome their problems, and it poses new ones of its own. We can start to see why by asking, where does the notion come from that Abraham is the standard by which each of those three traditions must be measured? Clearly not from those traditions themselves, for in them the notion is highly problematic, though in each case for somewhat different reasons. In Judaism, we have found that sometimes Abraham is interpreted as having observed the Torah and sometimes he is not. If the book of Genesis is to be the criterion, then clearly the Torah-observant interpretation must be disallowed, no matter which stratum of the book we use.[34] But how, without some quasi-Protestant (and very un-Jewish) notion of scriptural authority, can we set aside an idea that appears not only in classical medieval commentaries but in Talmudic tradition and even, for that matter, in older literature from Second Temple Judaism? Why, in a Jewish context, should texts that speak more highly of Israel in the time of Moses (that is, Israel with the full complement of the Torah's commandments) than of Abraham reverse those priorities?[35] Simply because Christianity and Islam doubt the value of those commandments and appeal to Abraham as evidence that they are not so important? If so, then as "a point of reference by which the later traditions of synagogue, church, and Umma, can and must be measured critically," Kuschel's Abraham is not in the least an honest broker: he is biased toward Christianity and Islam and against Judaism.

We can go further. Recall that in the book of Genesis there is one commandment that God specifically enjoins upon Abraham, who hastens to observe it—the commandment of ritual circumcision (Gen 17:9–14, 23–27). For various reasons, historical scholars of the Pentateuch date this text to a relatively late compositional stratum, the P, or Priestly, source. If Kuschel is right that "what is really common to all is the patriarch Abraham as he appears in the earliest strata of the traditions of Genesis," then clearly what all must affirm on the basis of their commonality is an uncircumcised Abraham.[36] What could fit better with the theology of the Christian apostle Paul, for whom Abraham, pronounced righteous before he was circumcised, serves as proof of the dispensability of the rite? "For in Christ Jesus neither circumcision nor uncircumcision counts for anything," wrote Paul; "the only thing that counts is faith working through love" (Gal 5:6).[37]

For Judaism, however, the matter looks very different. This is, after all, the tradition that speaks of adherents risking their lives—and suffering martyrdom—rather than abandoning the practice of ritual circumcision.[38] It is also the tradition in which an outstanding Talmudic authority is quoted as saying, "Great is circumcision, for no one involved himself in the commandments like Our Father Abraham, yet he was called 'blameless' only on account of circumcision."[39] And whereas Paul contrasts circumcision to "faith working through love" and sees the latter as decisive, the rabbinic text quotes that same Talmudic authority as saying, "Great is circumcision, for it is equivalent to all the commandments of the Torah" (b. Nedarim 32a). And so Kuschel's Abraham is once more a very un-Jewish one: he is essentially the Abraham of the Apostle to the Gentiles, a forerunner of Christianity more than of Judaism.

As for Islam, circumcision is practiced in that tradition as well, although it is neither mentioned in the Qur'an nor associated with Abraham (or performed on the eighth day of the boy's life, as required in Gen 17:12). But this does not mean that Kuschel's proposal for an Abrahamic confraternity of religions is any kinder to Islam than to Judaism. In fact, his requirement that all three Abrahamic religions defer to Genesis is one that Islam cannot possibly meet, since in that tradition, it will be recalled, the Hebrew Bible as it now exists does not have the status of authoritative scripture (Islam tends to attribute the passages in which the "peoples of the Book" contradict the Qur'an to Jewish or Christian tampering). Why should Muslims downplay or ignore the Qur'anic account of Abraham and Ishmael's founding (or refounding) of the Ka'ba, the shrine in Mecca that is the holiest site for Muslims, for example, in favor of a Jewish and Christian book that has not a trace of such a tradition?[40] Should we expect Muslims to marginalize the *hajj*, the mandatory pilgrimage to Mecca that is one of the Five Pillars of the faith, simply because it has no basis in the scriptures of the other two Abrahamic religions? And, finally, should outsiders expect Muslims to regard an account of Abraham's life as equally valid if it leaves out all mention of Mecca and its Ka'ba?[41]

And what, finally, of Christianity itself in Kuschel's thinking? Here we find good cause to wonder whether his use of Abraham is any fairer to his own tradition than it is to Judaism and Islam. Recall his claim that the version of Abraham to which he wants all to defer is that of "the earliest strata of the traditions of Genesis" and not that of the New Testament, Talmud, or Qur'an. Oddly, though, he also insists that in the scriptures of each of the three Abrahamic religions, "Abraham remains the primal image of faith."[42]

The problem is this: in all the strata of Genesis, what makes one a member of the Abrahamic family is not faith at all—there is no talk of conversion in Genesis—but rather birth into his lineage, chiefly the lineage that descends through only one of his eight sons, Isaac, and then through only one of Isaac's two sons, Jacob.[43] Now in Islam, this notion of Abrahamic identity through descent is explicitly denied. In the Qur'an, when God tells Abraham, "I am making you a spiritual exemplar to mankind," the latter replies, "And what about my posterity?" God responds: "My Covenant does not apply to the evil-doers" (2:124).

If this sounds familiar to the Christian reader, it is probably because of its resonance with New Testament texts similarly insistent that Abrahamic descent in the familial sense is of no account. Most pointed are words attributed to John the Baptist that we have already mentioned: "Do not presume to say to yourselves, 'We have Abraham as our ancestor'; for I tell you, God is able from these stones to raise up children to Abraham. Even now the ax is lying at the root of the trees; every tree therefore that does not bear good fruit is cut down and thrown into the fire" (Matt 3:9–10).[44] And as we saw in our last chapter, most of the time Paul makes Abrahamic descent (an all-important category for him) into a matter of faith, not birth. "Those who have faith are the descendants of Abraham," he writes, so that "it is not the children of the flesh who are the children of God, but the children of the promise are counted as descendants" (Gal 3:7; Rom 9:8).[45]

Kuschel's particular conception of the impartial Abraham, equally available in all three traditions, is in line with this classical Christian emphasis on faith:

> In all traditions Abraham shows what is most important for human beings before God: not legal religious achievements, but dedication to the will of God, a well-tried trust in God. Only in this way do human beings stand before God justified, are they in the truest sense of the word 'hanīf,' 'muslim.' Conversely, however, that means that Torah, Gospel and Qur'an are concretions of the faith of Abraham, attempts to revive it. They did not set out to replace the faith of Abraham by a religious system but to bring it to light for everyday human life. They seek to show in their own way that, like Abraham, Jews, Christians and Muslims have to do with a God who calls into being that which is not and expects from human beings only *emuna, pistis, islam*: dedicated trust.[46]

The Pauline resonance of Kuschel's supposedly neutral Abraham is patent. His phrase "legal religious achievements" unmistakably echoes the Christian apostle's "works of the law" (Gal 3:12). Kuschel's alternative to them, "well-tried trust" or "dedicated trust," echoes Paul's "faith," and the first sentence above is essentially a paraphrase of Paul's insistence in Galatians "that no one is justified before God by the law, for 'The one who is righteous will live by faith'" (3:11, quoting Hab 2:4), or as Paul would later summarize his position, "a person is justified by faith apart from works prescribed by the law" (Rom 3:28).

But note where Kuschel departs from this classic Christian thinking: he has dropped Jesus from the picture altogether and insisted that Jewish faithfulness (Hebrew, 'emunah) and Muslim submission (Arabic, islām) are equally effective in enabling "human beings [to] stand before God justified." They are, in other words, just as good as Paul's faith (Greek, *pistis*) in Jesus, by faith in whom, in the apostle's thinking, "the blessing of Abraham" finally comes to the Gentiles (Gal 3:14). For Kuschel, by way of contrast, "dedicated truth in God" is effective for Jews and Muslims no less than for Christians, who put their trust in the God who became flesh, suffered a cruel death, and rose in a glorious resurrection. The faith itself is what counts; the nature of the God in whom it is placed and the story that elicits it is of less importance, or none.

Where Paul preached faith in the God whose crucified son he raised from the dead, Kuschel just preaches faith in God. Even though we can clearly hear the traditional emphases within this new and supposedly more inclusive statement, it is nevertheless a major departure from classical Christian theology. Kuschel's thinking may seem to open things up for Jews and Muslims, especially since Paul and other New Testament authors found a forerunner of such faith in a man whom both religious Jews and Muslims revere. In reality, though, this restatement of the classical Christian emphasis on faith in more universal, or at least "Abrahamic," terms connects to the Abraham of Judaism and Islam less than Kuschel realizes.

To see why, let us begin with Islam.

In Muslim theology, it is very doubtful that "well-tried trust" or "dedicated trust," even if it is a trust in God, by itself makes one a *hanīf* or *muslim*, Arabic terms for, respectively, a thoroughgoing monotheist and one who has submitted, and, importantly, words the Qur'an actually employs to describe Abraham. The nature of the God in whom the trust is put and of the revelation he is thought to have given cannot be so easily set aside. From the beginning, Islam has seen itself not simply as restating but also as correcting Judaism and Christianity. Scholars who have examined the Muslim conception of Abraham thus argue that he appears in that tradition not only in continuity with but also in polemical opposition to Judaism and Christianity. In the Muslim view, as one of these scholars writes:

> The Jewish error was to over-elaborate the law, while that of the Christians was to worship the Messiah as an incarnated logos. Islam, by implication, is to be a *via media* between the exoteric and the esoteric, and this is the virtue associated with Abraham the *ḥanīf*.[47]

In the thinking of the Catholic theologian Karl-Josef Kuschel, however, the belief that Jesus was the word (Greek, *logos*) made flesh does not disqualify Christians from following faithfully in the footsteps of Abraham the *ḥanīf*. He asks Muslims, in effect, to ignore the key doctrine of the Incarnation in light of the Christians' *faith*.

There is room to doubt that many Christians will be sufficiently inclined to disregard their own scripture and tradition to accept the offer. And it is not hard to devise a response that a traditional Muslim might give to a traditional Christian who takes Kuschel's position:

> Do you really think that your unconditional trust in God enables you to be a *ḥanīf* and *muslim* like the prophet Abraham when you see Jesus not only as a prophet and messiah, as we do, but as the son of God as well? How long will you deny the manifest words of scripture, "It is not fitting for Allah [God] to have a son" and "He did not beget and is not begotten" (Qur'an 19:35; 112:3)? Have you not heard what the scripture calls your claim that "The Compassionate has taken to Himself a son"? It calls it a "shocking assertion, / From which the heavens are almost rent asunder, the earth is split and the mountains fall to pieces" (19:89–90)! Do you not know that the Qur'an tells us that Jesus denied his own divinity (5:116)? And how can you speak of salvation through faith in Christ crucified when we know, "They neither killed nor crucified him; but it was made to appear so unto them" (4:157)? Surely, yours is not the way of the prophet Abraham. For as the Qur'an tells us, "They say: 'If you become Jews or Christians, you shall be well-guided.' Say: 'Rather, we follow the religion of Abraham, who was upright and no polytheist'" (2:135). Your faith, unlike his, is

not a pure faith, and until you renounce your deviations, you will not be a *ḥanīf* or *muslim*, as he was.

However much the traditional Muslim may differ with Kuschel's notion that trust in God by itself moves one into the Abrahamic category, on one point the two can find themselves in substantial agreement. Recall that for Kuschel, it is "not legal religious achievements" that enable "human beings [to] stand before God justified." What enables them to do so is, again, trust in God. His "trust," we argued, is essentially identical to what the Christian apostle Paul called "faith," and for Paul (and almost all subsequent Christian tradition), faith stands in opposition to "the works of the law," if by the latter is meant the commandments of the Torah.[48] Now if we also remember that one key "Jewish error," according to Muslim tradition, is "to over-elaborate the law," we begin to sense an important and enduring commonality of two of the Abrahamic traditions—one that comes, however, at the expense of the third. For, according to both Christianity and Islam in their broad outlines, Judaism, by stressing the Torah and its commandments, has proven false to the religion of Abraham.

To his credit, Kuschel mentions the Jewish traditions that do not find in Abraham a practitioner of the whole Torah before it was revealed (as well as those that do).[49] He also acknowledges that in associating Abraham with conversion, Judaism finds in him "a connecting link between Israel and the nations, between Judaism and paganism," and not simply a paradigm for a thoroughgoing exclusivism. To Kuschel, though, these are minor exceptions to the grim character of rabbinic tradition. As he puts it in introducing that tradition, "orthodoxy left open just one crack in the system of halakhah."[50] Here, halakhah, the system of Jewish law, sounds like a prison; Kuschel's wording recalls Paul's equation of the Torah with slavery.[51] Not only does halakhah shut the world out; it also contradicts the universal import of Abraham.

In this reading, the movement from Abraham to Moses, or from the patriarchs to the Torah, is not a heightening of holiness and an extension of it to all aspects of life, a working out in detail of the sort of obedience that Abraham demonstrated, as it is in so much

Jewish thought. It is, rather, a narrowing, a sealing off of the wider perspective in which Israel's first patriarch lived his life. Although Kuschel does not use the word, he appears to find in halakhic religion a decline—one that, fortunately, is soon reversed in the aggressive Gentile mission of the early church. This becomes clear in his discussion of Paul's letter to the Galatian churches, in which, it will be recalled, the apostle argues strongly against Jewish law. "Indeed," Kuschel concludes, again echoing and quoting Paul, "through faith in Christ this divine blessing becomes really universal. . . . Abraham ceases to be the saving possession of Israel and is freed again really to become the 'father of many nations.'"[52]

In following Paul on these points, Kuschel closely associates three things—universalism, salvation, and freedom from law, secured through faith. What is curious, though, is that his own description of rabbinic theology undercuts that very association. "For in contrast to Christianity and like Islam," Kuschel observes, "Orthodox Judaism has never developed the notion that outside Israel there is no salvation . . . Here Noah plays an even more marked role than Abraham." The reason is simple: by observing the Seven Noahide Commandments, according to the rabbinic tradition, "the righteous from the non-Jewish people can receive a 'share in the world to come.'" "Thus," Kuschel goes on to say, "the existence of the Noachide commandments serves towards universal understanding and interreligious tolerance."[53]

But if that is so, then why should we see the emergence of the Torah-observant Abraham as narrowing Judaism and excluding outsiders from the possibility of salvation (to use the familiar Christian term)? If the Gentiles can find salvation without Abraham and without the Torah, what problem does the association of Abraham with the Torah and its 613 commandments pose for them? In sum, Kuschel recognizes that rabbinic Judaism has a different structure from that of ancient Christianity, as he understands it, and thus does not need to make Abraham serve the same goal as he does in Christianity—the goal, that is, of including Gentiles in the possibility of salvation. Yet he still faults the ancient Jews for claiming to be the exclusive descendants of Abraham (everyone, by contrast, is a descendant of Noah) and for making him a paradigm of halakhic observance.

Kuschel simultaneously restates an ancient Christian polemic against Judaism and recognizes that the polemic does not reckon with the actual structure of the theology against which it is directed. He sees the deep structural differences between the two religions but still wants them to give the same interpretation of Abraham.

Kuschel's proposal for an "Abrahamic ecumene," then, asks for fundamental change from all three Abrahamic communities, on the one hand, while on the other hand, he shows a bias toward one or two of the three.

Of Jews, it asks for a subordination of Talmudic tradition to the Hebrew Bible, and within the Hebrew Bible, it asks them to subordinate the material associated with Moses and Sinai to the Abrahamic narratives in the book of Genesis. But even within the book of Genesis, it asks Jews to subordinate later compositional layers to the earliest ones. It also asks them to ignore the fact that membership in the family of Abraham in all strata of Genesis comes by birth and not by faith. There, only the descendants of Abraham through Jacob inherit the covenant, and they are a flesh-and-blood people, not a religious communion.

Of Christianity, Kuschel asks that the unconditional trust in God that Christian tradition associates with Abraham be disengaged from the ancient proclamation for which it was seen as only an anticipation—faith in the proclamation that Jesus Christ was the Son of God and himself God incarnate, died by crucifixion in redemption of sin, and rose in glory. Kuschel wants his fellow Christians to believe that a trust like Abraham's is fully effective for salvation on its own and is equally available to those who do not subscribe to that central Christian proclamation. The Abraham of Genesis now reveals the true meaning of the Jesus of the New Testament and church tradition. In effect, this new Abraham becomes sovereign over Jesus.

Of Muslims, Kuschel asks that they subordinate their own scripture, the Qur'an, to that of alien religions, Judaism and Christianity, and that they equate faith, as Kuschel understands the term, with the status of the *ḥanīf* and the *muslim* that the Qur'an and Muslim tradition associate with Abraham. They must disregard the explicit Qur'anic attack on the elements in Christianity that speak of Jesus as God, the Son of God, or crucified and, instead, view Christian faith as the full equivalent of their own—and Abraham's—act of submission (*islām*).

In Kuschel's thinking, he has uncovered the common Abraham who stands at the origin and base of each of these three superficially different traditions, and he is calling them to drop or at least downplay those inauthentic beliefs and practices that divide them and to return to the way of their mutual founder. As we have been at pains to point out, however, the Abraham he offers them corresponds with the Abraham of none of their traditions, not even the one who appears in the earliest strata of Genesis. That Kuschel presents an Abraham to whom Jews, Christians, and Muslims can all object could conceivably be taken as a sign of the impartiality and objectivity of his theology. It can also, and more realistically, be taken as a sign of the high degree of wishful thinking underlying his program and the unlikelihood that the program will be brought about.

Nor is his Abraham so impartial after all. For, as we have seen, the enormous weight that Kuschel puts on Abraham's faith (rebranded as "a well-tried trust in God" and the like) privileges this Christian author's own religion at the expense of the other two traditions that he claims are equally Abrahamic. One can imagine the shoe on the other foot. Had Kuschel, for example, spoken of Abraham's uncompromising monotheism or his proactive opposition to iconography, he would have privileged themes well known in Jewish and Muslim tradition (and Muslim scripture) at the expense of Christianity. In that case, few people outside those traditions would have thought the Abraham he presented was neutral and equally accessible within each of the three religions. For Trinitarian Christians, whether Eastern Orthodox, Roman Catholic, or Protestant, would surely object to the proposition, as would members of any communion with a rich tradition of iconography.

There is another aspect in which Kuschel's Abraham proves far from neutral, and in this case, as in that of law, it is Judaism that is disadvantaged. This is the dimension of peoplehood, to which we must now turn.

First, however, we must recall some basic characteristics of all three Abrahamic religions that are too easily forgotten.

In chapter 4, we had occasion to note that in the ancient Mediterranean world monotheism was not unique to the Jews and Christians. There was also a pagan monotheism, exemplified, for example, by the Greco-Roman Stoic philosophers, who regularly spoke of God in the singular.[54] What this points to is the limitations of the term "monotheism," a category that covers too wide a swath of phenomena to be of much use in understanding any of them very deeply.

In the case of the Hebrew Bible, the key monotheistic element is not the number of deities but rather the exclusive allegiance that Israel owes to the LORD, their rescuer, liberator, and protector. The idiom of ancient Israelite monotheism is political, not philosophical; the focus is on the *service* that the people Israel owe to the divine personality with whom they are in a unique covenantal relationship.[55] The Deity whom they are to serve, then, is not simply nature writ large, an uncaring, impersonal force like fate or fortune; nor is it the depth dimension of life, or anything of the sort. He is rather an intensely personal being (though not a human being), active, caring, involved in history, and fully capable of entering into relationships with humans, including, and most important, the sort of familial relationships on which the biblical covenant is founded.

For, in the words of one scholar's definition, covenant is "a widespread legal means by which the duties and privileges of kinship may be extended to another individual or group, including aliens." Like adoption and marriage, whose language it borrows, covenant is a "means of ingrafting non-kin or distant kin into the lineage"—hence, the ubiquitous description of Israel in the Hebrew Bible as God's son, firstborn son, beloved son, or wife.[56] Consider as illustrations the words God instructs Moses to say to Pharaoh, "Israel is My firstborn son. I have said to you, 'Let My son go, that he may worship Me'" (Exod 4:22–23), or these words in Deuteronomy, which preface prohibitions on certain common practices, including matters of diet, "You are children of the LORD your God . . . a people consecrated to the LORD your God" (14:1–2).

This sort of language continues and reverberates throughout the Jewish tradition. Not coincidentally, it reverberates as well throughout Christian tradition as a description of the community of believers, beginning in the New Testament. Paul, for example, writes that

"God sent his Son . . . in order to redeem those who were under the law, so that we might receive adoption as children" (Gal 4:4–5). And both the Hebrew Bible and the New Testament can describe this relationship not only in terms of adoption, but even in terms of begetting. The Song of Moses can ask of the people Israel, "Is not He the Father who begot you?" (Deut 32:6), and the Gospel of John can say of those who receive Jesus and thus become "children of God" that they "were born, not of blood or of the will of the flesh or of the will of man, but of God" (1:13).[57] Finally, to vary the metaphor, just as prophets in the Hebrew Bible describe Israel in its ideal state as God's faithful and loving bride, some New Testament texts speak of the Church, again not coincidentally, in similar terms.[58] In both Jewish and Christian sources, the metaphors vary widely; the specialness that they aim to communicate does not.

It is essential to remember that in both its Jewish and its Christian settings, this act of adoption or marriage is viewed as a gift: no one becomes the son or the bride of God by right. Or, to put the same point differently, without God's special intervention, no community would have that precious status. The end of the passage from Deuteronomy quoted above states this unmistakably: "The LORD your God chose you from among all other peoples on earth to be His treasured people" (Deut 14:2). So does a New Testament letter attributed to Jesus's disciple Peter, though almost certainly written after the latter's death: "But you are a chosen race, a royal priesthood, a holy nation, God's own people, in order that you may proclaim the mighty acts of him who called you out of darkness into his marvelous light" (1 Pet 2:9).[59]

In Christian theology, as we have had occasion to note, the act of God that establishes this special relation of a human community to him is known as "election"; Jews are more likely to speak of it as "chosenness" and thus of a "chosen people." In chapter 1, we pointed out that the tendency among many modern Christians is to draw a contrast between Judaism and Christianity in which the Jewish notion of chosenness is judged to be parochial, tribal, or even racist and the Christian theology of election is either ignored or reinterpreted as progressive and universal in its own way: Christians want everybody to be among the elect, whereas the Jews think they alone have been granted that elevated status. The end of the New Testament verse quoted above can support this: You Christians have indeed been chosen, the author writes to his correspondents, but "in order that you may proclaim the mighty acts of him who called you out of darkness into his marvelous light."

Now, it is certainly correct that historically Christians have sought converts in ways Jews, in the main, have not. The obligation to do so can be found, most memorably, in words ascribed to Jesus after his resurrection from the dead, "Go therefore and make disciples of all nations, baptizing them in the name of the Father and of the Son and of the Holy Spirit" (Matt 28:19). But here again we must distinguish between universalism and a form of particularism that aspires to spread out universally, eliminating rival forms of particular identity. In the early Christian case, we are clearly dealing with the latter, with a community that hopes to include all peoples, and not with one that believes that all peoples are already one, as if everyone lives in the marvelous light and no one need be called out of darkness. There is also much room to doubt that the establishment of the Church as "a chosen race, a royal priesthood, a holy nation, God's own people" was thought to be purely instrumental, merely a means to proclaim God's mighty acts to others rather than an expression of his special love for those chosen.

If pagan monotheists found the notion of a personal, caring, and involved deity foreign and naive, one can easily imagine how they viewed election. For surely a god identified with nature, fate, or fortune is not only impersonal but also unconnected to any given community. Yet the God of the Jews and Christians cannot be long spoken of without reference to the particular group that he has established— his covenant partner, his son (whether by adoption or begetting), his firstborn, his treasured people, his beloved bride, his royal priesthood, his holy nation.

To Martin S. Jaffee, this communal aspect is the "essential marker" of the sort of monotheism represented by Judaism, Christianity, and Islam. So, alongside pagan or philosophical monotheism (which he calls "metaphysical" monotheism), Jaffee suggests we speak of "elective monotheism" in order to acknowledge the importance of election, too easily overlooked, to this phenomenon. "The essential marker of elective monotheism is not the uniqueness of God alone,"

Jaffee writes. "*Rather, it lies in the desire of the unique God to sum-mon from out of the human mass a unique community established in his name and the desire of that community to serve God in love and obedience by responding to his call.*"[60] In Judaism, that "unique com-munity" is called the people Israel. In Christianity, it is called the Church. In Islam, it is called the Umma, the body of the faithful who have submitted to God as he has commanded them to do.

A major difference, however, divides Judaism and Christianity from Islam, and it is a difference that Jaffee's useful term "elective monotheism" can cause us to miss. The problem does not lie in the emphasis in Islam on the community, for the difference between the insiders and the outsiders, between the believers themselves and the nonbelievers has come to be at least as pronounced in Islam as it is in the other two Abrahamic religions and is reflected in Muslim law and practice. To cite just an easily understood example, those in a state of ritual impurity must not touch a copy of the Qur'an itself. Since in the case of "non-Muslims . . . impurity is irremediable short of conversion to Islam," Michael Cook points out, "unbelievers, ac-cordingly, should never touch the Koran according to the majority view."[61] The difference, rather, lies in the understandings of the ori-gins of the community itself.

In the Jewish and Christian cases, as we have seen at length, the metaphors of sonship, adoption, begetting, and marriage dominate. The children of Abraham through Isaac and Jacob (but not Ishmael and Esau) are not only the covenant-partners of the LORD, the God of Israel; they are also his own children, whether through adoption, begetting, or promotion into the rank of the firstborn, or they are his beloved, through betrothal and matrimony. Despite the condi-tional note in the covenant theology that we explored in chapter 2, the people Israel does not forfeit this unique status when its members do evil, as indeed they do in much of the Hebrew Bible. The same dynamics of sonship to God or marriage to him are prominent in the characterization of the Church and its identity in early Christian-ity, and there, too, the Abrahamic descent of the Christian, brought about through Jesus, is a central idea.

In the case of Islam, by contrast, the language of sonship and de-scent is absent (though after his death, as we have noted, Muhammad himself comes to be viewed as a descendant of Abraham).[62] Indeed, as we have seen, God in the Qur'an is thought to have explicitly rejected Abraham's inquiry about whether his posterity can inherit his status as "spiritual exemplar to mankind": "He replied: 'My Covenant does not apply to the evil-doers'" (Qur'an 2:124).

The result is a striking contrast with the Jewish and Christian efforts to stake their own claim in the Abrahamic promise to the son of his who, according to Genesis, is the only one who will inherit his covenant.[63] Whereas Jews and Christians speak of "Abraham, Isaac, and Jacob," Muslim sources often interpose the name of Ishmael between the first two, to make a fourfold list that has no biblical precedent. While the Qur'an mentions Isaac seventeen times and Ishmael only twelve, the notion that one of the brothers takes precedence over the other is as alien to that scripture as it is natural to its Jewish and Christian antecedents.[64] This is the deeper implication of a point we made in chapter 3, that the Qur'an does not name the son Abraham set out to sacrifice, so that early Muslim interpreters arguing for his identification with Isaac and with Ishmael divided about evenly. The same point becomes more explicit in the Qur'anic rendering of Jacob's deathbed scene:

> Or were you present when Jacob was in the throes of death and said to his sons: "What will you worship when I am gone?" They replied: "We will worship your God and the God of your forefathers, Abraham, Isma'il and Isaac—the One God and to Him we submit." (Qur'an 2:133)

Here, Ishmael (Arabic, Isma'il) has become one of the forefathers, in no way less an heir than Isaac. The point, though, is not to claim that Ishmael's descendants are as much the heirs of the Abrahamic promise as Isaac's, as if the objective were some sort of Abrahamic egalitarianism. On the contrary, the underlying assumption is again one that denies the familial dimension of Abraham's identity altogether. God's covenant is not with the evildoers, whether they are Abraham's posterity or not. It is, rather, with all those, of whatever descent, who submit to God—or, to use the Arabic term with which the verse above ends, all those who are *muslim*.

A contrast with the version of the same legend that appears in the Talmud is instructive (*b. Pesachim* 56a). In the Jewish text, Jacob is fearful lest there be someone unfit among his children, "like Abraham, from whom Ishmael issued, or my father Isaac, from whom Esau issued." To reassure the dying patriarch of their unanimous fidelity to his God (and thus of his perfection over against his ancestors), the sons recite the first line of the affirmation known as the Shema': "Hear, O Israel! The LORD is our God, the LORD alone [or, 'is one']" (Deut 6:4). In this imaginative reading, "Israel" is not the people, as in the Shema', but Jacob himself, for whom Israel is, of course, an alternative name. The Israelites are possessed of a religious fidelity that their Ishmaelite and Edomite cousins lack (Edom being descended from Esau). In the Qur'anic adaptation, however, Ishmael is not a defector but a forefather, and Jacob's sons proclaim not only God's oneness but also their own submission, their *islām*, and this puts them in the same category as Abraham's first son.

We see here another important difference among the Abrahamic religions. Two of them, Judaism and Christianity, continue the focus in Genesis upon family and descent, even though each in its own way also allows those who cannot trace their lineage to Abraham to enter his family nonetheless and to belong to his covenant. The third, Islam, disclaims the familial dimension altogether and reinterprets covenant in ways that have nothing to do with the adoption metaphor but call instead for a new community made up of moral individuals who have unconditionally submitted to God. Morality and submission are, of course, also aspects of the Jewish and Christian concept of covenant and of the religious life more generally, but they do not, as in Islam, exhaust the meaning of covenant or relatedness to Abraham.

If the Qur'an can conceive of the earliest Israelites as *muslim*, it is not surprising that it also presents their first patriarch the same way, and in a fashion that directly relates to the vexed issue of how the new community conceives of the previous "religions of the Book":

65. O People of the Book, why do you dispute concerning Abraham, when the Torah and the Gospel were only revealed after him? Do you have no sense?
66. There, you have disputed concerning what you know; so why do you dispute concerning what you do not know? Allah knows and you do not know.

67. Abraham was neither a Jew nor a Christian, but a hanif
[i.e., a true monotheist] and a Muslim. And he was not one
of the polytheists.

68. Surely, the people who are worthiest of Abraham are
those who followed him, together with this Prophet and
the believers. Allah is the guardian of the believers!
(Qur'an 3:65–68)

At first glance, this passage may seem to endorse something like
the Protestant principle that scripture is the sole authority. Those
who are impatient with the whole midrashic presentation of Abraham, whether in a Jewish or a Christian mode, may resonate with the
Qur'anic insistence that the real patriarch never adhered to the distinctive theology of either community. A closer look discloses, however, that the passage is not calling for a return to the Abraham of
Genesis at all. It is not calling on Jews and Christians to see in Abraham the father of Isaac, the sole heir to his covenant and the sole son
through whom the chosen line descends, whether by biological descent (Judaism) or spiritual rebirth (Christianity). Rather, the Qur'an
sees in Abraham an uncompromising monotheist—in this it again
demonstrates its commonality with postbiblical Judaism—who thus
foreshadows the monotheistic prophet of its own time, Muhammad.
It is by way of following "this Prophet" that one proves worthy of
Abraham. Abraham was "neither a Jew nor a Christian" because he
was a Muslim.

Islam, in this thinking, is not a simple confirmation or extension
of the antecedent Abrahamic religions: it is also a correction of them.
Islam is the real "religion of Abraham," which the great patriarch be-
queathed to his sons, just as Jacob did two generations later (Qur'an
2:130–33).

All of this bears in a very direct but insufficiently noticed way upon
the claim of many today that Judaism, Christianity, and Islam constitute an Abrahamic family of religions. Only if communal membership is irrelevant to Abrahamic identity—only, that is, if membership
in any of the three communities is equivalent to membership in the
other two—could the claim be sustained. But to argue that is to deny

Jaffee's well-grounded point that "the essential marker of elective monotheism . . . *lies in the desire of the unique God to summon from out of the human mass a unique community established in his name.*" Similarly, to argue that all three speak of "the unique God" of Abraham is also not correct, even apart from the inconvenient truth that Jews and Muslims have historically held some doubts about whether Christianity is fully monotheistic. Rather, once again the thorny question of "the unique community" is essential and unavoidable, even though the whole modern discourse of Abrahamic religion is awash in efforts to avoid it.

Consider, as a first example, the words of Abraham's Path quoted at the beginning of this chapter: "Three and a half billion people—over half the human family—trace their history or faith back to Abraham, considered the father of monotheism." At face value (leaving aside the exact figure), the statement is unexceptionable, in fact, innocuous: Who would deny that billions of people do what these words say they do? A second look, though, turns up problems. Are history and faith equally legitimate connections to Abraham? If so, then polytheists or atheists who trace their history back to him would be no less worthy members of the Abrahamic community than the devout, and the point about Abraham as "the father of monotheism" would be irrelevant. But if monotheism really is the key factor, then why focus on Abraham at all and not on Adam and Noah, for example, both of whom are monotheists in those three traditions (in Islam they are prophets, to boot)?

None of the three traditions conceives of Abraham as the first person ever to perceive and worship the true God. In Judaism and Islam, from which the idea of a "father of monotheism" is drawn, Abraham *rediscovers* the lost truth; he is not the first to know it. What Abraham fathers is not monotheism. Rather, he fathers—and here we must differentiate Judaism and Christianity from Islam—that "unique community" whose importance Jaffee astutely underscores. In the Jewish case, the fathering is quite literal; Jews belong to his family by descent, whatever may be their allegiance to monotheism or the degree of their faith in the God of Abraham. Jewish saints and Jewish sinners, the observant and the nonobservant, are equally members of the Abrahamic people.

The wording of Abraham's Path, "history or faith," thus falls short of a full recognition of the place of descent and familial origins in traditional Jewish thinking. The same wording fails to do justice to the Christian view as well, since at least for the powerful Pauline trajectory within the Christian tradition, it is faith and faith alone by which God's grace allows Gentiles to be engrafted into the Abrahamic family; history and monotheism cannot make a Gentile into a descendant of Abraham.

In brief, the Abraham's Path document mixes the theologies of the various Abrahamic religions together in a way that does not adequately respect the distinctive claims of any of them. With its mention of monotheism, it favors Islam and perhaps Judaism above Christianity. With its mention of faith, it favors Christianity (and perhaps Islam) over Judaism. With its mention of fatherhood, it favors Judaism and Christianity over Islam, though the absence of any acknowledgment of lineage alongside history and faith is problematic for Judaism. In the overall impression left by the document, all that matters is that Jews, Christians, and Muslims talk a lot about Abraham, and this alone should compel them to accept and affirm each other. What they actually say about Abraham, how they make a connection to him, and what the identity is of "the unique community" with which he is associated—these issues, central to the foundational literatures of all three traditions, are accounted as of no, or at best secondary importance. If the people actually walking along that path and talking of Abraham are reasonably well informed about their own traditions, it will not take long for the very dimensions that the document has suppressed to return in force.

This effort to stress monotheism at the expense of election is not unique to Abraham's Path; it pervades today's discourse of the three Abrahamic religions. We have already seen it in Bruce Feiler's interpretation of Abraham as "the first person to understand that there is only *one* God" and his claim that "Abraham belongs to all humanity" because "the carefully balanced message of the Abraham story [is] that God cares for all his children." In a more learned way, Karl-Josef Kuschel moves in much the same direction. For him, too, "at the beginning of all three religions lies a source of peace which time and again has been and still is obscured on all sides by fanaticism and exclusiveness. This source is called Abraham" (Genesis 14, in which Abraham engages in and wins a war against four Mesopotamian kings, is obviously not the center of Kuschel's thinking).

Again and again, though, that pesky problem of communal particularity keeps cropping up. "Jews, Christians and Muslims are doggedly persisting in their exclusivisms," Kuschel laments, "and are therefore incapable of ecumenical brotherhood and sisterhood."[65] And what brought about this fall from the Edenic world of grace and peace into one in which the Abraham peoples are doggedly persisting in their own exclusive identities? For Kuschel, it was a process of "the politicizing of Abraham between the Testaments," or, to put it in Jewish terms, the period of the Second Temple. At this point, and owing to that unfortunate political turn, "Israel proudly calls itself the 'descendants of Abraham' or the 'people of the God of Abraham'" and "a tendency towards an exclusivity of salvation is unmistakable."[66]

What this misses, of course, is that already in Genesis the covenant and its land promise go from Abraham to Isaac (and not to Ishmael or Abraham's other six sons) and then to Jacob (and not to Esau). As we have repeatedly seen, despite the assumptions made by advocates of an Abrahamic fraternity of religions, the Hebrew Bible always associates Abraham with communal particularity. This feature was not the invention of later Jewish interpreters of Genesis, nor does the fact that multiple kin-groups descend from Abraham, just as he was promised, imply that they are all equally the heirs of the promises to him and the covenant with him.[67]

In addition, Kuschel misses the crucial fact that election in the Hebrew Bible is not the same thing as "salvation" in Christian theology; peoples outside the Abrahamic covenant are not outside the care and concern of God, doomed, or damned. Abrahamic particularity in no way precludes a belief in the universality of God and the possibility of universal salvation.

Despite its lavish use of biblical and Qur'anic language, the position that underlies the discourse of the three Abrahamic religions is actually a version of religious humanism, one that is heavily invested in a vision of human unity. Whatever the value of this line of thinking, its choice of Abraham as its focus is disastrously misplaced. To deploy, as the focus of a vision of universality, a figure who in both the Hebrew Bible and the New Testament represents election is unwise at best.

In the Jewish case, it is particularly inappropriate, since Abraham is thought of as the "the first of the converts" (*b. Chagigah* 3a) and serves as the father of all converts to Judaism, just as Sarah serves as their mother. As Alon Goshen-Gottstein puts it, "There would be something contradictory in the same figure both enabling entry into Judaism and validating other religions outside Judaism." If Abraham is the father of everybody, the claim that he is the father of the Jewish people—or, for that matter, of those who believe in Jesus—would be at best a pointless tautology. That Jews and Christians both call upon Abraham as father does not mean he is equally the father of both communities; it means only that each community believes he is their own father.

Nor does the mere existence of a belief make it true. To quote Goshen-Gottstein a second time, "To describe Christianity as 'Abrahamic' is thus implicitly to accept the Christian theological position. This is certainly more than simple description."[68] The indisputable fact that a plurality of religions appeals to Abraham does not at all warrant the prescriptive claim that each religious community should regard the appeal of the others as legitimate. That can only be done by reference to the norms of the individual tradition. There is no neutral Abraham to whom appeal can be made to set aside the authoritative documents and traditions of the separate Abrahamic religions.

Nothing we have said above should be taken to deny the obvious fact that Judaism, Christianity, and Islam are related religions whose common character readily becomes apparent when they are compared to Hinduism, for example, or to Buddhism. These three traditions have roots in the Hebrew Bible, reverence for the figure of Abraham, and complex patterns of influence among them. That influence, it must also be noted, is not unidirectional, as if it flowed only from Judaism to Christianity and from those two to Islam. Christianity, for example, may have helped bring about the high status that the Aqedah holds in rabbinic tradition, where it sometimes seems to serve as the Jewish answer to the Crucifixion.[69] Islam, too, has influenced Judaism, as in the borrowing by medieval Jews of the Muslim legend that Abraham's birth had been prophesied, to cite one of many instances.[70]

These interactions are well known to scholars of the material and encourage the correct perception that each tradition is best studied in a wider context that takes respectful account of others in its cultural world. The alternative is the traditional practice of treating one's own religion as if it either existed in a vacuum, superseded its predecessors, or so surpassed its contemporaries that they need not be considered, except perhaps as foils against which the splendor of the true faith can shine all the more. For critical historians of Judaism, Christianity, and Islam, as for fair-minded adherents of any of those traditions, this kind of traditionalism is indefensible. It is to the credit of those who speak of "Abrahamic religions" that they bring to mind the historical interconnections of which thoroughgoing religious traditionalists are unaware or which they prefer to forget.

A question arises, however, that historians, for their part, likewise prefer not to entertain; indeed, many run from it. The question is this: Must all forms of discourse conduct themselves according to the rules of critical historical study? If so, then it is hard to see how any coherent religious commitment could be sustained, for historical investigation cannot disclose the higher reality, the suprahistorical truth, as it were, on which such a commitment is based. Historians can tell us that many people have thought God spoke to them. Whether God did speak to them is another matter, and one that historians find themselves impotent to address, let alone to resolve.

For historians, the path of least resistance is usually just to ignore such questions. Unfortunately, in practice that path usually amounts to treating the various traditions as equally true or as equally false. In other words, the exclusion of theological considerations is not a neutral move. For when historical inquiry is given a monopoly in the discussion, and all reference to suprahistorical realities is ruled out of bounds, what results (whether intended or not) is a historical relativism at odds with all religious commitments—and hence with the long-term survival of all religious traditions.

Fortunately, most of those who speak of "Abrahamic religions" do not subscribe to such unyielding historical relativism. If they did, they could hardly celebrate Abraham for his monotheism, as they are wont to do. For if it is a historical fact that some people and some cultures are monotheistic, while others are not, and if historical investigation alone cannot determine which position is closer to the truth, then what is so self-evidently good about Abraham's having faulted his family and townsmen for their idolatry? Surely the more tolerant approach would have been one of agnosticism about the suprahistorical reality that is God or the gods. "Maybe your gods exist," Abraham might have said, "or maybe they don't. Maybe there is only one God, maybe more than one. We do not and cannot know. So, if you tell me you are worshipping real gods, I have no choice but to accept your own self-understanding. Maybe we are all wrong, and an impersonal, uncaring force, like fate or nature, governs the world. There is no way to know. We should just accept each other and recognize that each person's beliefs are right for him but not for everybody."

Those who speak of three equally Abrahamic religions are both unlike and like this relativistic—and totally fictive—Abraham. Unlike him, they do speak of an encompassing truth that transcends particular communities—the truth of the one saving God who orders nature and history according to his will, a central feature of Judaism, Christianity, and Islam alike. But like the relativistic Abraham, they also regard people's self-description as accurate and in fact unassailable: If you say you are the progeny of Abraham, you must be right. If Christians, for example, say their faith in Jesus Christ has made them into Abraham's descendants and heirs to his promise, the Jews therefore have no choice but to accept this; anything else is a denial of the Abrahamic message. And if Muslims say that the identity of Abraham's progeny is irrelevant anyway and contradicts God's explicit message to him, Jews and Christians have no choice but to accept the truth of that, too; anything else would involve substituting their own scriptures for the Qur'an, as if one were truer than the other.

And so, we find in the claim that there are three equally Abrahamic religions a strange mixture of positions, one that enters transcendent or suprahistorical claims and one that rejects them. This is in itself a troubling incoherence. At least as troubling, however, is the position that rejects transcendent claims but then requires the individual Abrahamic religions to renounce central aspects of their own tradition, even of their own understanding of Abraham, in favor of an all-embracing—and entirely fictive—Abraham of its own devising.

To the extent that the term "Abrahamic" serves simply as a convenient rubric under which to group Judaism, Christianity, and Islam (like "monotheistic" and "prophetic," each of which also has its drawbacks), it is relatively innocent. Unfortunately, as we have seen, a much stronger use of the term is now widespread, one that, in effect, creates a new religion that both encompasses these three and supersedes them.

The advocates of this new pan-Abrahamic religion, as we have seen, tend to point to the divine promise that the patriarch would become "the father of a multitude of nations" (Gen 17:5) in support of their central claim: namely, that there is a family of equally Abrahamic religions that must not only recognize their historical connection with one another but grant one another full legitimacy. Yet here is the key point: neither the Hebrew Bible nor the New Testament speaks of the revered patriarch as the father of a multitude of *religions* at all.

This not-so-subtle conversion of "nations" to "religions" has a pedigree of its own. It reflects both the Christian claim that faith in Jesus engrafts the Gentile into the Abrahamic lineage and the Muslim claim that it is the spiritual act of *islām* (submission to God) that the Abrahamic paradigm requires, so that national or communal identity is irrelevant. From the traditional Christian perspective, however, the notion that anything *other* than faith in Jesus Christ could bring a Gentile into the Abrahamic family and covenant would be quite bizarre: as we saw in chapter 5, whether Jews without Christian faith remain in that covenant is itself less than completely resolved in the New Testament.

From the traditional Jewish point of view, it is correspondingly doubtful that anyone other than the Jewish people can legitimately claim the status of descendants of Abraham. The Mishnah, the early rabbinic collection of laws (it was put together around 220 C.E.), provides a telling example. The text in question deals with a Jew who has taken a vow not to "derive any benefit from the progeny of Abraham." Such a person is indeed "forbidden to derive benefit from Israelites but permitted to do so from Gentiles." The implication is clear: the fact that

Abraham has non-Jewish descendants is theologically and legally irrelevant. Indeed, the same passage goes so far as to stipulate that one
who has vowed to deny himself benefit derived "from those who are
circumcised" is forbidden to derive benefit "from the uncircumcised
of Israel but permitted to do so from the circumcised of the Gentiles"
(*m. Nedarim* 3:11).

The reason the Mishnah gives is that in the Hebrew Bible, "uncircumcised" is simply a synonym for a non-Jew. An uncircumcised
Jew is still a Jew, and a circumcised Gentile is still a Gentile. In his
own codification of this law, Maimonides makes it explicit that one
who vowed to have no benefit "from the progeny of Abraham" is permitted to derive benefit from the descendants of Ishmael and Esau,
Abraham's son and grandson, respectively. The proof Maimonides
cites is that God explicitly told Abraham that "it is through Isaac that
offspring shall be continued for you," thus eliminating the older half
brother Ishmael, while Isaac, in turn, said to Jacob, "May He grant
the blessing of Abraham to you and your offspring," thus eliminating
Jacob's older brother Esau (Gen 21:12; 28:4).[71] The point is unmistakable: Only the Jews are in the Abrahamic family. Muslims and
Christians—understood in the Middle Ages as the Ishmaelites and
Edomites, respectively—fall outside it.[72]

This line of thought emphatically does not imply that Gentiles
have no valid knowledge of the God whom Jewish tradition associates with Abraham; nor does it suggest that they cannot have a
portion in the World-to-Come. It asserts only that Gentiles are not
members of the Abrahamic *family*. To the extent that their religion
requires monotheism and good deeds, they are surely commendable. According to the classical Jewish theology, faithful adherence
to monotheism and the practice of good deeds do not graft Gentiles
into the family of Abraham. They make them admirable descendants
of the common fathers of the human race, Adam and Noah. They do
not make them descendants of Abraham or heirs to his promise.

If neither Judaism nor Christianity has traditionally spoken of
the other community as equally Abrahamic, the matter is more complicated in the case of Islam. Consider again this verse from the Qur'an:
"O People of the Book, why do you dispute concerning Abraham,

when the Torah and the Gospel were only revealed after him?" (3:65). With this, the prophet assumes that the two scriptural communities of Arabia in the seventh century C.E. wish to be faithful to their common antecedent, Abraham—and not, exclusively, to Moses or Jesus. Each community is not only scriptural, a "people of the Book," but also Abrahamic. The problem is that Jews and Christians have both falsified Abraham, anachronistically seeking to harmonize him with their own religions of Torah or Gospel, or, to put it differently, absorbing Abraham into their scriptures rather than allowing him to be independent of them and, importantly, sovereign over them.

At first, this seems simply to state in a religious idiom the valid historical insight that Second Temple and rabbinic Judaism and the early church read the patriarch in ways one would never guess from Genesis alone (as a fierce monotheist, for example, or an implacable enemy of religious iconography, a Torah-observant Jew, or a Gentile justified and saved by his faith alone). In point of fact, though, the Qur'an is not asking for a return to the Abraham of Genesis at all. Rather, it is asking for fidelity to the message of Muhammad himself, understood as Abraham's final successor in the chain of prophets that he culminates: "Surely, the people who are worthiest of Abraham are those who followed him, together with this Prophet and the believers" (3:68). Judaism and Christianity are religions that revere Abraham but have distorted his message; Islam is "the religion of Abraham" (2:135). It is what Judaism and Christianity ought to be— and were in the time of their common patriarch.

In this, the Muslim use of Abraham reminds us of Paul's, for the Christian apostle had also thought that the Christ Event made the message of the Abraham story available anew: now Gentiles could be justified without the Torah and its commandments. In that sense, both Christianity and Islam may be termed *Abrahamic restoration movements*. Christianity (at least in Paul's highly influential articulation of it) seeks to restore the Abrahamic mode of being religious over against the Mosaic distortion of it. Islam seeks to restore the Abrahamic mode over against both Judaism and Christianity, against Torah and Gospel alike. But whereas Paul found in Abraham a foreshadowing of what would eventually become available through the Gospel, the Qur'an presents its message as itself "the religion of Abraham": Abraham was a Muslim. And, indeed, any student of the Jewish and Christian Bibles and the Qur'an can see that it is in the Qur'an that Abraham receives the most attention and is the most central. The very appeal to Abraham—and not, say, to Jacob, Moses, or David, all of whom appear in each of the three scriptural collections—has a certain Muslim feel to it. Imagine the difference if we referred to these three related religions as "Mosaic" instead and challenged them to live up to their Mosaic heritage.

All this helps explain why it was a Western scholar of Islam who proved to be so central in the emergence of the idea that there are the three equally Abrahamic religions. That scholar was Louis Massignon (1883–1962), a distinguished French Arabist who was also a devout Roman Catholic with a mystical bent.[73] Massignon was so enamored of Abraham that "he formally dedicated his life to St Abraham; when he officially took the habit as a third order Franciscan in November of 1931 he adopted the religious name 'Abraham.'" Eventually, he received special permission to transfer from the Western rite of the Roman Catholic Church to its Middle Eastern (Melkite) rite, of which he became a priest.[74] This enabled him to say mass in Arabic rather than in Latin, as was the norm in the Western Church at the time.

Massignon found a way, as it were, to become a Middle Easterner without ceasing to be a devout Roman Catholic. In fact, in Massignon's idiosyncratic theology, Abraham is not simply a Christian saint but also one who transcends Christianity precisely because his memory is venerated in two other religious traditions. "More than any other defender of lost causes," he wrote in 1949,

> Abraham is an intercessor. For the other saints who can cure us of despair merely cauterize our transitory wounds whereas Abraham continues to be invoked as their Father by twelve million circumcised Jews, who aspire to take possession for themselves alone of the Holy Land which was long ago promised to him, and four hundred million Muslims who trust patiently in his God through the practice of their five daily prayers, their betrothals, their funerals,

and their pilgrimage. The Jews have no more than a hope, but it is Abrahamic. The Muslims have no more than a faith, but it is Abraham's faith in the justice of God (beyond all human illusions).[75]

But Massignon was enamored of more than just Abraham. He was also enamored of Islam (though not of Judaism), and not simply in the way scholars often love the material they study. For in Louis Massignon's personal theology, the Muslim tradition was not just a fascinating and worthwhile object of study; it was a revelation of God that enriched—but did not displace—the Catholic revelation on which his own life came to be based. In Islam he found a disclosure of God's nature that he thought complemented the Christian message: "I say that we are several in France to have received in the Arabian desert this summation of Islam which is a grace, which made us find God again, in His Christ, there to adore His transcendence . . . and that this summation is an authentic mission of Islam."[76]

It is highly doubtful, of course, that Massignon ever effectively confronted the conflicting truth claims of the two religions. What is clear is that in his mature thinking he both accepted Islam as Abrahamic—and thus legitimate—and sought to incorporate it within his own Catholic mysticism. He called upon his fellow Christians to "dedicate themselves to the salvation of their brothers [the Muslims] and, in that hope to give to Jesus Christ on behalf of their brothers, the faith, adoration, and love that an imperfect knowledge of the Gospel does not allow them to give themselves." But "salvation," in his terminology, "does not necessarily mean an external conversion."[77]

If Massignon thought that Muslims could undergo some sort of internal conversion to Jesus without converting to Christianity—itself a rather strange idea—it was from Islam, conversely, that he adopted the notion of three coequal Abrahamic religions. "The Muslim," he wrote, "who believes in the original equality of the three Abrahamic religions, Israel, Christianity, Islam, knows that they refer to the same God of truth."[78] Given the traditional Muslim view of the Trinity, this is, of course, not always quite the case. It is also misleading to say that Islam "believes in the original equality of the three Abrahamic religions." A more accurate statement would be that Islam has historically believed that all three religions can be faithful to Abraham provided they do not contaminate his message of *islām* (submission to God) with the later and divisive distortions that they falsely regard as normative. Louis Massignon may have thought that Islam was the religion of Abraham in a way that did not negate Christianity, and perhaps some of his Muslim friends did as well.[79] But committed as he was to the proposition that "Saint Abraham" was a Christian, at some level he surely knew that in Muslim theology it is Islam itself that is the "religion of Abraham," not the other peoples of the Book who quarrel unproductively over the common patriarch.[80]

However Massignon sorted out the relationship of Christianity and Islam, or failed to, it is not far from his understanding of Abraham to the common view today that they, along with Judaism, are all coequally Abrahamic and that none of them has a more perfect or more imperfect knowledge of the God of Abraham than the others do. Thus, a devout Christian Islamophile took a position that originated in a Muslim critique of Judaism and Christianity and, perhaps not altogether wittingly, helped transform it into a claim that the God of Abraham and the message of the story of Abraham are equally available in all three traditions and to members of all three communities. As we have seen, however, this requires an "internal conversion" of its own—a conversion from the view of Abraham particular to each community and based on its scriptures to the view that each tradition is as authentically Abrahamic as the other two.

Before we conclude, it is important to review wherein the failure of the notion of three coequal Abrahamic traditions does and does not lie. It surely does not lie in the intention that usually motivates it, to bring about peace and understanding among Jews, Christians, and Muslims. That is an indisputably worthy goal, and the respectful study by members of any of these groups of the scriptures and traditions of the other two can definitely advance it and has already done so. (Whether the scriptures and traditions about Abraham should be stressed over others is a more complicated question.)

Nor is there a problem with the idea that all human beings are brothers and sisters under the fatherhood of the one God who created them all. This idea is a rather obvious implication of the biblical and Qur'anic notion that all human beings are descended from

Adam and Eve (even though all three traditions have sometimes found ways to deny the full humanity of outsiders). The Mishnah makes the point well. In the beginning, God created only one man, it says, precisely so that no one could say to anybody else, "My father is greater than your father!" (*m. Sanh.* 4:5).

The weakness of the notion that Judaism, Christianity, and Islam are all equally Abrahamic also does not lie in the idea that Abraham is an important figure in the scriptures and traditions of each community. Although he is not equally important to each tradition—as we have seen, he is most central to Islam—both a significant overlap in the interpretive traditions about him and a complicated pattern of influences and responses across traditions exist. Knowledge about Abraham in one tradition alone therefore falls far short of full historical knowledge about Abraham.

What, then, are the salient shortcomings of the idea that there are three equally Abrahamic traditions? We have already seen one of them—its neglect of the great importance of communal specificity to each of the traditions and especially of the doctrine of election in Judaism and Christianity. In those two traditions, while Adam and Noah are the fathers of universal humanity, Abraham for the most part is seen as the father of the chosen community alone. That he is to be "the father of a multitude of nations" (not religions) does not obviate the explicit affirmation in the same chapter of Genesis that God's covenant is with Isaac and not with the ancestors of the other Abrahamic lineages (17:5, 21). In Islam, where Abraham is not the father of the faithful (and where descent is in that sense theologically irrelevant), he is a believer and a prophet who is eminently worthy of emulation. And the best way to emulate him is not by observing the Torah or the Gospel (admirable as those both may be) but by following Muhammad, the prophet whom he so clearly foreshadows and who, like Abraham, restored the original, natural religion of humanity that idolaters, Jews, and Christians, all in their different ways, had lost.

Earlier, we also saw that the idea of three equally Abrahamic religions fails in its naive attempt to move from a historical observation to a normative claim—from the observation that the three traditions speak of Abraham in ways that resonate across communal boundaries to the claim that the communal boundaries have no ultimate significance. Ironically, this misses one of the most salient historical characteristics of all three Abrahamic traditions—their disbelief in the very proposition that each is equally as Abrahamic as the other two.

Beneath this failure lies the unwarranted conviction that there exists a neutral Abraham who can be made to serve as a control on the Abrahams of the three traditions that are thought to derive from him. As we saw in our introduction, the historical record, as uncovered by archaeology and its kindred sciences, does not support that claim, just as it does not offer external confirmation for the theologies of Abraham that appear in the authoritative texts of the three traditions themselves. Despite the popularity of that claim today, there is good reason to believe that the neutral Abraham who is beyond text, beyond tradition, and beyond history will not overwhelm the figure attested in the complex and endlessly fascinating texts of the historical traditions. For the question of who Abraham's heirs are and how they inherit his legacy is internal to each of these three related yet distinct traditions. Rather than inventing a neutral Abraham to whom these three ancient communities must now hold themselves accountable, we would be better served by appreciating better both the profound commonalities and equally profound differences among them and why the commonalities and the differences alike have endured and show every sign of continuing to do so.

# Notes

## Epigraph

1. I have changed the NJPS to make the meaning clearer and to improve the English style in these two verses.

## Introduction

1. *b. Bava Batra* 91a–b.

2. Gen 11:26–25:18. A good example of such a translation is *Tanakh: The Holy Scriptures* (Philadelphia: Jewish Publication Society, 1985). It can be found in *The Jewish Study Bible*, ed. Adele Berlin and Marc Zvi Brettler (New York: Oxford University Press, 2004). The author of the present discussion is also responsible for the annotations to Genesis in that volume. Unless otherwise noted, all translations from the Hebrew Bible/Old Testament in this book are taken from *Tanakh*, except for those cited within an excerpt from another source.

3. See Avigdor Shinan, "The Various Faces of Abraham in Ancient Judaism," in *Abraham in the Three Monotheistic Faiths* (Jerusalem: Palestinian Academic Society for the Study of International Affairs, 1999), 6–10.

4. Unless otherwise noted, all citations from the New Testament are taken from the New Revised Standard Version (NRSV). In this instance, and whenever these verses are cited throughout this volume, I have changed the NRSV "believe" to "have faith" and its "ancestor" (the rendering of Greek *pater*) to "father." The importance of both faith and fatherhood will become clear in the ensuing chapters. Note also that when Paul uses the Greek verb in question (*pisteuo*), he is talking about something more than a cognitive act.

5. As Paul reads it, Gen 15:6 records God's pronouncement that Abraham's faith made him righteous, whereas the commandment of circumcision does not appear until two chapters later.

6. See Y. Moubarac, *Abraham dans le Coran: L'histoire d'Abraham dans le Coran et la naissance de l'Islam* (Paris: Librairie Philosophique J. Vrin, 1958).

7. All quotations from the Qur'an in this volume are taken from Majid Fakhry, *An Interpretation of the Qur'an* (Washington Square: New York University Press, 2000).

8. *Gen. Rab.* 44:15, on Gen 15:9.

9. 2 Chr 3:1.

10. The Mormon Book of Abraham is no exception. See Richard Lyman Bushman, *Joseph Smith: Rough Stone Rolling* (New York: Vintage Books, 2005), 285–93 (especially 291–92) and 452–58.

11. See, for example, John Van Seters, *Abraham in History and Tradition* (New Haven: Yale University Press, 1975), 5–122. Among the more useful recent discussions of the historical issue are Wayne T. Pitard, "Before Israel: Syria-Palestine in the Bronze Age," in *The Oxford History of the Biblical World*, ed. Michael D. Coogan (New York: Oxford University Press, 2000), 33–77; Ronald Hendel, *Remembering Abraham: Culture, Memory, and History in the Hebrew Bible* (New York: Oxford University Press, 2005), 44–55; and, from a more conservative viewpoint, Iain Provan, V. Philips Long, and Tremper Longman III, *A Biblical History of Israel* (Louisville, Ky.: Westminster John Knox Press, 2003), 107–21.

12. As in Justin Martyr, *Dialogue with Trypho* 113:4–7 (and compare John 8:56). See Jeffrey S. Siker, *Disinheriting the Jews: Abraham in Early Christian Controversy* (Louisville, Ky.: Westminster John Knox Press, 1991), 167.

13. Qur'an 2:125.

14. Gen 17:25; 21:8.

15. An accessible recent introduction to the complex issues involved in source criticism is Jean-Louis Ska, *Introduction to Reading the Pentateuch* (Winona Lake, Ind.: Eisenbrauns, 2006).

16. *Gen. Rab.* 53:13.

17. Gen 12:10–20 and 20:1–18; 15:1–21 and 17:1–27; 17:15–19 and 18:9–13; 16:4–16 (where Ishmael is still in utero) and 21:9–21.

18. I have provided some thoughts about how this might appear in "The Eighth Principle of Judaism and the Literary Simultaneity of Scripture," in Jon D. Levenson, *The Hebrew Bible, the Old Testament, and Historical Criticism: Jews and Christians in Biblical Studies* (Louisville, Ky.: Westminster John Knox, 1993), 62–81.

19. See Marc B. Shapiro, *The Limits of Orthodox Theology: Maimonides' Thirteen Principles Reappraised* (Portland, Ore.: Littman Library of Jewish Civilization, 2004), 91–121.

20. Though they may be sawing off the branch on which they are perched. See my essay on "Historical Criticism and the Fate of the Enlightenment Project," in *The Hebrew Bible, the Old Testament, and Historical Criticism*, 106–26.

## Chapter One

1. Ramban to Gen 12:1.

2. Gerhard von Rad, *Genesis: A Commentary*, rev. ed., Old Testament Library (Philadelphia: Westminster Press, 1972), 153–54.

3. I have slightly changed the NJPS translation of the first verse in order to reflect the fact that there are three, not two nouns describing that from which Abram is to go forth. This point will figure in our discussion of the Binding of Isaac in chapter 3.

4. Note that the rare combination *harbah 'arbeh* occurs only three times in the Tanakh—once in connection with the punishment of Eve (Gen 3:16) and twice in connection with the offspring of Abraham (16:9; 22:17). The phrase means something like "I will greatly multiply," though the NJPS unfortunately renders it differently in each instance.

5. Jon D. Levenson, *The Death and Resurrection of the Beloved Son: The Transformation of Child Sacrifice in Judaism and Christianity* (New Haven: Yale University Press, 1993), 84.

6. In v. 7, I have rendered *chashaq* as "took a passion" rather than the blander "set His heart" of the NJPS, and in v. 8, I have translated the Hebrew *'ahavat* as "loved" rather than "favored" for the same reason.

7. Gen 10.

8. *Emunot ve-Deot* 3:7.

9. Compare Ps 27:10.

10. The combination of the sources underlying the Torah introduces a complication here. Since the Torah reports Abram's father's death before the son is commanded to leave his father's household (Gen 11:32), we have the impression that Abram left only after Terah had passed away. The problem is that if Terah lived to be 205, as that verse says, but had begotten Abram when he was 70, as 11:26 seems to say, and Abram was 75 when he set out from Haran (12:4), then Terah lived 60 years after his son's departure. Modern historical critics often solve the issue by attributing 11:28–30 to one antecedent source (J) and 12:4b–5 to another (P). An ancient midrash solves it with a homiletical point: "The wicked," it says, "are called 'dead' in their own lifetimes" (*Gen. Rab.* 39:7).

11. Gen 15:4.

12. In support of the reciprocal or reflexive translation, one might note the use of the *hitpa'el* rather than the *niph'al* stem in the closely parallel wording of Gen 22:18 and 26:4. The philological issues here are complicated and controverted (for example, the more distant parallel in Jer 4:2 suggests that even the *hitpa'el* can convey the passive rather than the reciprocal or reflexive sense).

13. For a fine defense of this interpretation, see Erhard Blum, *Die Komposition der Vätergeschichte*, Wissenschaftliche Monographien zum Alten und Neuen Testament 57 (Neukirchen-Vluyn: Neukirchener Verlag, 1984), 349–59, and note especially Blum's citation of Ps 72:17 in support of it (351).

14. R.W.L. Moberly, *The Theology of the Book of Genesis* (Cambridge, U.K.: Cambridge University Press, 2009), 152. The whole discussion on 148–56 has much aided me in understanding Gen 12:3.

15. I have again replaced the NRSV "believe/believed" with "have/had faith." See introduction, note 4, in this volume.

16. For example, *b. Shab.* 97a. It must be remembered that the rabbis come *after*, not before Paul, though the theology they represent has older roots in Second Temple Judaism. In our construction of a debate between him and them, we intend no implication that Paul somehow presupposed rabbinic thinking or broke off from it.

17. I have again changed "believe" (NRSV) to "have faith." See introduction, note 4, above.

18. Siker, *Disinheriting the Jews*, 150 (also for the Barnabas translation).

19. Ibid., 169, translating *Dialogue with Trypho* 16:2–4.

20. Note, however, that not all Christians held the pernicious theology in question, and the threat of "Judaizing" remained alive.

21. H. H. Rowley, *The Biblical Doctrine of Election* (London: Lutterworth, 1950), 162, 164, quoted in Joel S. Kaminsky, *Yet I Loved Jacob: Reclaiming the Biblical Doctrine of Election* (Nashville, Tenn.: Abingdon Press, 2007), 4.

22. The one possible exception involves the Binding of Isaac. See chapter 3 in this volume.

23. Gen 41; 47:7; Dan 2–4; Esth 2:21–23.

24. Yehuda Shaviv, *Perush ha-Torah le-Rabbenu Yitschaq Abarbanel* [in Hebrew] (Jerusalem: Horev, 5767/2007), 340 (my translation). See also Moshe Greenberg, "To Whom

and for What Should a Bible Commentator Be Responsible?," in *Studies in the Bible and Jewish Thought* (Philadelphia: Jewish Publication Society, 5755/1995), 240. I thank Walter Moberly for bringing this article to my attention.

25. Maimonides, *Mishneh Torah, hilkhot teshuvah* 3:5.

26. Joel S. Kaminsky, *Yet I Loved*, especially 107–36.

27. I owe the term "pro-elect" and the example of Rahab to my student, Rachel Billings.

28. Regina M. Schwartz, *The Curse of Cain: The Violent Legacy of Monotheism* (Chicago: University of Chicago Press, 1997), 18–19, 20.

## Chapter Two

1. *b. Yevamot* 79a, quoting Gen 18:19. I have filled out the rest of the biblical quote in order to bring out the identification of "the way of the Lord" and "what is just and right" with the doing of charity, as argued later in this chapter.

2. Burton L. Visotzky, *The Genesis of Ethics* (New York: Crown, 1996), 27.

3. Ramban to Gen 12:10.

4. Barry L. Eichler, "On Reading Genesis 12:10–20," in *Tehillah le-Moshe*, ed. Mordechai Cogan et al. (Winona Lake, Ind.: Eisenbrauns, 1997), 33, 37–38.

5. Gen 41:53–57; 46:5–6; Exod 1:15–22; Exod 5–11; 12:29–36.

6. In v. 9, I have chosen the alternative translation noted as more literal in the NJPS, "Please separate from me," over the preferred rendering in that edition, "Let us separate."

7. Gen 18–19.

8. Gen 19:30–38.

9. For example, *b. Shab.* 97a.

10. The E, or Elohistic, source, interpolated by a redactor into the surrounding J, or YHWHistic narrative (in accordance with the ancient pronunciation of the letter *vav* as a *w*, the consonants of the divine name are often transliterated as YHWH, rather than YHVH).

11. That the Abrahamic covenant protects the promise is perhaps symbolized as well by v. 11, in which "Birds of prey came down upon the carcasses, and Abram drove them away." Were it not for Abram, in other words, the covenant granting the land to his descendants would have died aborning.

12. Here and in Gen 16:6 (below), I have substituted "slave woman" for "maid" (NJPS), which fails to convey adequately the key point that Hagar is a slave.

13. Gen 30:1–13.

14. Not "as a concubine," as the NJPS version misleadingly renders *le'ishshah*.

15. See Paul R. Williamson, *Abraham, Israel, and the Nations: The Patriarchal Promise and Its Covenantal Development in Genesis*, in *Journal for the Study of the Old Testament*, Supplement Series 315 (Sheffield, U.K.: Sheffield Academic Press, 2000), especially 206 and 255–56.

16. See Nahum M. Sarna, *Genesis*, Jewish Publication Society Torah Commentary (Philadelphia: Jewish Publication Society, 5749/1989), 124.

17. Gen 17:7–8.

18. I have changed "ancestor" (NRSV) to "father" in Rom 4:11 to reflect more accurately the Greek *patera* and the intertextual resonances with our texts in Genesis.

Similarly, I have again changed "believe" to "have faith" in order to capture the critical fact that Paul is not talking about the acceptance of an opinion, as "believe" might imply. Gal 3:14 picks up language from Gen 28:4.

19. Moses ben Maimon, "Letter to Obadiah the Proselyte," in *A Maimonides Reader*, ed. Isadore Twersky (New York: Behrman House, 1972), 475–76, here 475.

20. The idea that fatherhood here refers to covenantal lordship, as argued by Williamson (*Abraham, Israel*, 157–58), is quite unlikely.

21. That both texts are generally recognized by historical critics as stemming from P adds likelihood, though hardly certainty, to the hypothesis.

22. E.g., Gen 20:4 and Ps 43:1.

23. Gen 25:1–4.

24. Contra Williamson, *Abraham, Israel*, 157–58, and Desmond T. Alexander, whom he quotes there. The verses are Gen 17:4–5, 15–16.

25. Sozomène, *Histoire Ecclésiastique*, Books 1–2, Greek text ed. J. Bidez, introd. Bernard Grillet and Guy Sabbah, trans. André-Jean Festugière, annot. Guy Sabbah, Sources Chrétiennes (Paris: Les Éditions du Cerf, 1983), 247.

26. Williamson's argument (*Abraham, Israel, and the Nations*, especially 78–95) that these are meant to be read as two distinct covenants is unpersuasive.

27. The first covenant text comes (with the exception already noted) from the source historical critics call J, and the second, from P (the Priestly source). J is also responsible for chapter 16, and E for the expulsion of Ishmael and Hagar in Gen 21:9–21.

28. See Lev 26:14–38 and Deut 28:15–68.

29. Exod 19:8.

30. Chapter 18 is J, but 17 is P, almost certainly the later document.

31. Compare the definition of Ezekiel's role in Ezek 33:1–9.

32. I have changed "deal justly" (NJPS) to "practice justice" in v. 25 to make the play on the Hebrew words clearer.

33. Moshe Weinfeld, *Justice and Righteousness in Israel and the Nations: Equality and Freedom in Light of Social Justice in the Ancient Near East* [in Hebrew] (Jerusalem: Magnes Press, 1985).

34. See note 1 above.

35. Gen 20.

36. The first source is J; the second is E. Gen 20:18, the only place that the four-letter proper name of the God of Israel (rendered as "the Lord") appears in that chapter, is often seen as an exception to its Elohistic authorship.

37. Gen 11:29.

38. Ramban to Gen 20:12. Ramban's wording suggests that he was not persuaded that Abraham was being truthful. Another (and earlier) commentator, Rabbi Abraham ibn Ezra (1089–1167), explicitly interprets the patriarch's words here as a falsehood called for by the situation.

## CHAPTER THREE

1. *Gen. Rab.* 56:8.

2. The translation of Gen 22 in this chapter generally follows the NJPS, but with adjustments in places.

3. The translation departs from the NJPS in order to bring out the fact that there are three terms indicating what Abram must leave.

4. See, for example, Lev 1.

5. *Jewish Study Bible* (ed. Berlin and Brettler), 207, 206.

6. On this, see, for example, Exod 22:28–29, and the discussion in Jon D. Levenson, *The Death and Resurrection of the Beloved Son: The Transformation of Child Sacrifice in Judaism and Christianity* (New Haven: Yale University Press, 1993), 3–17. The objection that not Isaac but Ishmael is Abraham's firstborn son assumes that the status derives from the father, not the mother (rabbinic law assumes the latter, as Exod 13:15 conceivably does as well), and that Ishmael's birth from a foreign slave serving as a surrogate mother for Sarah does not disqualify him. Both assumptions, but especially the latter, are open to much doubt. Note that Ishmael is never described in the Hebrew Bible as Abraham's "firstborn."

7. See 1 Sam 1:19b–28.

8. I have rendered the quotation from Gen 21:12 according to the NRSV rather than the NJPS in order to capture the Greek form of the quotation more accurately.

9. I have changed "trust" (NJPS) to "faith," which resonates better with the discourse of the Letter to the Hebrews.

10. The book, usually known as ben Sira in Jewish circles, is known in Christianity as Sirach or Ecclesiasticus.

11. The translations from ben Sira and 1 Maccabees are from the NRSV. The same relocation can be found in the New Testament in James 2:21–23.

12. For example, *b. Shab.* 97a.

13. See 1 Sam 1:3.

14. As in Gen 23:7–9; Isa 44:17; or 2 Chr 20:18.

15. Ezek 20:25–26.

16. I have changed the NJPS "walked off" in v. 6 and "walked on" in v. 8 to "walked along" in both instances. The Hebrew expression is, in fact, identical in the two verses.

17. The doubling of the second *n* and the resultant shortening of the preceding vowel are not semantically significant.

18. Claus Westermann, *Genesis 12–36: A Commentary* (Minneapolis: Augsburg, 1985), 359. I thank Professor Terence E. Fretheim for drawing this reference to my attention in a paper he gave at Augustana College on April 14, 2010.

19. See, for example, *Gen. Rab.* 56:7, Saadya, and Chizquni.

20. Note the play on the two roots in Gen 20:10–11 as well.

21. See Bill T. Arnold, "The Love-Fear Antinomy in Deuteronomy 5–11," *Vetus Testamentum* 61 (2011): 551–69, especially 562–67.

22. See Jon D. Levenson, *Sinai & Zion: An Entry into the Jewish Bible* (San Francisco: Harper & Row, 1987), 28–29, 75–86. For the rich resonance of this in the ancient world, see also William L. Moran, "The Ancient Near Eastern Background of the Love of God in Deuteronomy," *Catholic Biblical Quarterly* 23 (1963): 77–87.

23. I have changed the NJPS "revere" to "fear" to highlight the fact that the same verb is used here as in Gen 22:12, and I have rendered *uvqolo tishma'u* as "obey only His orders" so as to highlight the connection to the same Hebrew expression in 22:18.

24. See, for a recent example, James L. Kugel, *How to Read the Bible: A Guide to Scripture, Then and Now* (New York: Free Press, 2007), 132. The Aqedah, he writes, "would seem to have a clear etiological message: our God does *not* demand that we sac-

rifice our children to Him. The one occasion on which He seemed to do so turned out to be only a 'test': ever afterward, we have sacrificed animals . . . [I]ts original purpose was less to commemorate Abraham's piety than to explain Israel's curious abstention from the practice of child sacrifice."

25. R.W.L. Moberly, "The Earliest Commentary on the Akedah," *Vetus Testamentum* 38 (1988): 302–23.

26. Gen 12:7; 13:14–17; 15:18–19; 17:8.

27. This analysis essentially follows Richard Elliott Friedman, *The Bible with Sources Revealed: A New View into the Five Books of Moses* (San Francisco: HarperSanFrancisco, 2003), 65. See, too, Bruce Zuckerman, *Job the Silent: A Study in Historical Counterpoint* (New York: Oxford University Press, 1991), 18–20. Also noteworthy is a book that reasons similarly but comes to the diametrically opposite conclusion—that Abraham refused to sacrifice his son, substituting a ram instead, and the notion that an angel called off the sacrifice was later interpolated to cover up Abraham's heroic disobedience: Omri Boehm, *The Binding of Isaac: A Religious Model of Disobedience* (New York: T&T Clark, 2007).

28. In the Hebrew, only the word for "foes" is different.

29. Probably the only direct reference to the Aqedah is Gen 26:5, which seems to echo the end of 22:18. On the Aqedah in Second Temple and rabbinic Judaism, see Shalom Spiegel, *The Last Trial: On the Legends and Lore of the Command to Abraham to Offer Isaac as a Sacrifice* (Woodstock, Vt.: Jewish Lights, 1993; the original Hebrew version was published in 1950) and Levenson, *Death and Resurrection*, 173–99.

30. 2 Chr 3:1.

31. On the different versions and ascriptions of this midrash in rabbinic literature, see Spiegel, *Last Trial*, 90–91. In this chapter, I have reused with permission parts of my essay "The Akedah in Four Traditions," and my response to an essay by Professor Terence E. Fretheim to be published in a volume edited by Murray Haar and published by Wipf and Stock.

32. See Levenson, *Death and Resurrection*, 183–87, and Jane Kanarek, "He Took the Knife: Biblical Narrative and the Formation of Rabbinic Law," *Association for Jewish Studies Review* 34 (2010): 65–90.

33. I thank my colleague, Professor Bernard Septimus, for his assistance on the question of the origins of the Aqedah in the daily liturgy.

34. All the translations from Jubilees in this book are taken from that of O. S. Wintermute in *The Old Testament Apocrypha*, ed. James H. Charlesworth (Garden City, N.Y.: Doubleday, 1985), 2:52–142.

35. Jub 15:15; Exod 12:6.

36. More on this in chapter 5.

37. Jub 48:2–4 (interpreting Exod 4:24–26), 9, 12, 15–19. The notion that the Aqedah originated in an accusation within the divine council carries over into rabbinic tradition (for example, *Gen. Rab.* 55:4), as does the notion that a devil tried to prevent the sacrifice from taking place (for example, *Gen. Rab.* 56:4, 5).

38. See Levenson, *Death and Resurrection*, 3–52.

39. *Gen. Rab.* 56:9. See also Spiegel, *Last Trial*, 56–59, and Kanarek, "He Took," 81n54.

40. "Medabber bitsdaqah," an acrostic of its author's name (Simon bar Isaac), recited on the second day of Rosh Hashanah.

41. *b. Rosh. Hash.* 11a.

42. *JA* 1:227; *Gen. Rab.* 56:8.

43. For example, Lev 20:2–6; Deut 12:29–13:1; Jer 19:1–6; Ezek 20:21–26.

44. All citations from 4 Maccabees are taken from the NRSV.

45. See Edward Kessler, *Bound by the Bible: Jews, Christians and the Sacrifice of Isaac* (New York: Cambridge University Press, 2004), and Levenson, *Death and Resurrection*, 200–19.

46. The words from Exod 12:46 are from the NRSV translation of John 19:36, rather than the NJPS, in order to capture the evangelist's sense.

47. Which verse Paul has in mind is unclear. The term appears in Gen 12:7, 15:5, 17:8, and 22:17.

48. The verse seems to have Gen 28:3–4 in mind; only there do we find the expression "blessing of Abraham" (v. 4).

49. Melito of Sardis, *On Pascha: With the Fragments of Melito and Other Material Related to the Quartodecimans*, trans. Alistair Stewart-Sykes (Crestwood, N.Y.: St. Vladimir's Seminary Press, 2001), 76 (this is from fragment 9). See also Kessler, *Bound by the Bible*, 108–11.

50. Melito of Sardis, *On Pascha*, 46–47.

51. Qur'an 37:99–113.

52. Note that a late midrashic text also presents the initial command to Abraham as a night vision (*Pirqé de-Rabbi Eliezer* 31), though the direction of influence is unclear. The similarity is noted in Bat-Sheva Garsiel, "The Quran's Depiction of Abraham in Light of the Hebrew Bible and Midrash," in *The Convergence of Judaism and Islam: Religious, Scientific, and Cultural Dimensions*, ed. Michael M. Laskier and Yaakov Lev (Gainesville: University Press of Florida, 2011), 57.

53. See Reuven Firestone, "Abraham's Son as the Intended Sacrifice (*al-dhabīḥ*, Qur'ān 37:99–113): Issues in Qur'ānic Exegesis," *Journal of Semitic Studies* 34 (1989): 95–131, especially the chart showing the "Opinions of the Traditionists regarding who was the Intended Sacrifice" on 127; *Journeys in Holy Lands: The Evolution of the Abraham-Ishmael Legends in Islamic Exegesis* (Albany: State University of New York Press, 1990), 135–59 (the same chart appears here on 170–78); and "Merit, Mimesis and Martyrdom: Aspects of Shiʿite Meta-historical Exegesis on Abraham's Sacrifice in the Light of Jewish, Christian and Sunnite Traditions," in *The Faith of Abraham: In Light of Interpretation throughout the Ages* [in Hebrew], ed. Moshe Hallamish, Hannah Kasher, and Yohanan Silman (Ramat-Gan: Bar-Ilan University Press, 2003), 95–101.

54. Firestone, "Abraham's Son," 126, 128, and *Journeys*, 149–51. For some contrary considerations, see Moubarac, *Abraham dans le Coran*, 87–90.

55. Firestone, *Journeys*, 137. (The scholar was al-Thaʿlabi.) Yvonne Sherwood notes a related development on the Jewish side. The *Pirqé de-Rabbi Eliezer*, which was compiled after the rise of Islam, has become "more zealous about effecting the disinheritance of Ishmael and his sons." Yvonne Sherwood, "Binding-Unbinding: Divided Responses of Judaism, Christianity, and Islam to the 'Sacrifice' of Abraham's Beloved Son," *Journal of the American Academy of Religion* 72 (2004): 821–61, here 831. For a detailed discussion of the complexities in these texts, see Carol Bakhos, *Ishmael on the Border: Rabbinic Portrayals of the First Arab* (Albany: State University of New York Press, 2006), 96–104.

56. Immanuel Kant, *Religion and Rational Theology*, trans. and ed. Allen W. Wood and George Di Giovanni (Cambridge, U.K.: Cambridge University Press, 1996), 283. The passages are from *The Conflict of the Faculties*, 7:63.

57. Of course, Kant's goal is not to explicate Gen 22 but to use it to illustrate the ethical inadequacy of a morality based on divine commandments. Even so, the difficulties are large. On the Jewish problems with the framework that Kant presupposes in criticizing divine command ethics, see Emil L. Fackenheim, *Encounters between Judaism and Modern Philosophy: A Preface to Future Jewish Thought* (Philadelphia: Jewish Publication Society of America, 1973), 31–77. A Christian counterpart can be found in John E. Hare, *God's Call: Moral Realism, God's Commands, and Human Autonomy* (Grand Rapids, Mich.: Eerdmans, 2001).

58. The claim that the essence of sacrifice is killing, which is advocated by many prominent scholars, has now come under serious attack. See Kathryn McClymond, *Beyond Sacred Violence: A Comparative Study of Sacrifice* (Baltimore: Johns Hopkins University Press, 2008). She notes on the basis of Jewish and Hindu materials that much sacrifice involves no slaughter at all; a parade example is the *minchah*, or vegetal offering, in Lev 2.

59. In his great book on the Aqedah, the mid-nineteenth-century Danish philosopher Søren Kierkegaard challenges Kant in some ways but in others simply assumes Kant's position. Thus, he can write, "The ethical expression for what Abraham did is, he would murder Isaac; the religious expression is, he would sacrifice Isaac." Søren Kierkegaard, *Fear and Trembling* (Garden City, N.Y.: Doubleday Anchor, 1954), 41. The problem, though, is that Kierkegaard still thinks of sacrifice as unethical (that is, the religious name for murder) and therefore sees it as justified only if ethics is suspended (his famous "teleological suspension of the ethical"). He misses the possibility that the message of the Aqedah has to do with a domain that is neither confined to ethics (as Kant would have it) nor equivalent to the overriding of ethics. See Fackenheim, *Encounters between Judaism and Modern Philosophy*, 53–70. Note especially this observation: "whereas Kant bids Jewish thought to reject even the original *Akedah*, Kierkegaard demands of Jewish thought the eternal perpetuation of its possibility. Whereas Kant will not let the Torah rest on Abraham's merit, Kierkegaard would rob us of the Torah, which forbids child sacrifice" (63).

60. See Jon D. Levenson, "Abusing Abraham: Traditions, Religious Histories, and Modern Misinterpretations," *Judaism* 47:3 (1998): 259–77. That article was written before the appearance of the prime example of the genre, Carol Delaney, *Abraham on Trial: The Social Legacy of Biblical Myth* (Princeton: Princeton University Press, 1998).

61. Sherwood, "Binding," 822–24 (the quote is on 824).

62. Delaney, *Abraham on Trial*, 40, 46, 55–56, 63.

63. To Sherwood's well-stated observation ("Binding," 845), "far from being unequivocal scripts for actions, religious scriptures give rise to writing and performances through which it is possible (and often desirable) to inherit delicately, ambiguously," it should be noted that at least in the cases of Judaism and Islam, scriptures are embedded in traditions that govern through law (and usually without delicacy or ambiguity) what actions may and may not be performed on the basis of them.

64. For example, Deut 12:2–28. I leave aside the special case of the offering of paschal lambs on the Temple Mount, which some rabbinic authorities approve.

65. A rich bibliography on jihad has developed in recent years. See, for example, Rudolph Peters, *Jihad in Classical and Modern Islam: A Reader*, 2nd ed. (Princeton: Markus Wiener Publishers, 2005); Michael Bonner, *Jihad in Islamic History: Doctrines and Practice* (Princeton: Princeton University Press, 2006); and Ella Landau-Tasseron, "Is *jihād* Comparable to Just War? A Review Article," *Jerusalem Studies in Arabic and Islam* 34 (2008): 535–50. I thank David Powers for his bibliographic help on the topic of jihad.

## CHAPTER FOUR

1. See 8:3. All translations from the Apo Abr are those of R. Rubinkiewicz (revised by H. G. Lunt) in *The Old Testament Pseudepigrapha*, ed. Charlesworth, 1:689–705.

2. I have replaced the first choice of the NJPS "between two opinions" with "between the two boughs" in order to capture the metaphor more graphically. The NJPS suggests "on the two boughs" as an alternative.

3. For example, Exod 22:19 and 23:24; Deut 12:3.

4. For instance, Judg 11:24; Mic 4:5; Ps 95:3.

5. See especially Isa 44:6–22.

6. See, for example, Exod 5:2 and 9:13–21.

7. Frank Moore Cross, *Canaanite Myth and Hebrew Epic: Essays in the History of the Religion of Israel* (Cambridge, Mass.: Harvard University Press, 1973), 50–52, here 51–52.

8. See Cross, *Canaanite Myth*, 3–75, especially 3–12; Joseph Blenkinsopp, "Abraham as Paradigm in the Priestly History in Genesis," *Journal of Biblical Literature* 128 (2009): 225–41; and Rainer Albertz, *A History of Israelite Religion in the Old Testament Period* (Louisville, Ky.: Westminster John Knox, 1994), 1:25–39.

9. This is according to manuscript S and C. See *The Old Testament Pseudepigrapha*, ed. Charlesworth, 692.

10. Jerome (347–420 C.E.) reports that the Jews had a tradition of Abraham surviving the fire, but does not dwell on the theme. See C.T.R. Hayward, *Saint Jerome's "Hebrew Questions on Genesis"* (Oxford: Clarendon Press, 1995), 43, on Gen 11:28.

11. See John Kaltner, *Ishmael Instructs Isaac: An Introduction to the Qur'an for Bible Readers* (Collegeville, Minn.: Liturgical Press, 1999), 106–11.

12. See Thorkild Jacobsen, "The Graven Image," in *Ancient Israelite Religion: Essays in Honor of Frank Moore Cross*, ed. Patrick D. Miller Jr., Paul D. Hanson, and S. Dean McBride (Philadelphia: Fortress Press, 1987), 15–32. Even in the case of Israelite worship, the absence of an icon of the Deity should not distract us from the rich iconography of the Temple and the awareness that those who worshipped there associated the iconography with the presence of God.

13. J. H. Lesher, *Xenophanes of Colophon: Fragments; A Text and Translation with a Commentary* (Toronto: University of Toronto Press, 1992), 85, 89, 90.

14. Emilio Gabba, *Greek Knowledge of Jews up to Hecataeus of Abdera* (Berkeley, Calif.: Center for Hermeneutical Studies, 1981), 6. No claim is made here that the encounter between the Jew and Aristotle actually took place. The point, rather, is the cultural perception that underlies the story.

15. Ibid., 5.

16. Josephus, *JA*, Books 1–3, Loeb Classical Library, no. 242 (Cambridge, Mass.: Harvard University Press, 1930), 77, 81. Abraham as philosopher is one aspect of the broader Hellenistic Jewish conception of Abraham as culture-bringer. See Günter Mayer, "Aspekte des Abrahamsbildes in der hellenistisch-jüdischen Literatur," *Evangelische Theologie* 32 (1972): 118–27.

17. Josephus, *JA*, 1:156 (p. 77 in the translation referenced in note 16).

18. See Louis H. Feldman, "Abraham the Greek Philosopher in Josephus," in *Transactions and Proceedings of the American Philological Association* 99 (1968): 146–47.

19. *De Natura Deorum*, 2:5. The translation is taken from Cicero, *De Natura Deorum* [and] *Academica*, trans. H. Rackham, Loeb Classical Library 268 (Cambridge, Mass.: Harvard University Press, 1933), 137–38.

20. *Philo*, trans. F. H. Colson, Loeb Classical Library 289 (Cambridge, Mass.: Harvard University Press, 1935), 39, 41; other references to Philo are also to this edition. My discussion of Philo draws upon my booklet, "Monotheism and Chosenness: The Abrahamic Foundation of Judaism and Roman Catholicism; The Joseph Cardinal Bernardin Jerusalem Lecture, March 26, 2009" (Chicago: American Jewish Committee [Chicago office], the Archdiocese of Chicago, and the Jewish United Fund of Metropolitan Chicago, 2010), 15–16.

21. James L. Kugel, *Traditions of the Bible: A Guide to the Bible as It Was at the Start of the Common Era* (Cambridge, Mass.: Harvard University Press, 1998), 249.

22. In these remarks, I am commenting only on the texts quoted and not intending to imply anything about the rest of the work of their authors.

23. I thank my colleague, Professor Bernard Septimus, for his invaluable assistance in dealing with the variants of this midrash in rabbinic literature and for suggesting "Israel is not subject to the stars" as the best translation of the famous phrase *'eyn mazzal leyiśra'el*.

24. See Pierre Hadot, *Philosophy as a Way of Life: Spiritual Exercises from Socrates to Foucault* (Malden, Mass.: Blackwell Publishing, 1995). On the possible interest in Abraham among pagans in antiquity, see Yehuda Liebes, *Ars Poetica in Sefer Yetsira* [in Hebrew] (Jerusalem and Tel-Aviv: Schocken, 2000), 80–93.

25. The translation from the "Letter to Obadiah the Proselyte," including the biblical quote, is taken from Twersky, *Maimonides Reader*, 475.

## CHAPTER FIVE

1. *Mekhilta de-Rabbi Ishmael, beshallach* 7.

2. When it became possible to convert—that is, to change one's communal affiliation in response to the new perception—is a more complicated matter and much discussed by scholars.

3. *On Abraham*, 70; *Gen. Rab.* 54:6.

4. On this issue within the Hebrew Bible itself, see Moberly, *The Old Testament*.

5. Compare, for example, Amos 3:1–8, especially v. 7.

6. H. B. Huffmon, "The Treaty Background of Hebrew Yada," *Bulletin of the American Schools of Oriental Research* 181 (1966): 31–37, especially 34, and H. B. Huffmon and S. B. Parker, "A Further Note on the Treaty Background of Hebrew Yada," *Bulletin of the American Schools of Oriental Research* 184 (1966): 36–38.

7. Beate Ego, "Abraham als Urbild der Toratreue Israels: Traditionsgeschichtliche Überlegungen zu einem Aspekt des biblischen Abrahamsbildes," in *Bund und Tora*, ed. F. Avemarie and H. Lichtenberg, Wissenschaftliche Untersuchungen zum Alten und Neuen Testament 92 (Tübingen: J.C.B. Mohr, 1996), 25–40, here 33.

8. I have departed from the NJPS rendering of Gen 22:18 in order to bring out the fact that the Hebrew wording is almost identical to that of Gen 26:5. On the theology in question, see chapter 3 in this volume.

9. Gen 12:1; 17:9–14 and 23–27; 21:12; 22:1–19.

10. The Deuteronomic affinity of Gen 26:5 has long been recognized. See Georg Winter, "Die Liebe zu Gott im Alten Testament," *Zeitschrift für die alttestamentliche Wissenschaft* 9 (1889): 221.

11. I have treated the overall subject of this chapter in Jon D. Levenson, "The Conversion of Abraham to Judaism, Christianity, and Islam," in *The Idea of Biblical Interpretation: Essays in Honor of James L. Kugel*, ed. Hindy Najman and Judith H. Newman (Boston: Brill, 2004), 3–40. Some of the material in the current chapter appears in my book *Abraham between Torah and Gospel*, Père Marquette Lecture in Theology 2011 (Milwaukee, Wisc.: Marquette University Press, 2011). On this point, see 18–21. Especially helpful to me have been Ego, "Abraham als Urbild," and Joseph P. Schultz, "Two Views of the Patriarchs: Noahides and pre-Sinai Israelites," in *Texts and Responses: Studies Presented to Nahum M. Glatzer on the Occasion of His Seventieth Birthday by His Students*, ed. Michael A. Fishbane and Paul R. Flohr (Leiden: Brill, 1975), 43–59.

12. Jub 6:17–19; Exod 23:16.

13. Jub 12:25–27. See, more generally, Gary A. Anderson, "The Status of the Torah before Sinai: The Retelling of the Bible in Jubilees and the Damascus Covenant," in *Dead Sea Discoveries* 1 (1994): 1–29; Ego, "Abraham als Urbild"; and Bradley C. Gregory, "Abraham as the Jewish Ideal: Exegetical Traditions in Sirach 44:19–21," *Catholic Biblical Quarterly* 70 (2008): 66–81, especially 69–72.

14. For a list of passages in Jewish pseudepigrapha in which the patriarchs observe the Torah, see Schultz, "Two Views," 45.

15. The translations are taken from *Philo*, 7, 133, and 135.

16. The unwritten law to which Philo refers, it must be noted, is not the same as the Oral Torah so central to Talmudic tradition, in which it appears as the binary opposite of the Written Torah. For the Oral Torah is learned from teachers and passed on from master to disciple over the generations, whereas for Philo the heroes of Genesis "were not scholars or pupils of others, nor did they learn under teachers what was right to say or do" but rather regarded "nature itself [as] the most venerable of statutes." Elsewhere, however, Philo does see Abraham as learning from a teacher and thus inferior to Isaac, who, as Ellen Birnbaum puts it, "acquires his self-taught knowledge from God." See her book, *The Place of Judaism in Philo's Thought*, Brown Judaic Series 290, Studia Philonica Monographs 2 (Atlanta: Scholars Press, 1996), 56–57. I thank Dr. Birnbaum for her expert advice on matters Philonic.

17. For reasons to doubt that the passage is original to the Mishnah, see J. N. Epstein, *Introduction to the Mishnaic Text* [in Hebrew], 3rd ed. (Jerusalem: Hebrew University Magnes Press, 2000), 2:977. That there were apparently two ancient rabbis named Nehorai, one Tannaitic (that is, early) and one Amoraic (later) makes it difficult to know which one is associated with the passage about Abraham here, even if one assumes that Rabbi Nehorai is still the speaker. See Ch. Albeck, *Introduction to the Talmud, Babli and Yerushalmi* [in Hebrew] (Tel-Aviv: Dvir, 1969), 188. I have been helped on these matters by a seminar paper by Yonatan Miller, "Abraham's Observance of the Law: Reconsidering the Rabbinic Evidence" (December 9, 2010) and thank Mr. Miller for his assistance.

18. Note the Talmudic statement that "until Abraham there was no old age" (*b. Bava Metsia* 87a).

19. He is first described as "old" in Gen 18:11, in which Sarah is the first woman so described. Abraham's death notice is given in Gen 25:8, and his new family with Keturah is reported in Gen 25:1–2.

20. See *b. Bava Batra* 16b.

21. For example, *Deuteronomy Rabbah* 1:25; *b. Nedarim* 32b; *b. Bava Metsia* 87a.

22. See Mircea Eliade, *Myth and Reality* (New York: Harper and Row, 1963), 21–38.

23. To put it in historical-critical terms, the association of circumcision with Abraham is peculiar to P. (Gen 21:4, which refers to chapter 17, is also ascribed to P.)

24. I have rendered the word "kidneys" in conformity with what I take to be Rabbi Shimon bar Yochai's understanding. The passage is a midrash on Ps 1:2b.

25. Much literature on Abraham in early Christianity exists. Good places to begin are Siker, *Disinheriting*, and Marvin R. Wilson, "Our Father Abraham: A Point of Theological Convergence and Divergence for Christians and Jews," in *Jews and Christians: People of God*, ed. Carl E. Braaten and Robert W. Jenson (Grand Rapids, Mich.: Eerdmans, 2003), 41–64.

26. For example, see Luke 13:28–29 and 16:19–31.

27. See Joshua Trachtenberg, *The Devil and the Jews: The Medieval Conception of the Jew and Its Relation to Modern Antisemitism* (New Haven: Yale University Press, 1943).

28. Exod 3:13–14, where the Hebrew *'ehyeh* has traditionally been rendered "I am," as it is in the Septuagint (*ego eimi*, the same words that appear in John 8:58).

29. For example, Gal 2:16.

30. And one should not assume Paul won a complete victory. Note that the apostles meeting in Acts 15 are reported to have decreed that some minimal mitsvot do indeed apply to Gentile converts (vv. 20, 29) and contrast Gal 2:10. I thank Professor Gary A. Anderson for reminding me of this issue.

31. See introduction, note 4, in this volume. The other long reflection on Abraham in the Pauline corpus is Rom 4.

32. It bears mention that because Gen 15:6 does not specify the subject of its second verb, it is open to a radically different translation: "And he put his trust in the LORD and reckoned it as righteousness to him." On this rendering, it is Abraham who is doing the reckoning, trusting the LORD because he finds him to be righteous and his promise therefore reliable. See especially the commentary of Nachmanides (Ramban) on the verse. For a list of others who understand it similarly, see Ruth ben-Meir, "Abraham in Nahmanides' Thought," in *Faith of Abraham* [in Hebrew], ed. Moshe Hallamish, 156.

33. Various forms of the promise appear in Gen 12:3, 18:18, and 22:18, though the wording of none of them corresponds exactly to the wording in Paul's citation in Gal 3:8.

34. Most memorably in Krister Stendahl, "The Apostle Paul and the Introspective Conscience of the West," in *Paul among Jews and Gentiles* (Philadelphia: Fortress Press, 1976), 78–96. The essay was first published in English in *Harvard Theological Review* 56 (1963): 199–215. See also E. P. Sanders, *Paul and Palestinian Judaism: A Comparison of Patterns of Religion* (Philadelphia: Fortress Press, 1977), 431–556, especially 442–47.

35. On the Torah as offering a bill of indictment but no possibility of acquittal (available exclusively through Jesus), see Rom 5:12–21, for example.

36. Sanders, *Paul*, 446.

37. See, for example, Sanders, *Paul*, especially 474–511; James D. G. Dunn, *Jesus, Paul and the Law* (Louisville, Ky.: Westminster John Knox, 1990), 215–41, and *A Commentary on the Epistle to the Galatians* (London: A&C Black, 1993), especially 168–80; and Daniel Boyarin, *A Radical Jew: Paul and the Politics of Identity* (Berkeley: University of California Press, 1994), 136–43.

38. Paul's understanding of Deut 21:23 is intended to advance his claim that the crucifixion of Jesus absorbed the curse of the law and thus opened up an avenue to bless-

ing. NJPS renders these words (from a law that forbids leaving the corpse of an impaled person on the stake overnight) thus: "For an impaled body is an affront to God." Paul picks up the phrase "the blessing of Abraham" from Gen 28:4.

39. Dunn, *Jesus, Paul*, 232, 248. In this discussion, I have been aided by John M. G. Barclay, " 'Neither Jew nor Greek': Multiculturalism and the New Perspective on Paul," in *Ethnicity and the Bible*, ed. Mark G. Brett (Leiden: Brill, 1996), 197–214.

40. Boyarin, *Radical Jew*, 6, 7.

41. On the complex question of ethnicity in early Christianity, two innovative recent studies need more attention than they have received outside the academy. On the general categories of ethnicity and universality in early Christianity, see Denise Kimber Buell, *Why This New Race? Ethnic Reasoning in Early Christianity* (New York: Columbia University Press, 2005). On Paul in particular, see Caroline Johnson Hodge, *If Sons, then Heirs: A Study of Kinship and Ethnicity in Paul's Letters* (New York: Oxford University Press, 2007).

42. 1 Cor 15:20–22; Rom 5:12–21.

43. Paula Fredriksen, "Judaizing the Nations: The Ritual Demands of Paul's Gospel," *New Testament Studies* 56 (2010): 232–52, here 243–44. Fredriksen (243n27) notes that Rom 9:7 might suggest that the "Gentiles-in-Christ" are also descended from Isaac. The point, nonetheless, stands that it is Abraham, the father of many nations, rather than Jacob/Israel, the father of the one chosen nation, on whom Paul focuses and into whose lineage he thinks the Spirit of Jesus has grafted the Gentiles.

44. See, for example, Isa 2:2–4, Zech 14:16–21, and Ps 86:9.

45. In recent decades, the classical Christian view—that Paul sees the Torah in only negative terms and sought to replace it altogether with the gospel—has receded in the world of professional biblical scholarship (less so elsewhere). On this, with special reference to Abraham, see Jeffrey S. Siker, "Abraham, Paul, and the Politics of Jewish Identity," *Jewish Studies Quarterly* 16 (2009): 56–70. There is much of value in the so-called "new perspective" on Paul, especially in its placement of the apostle's thinking within the culture of Judaism as it stood in his time and its dismantling of simpleminded stereotypes about Judaism and the Jews. Some scholars, however, go so far as to interpret Paul as finding no fault with Judaism at all but simply wanting to open up an equivalent path for Gentiles, so that Judaism and Christianity are simply variations of the same religion directed at different social groups. See, for example, Lloyd Gaston, *Paul and the Torah* (Vancouver: University of British Columbia Press, 1987) and John Gager, *Reinventing Paul* (New York: Oxford University Press, 2000). My own view is that this latter claim is too extreme. Paul saw the gospel as the only path to salvation for Jews and Gentiles alike and did not believe that the Torah and its norms were an acceptable equivalent for anybody. On this, see Jeffrey S. Siker's review of John Gager, *The Origins of Anti-Semitism*, in *Union Seminary Quarterly Review* 41 (1983): 63–65, and his "Abraham, Paul," 67–68.

46. The contrast was most memorably and most brilliantly developed by Leo Baeck. See his *Judaism and Christianity: Essays by Leo Baeck* (New York: Atheneum, 1970), chapter 3 ("The Faith of Paul") and especially chapter 5 ("Romantic Religion").

47. H. L. Mencken, "The Divine Afflatus," reprinted in *A Mencken Chrestomathy*, ed. H. L. Mencken (New York: Knopf, 1949), 443. The essay was originally published in the *New York Evening Mail*, Nov. 16, 1917.

48. This is not to imply that Paul in any way slights the ethical dimension. See, for example, Gal 5:9–6:13 or 1 Cor 5–6.

49. I have departed from the NRSV translation of Gen 15:6 in order to bring out the use made of it in this passage. The idea of Abraham as the "friend" (or lover) of God is taken from Isa 41:8. My discussion of the Letter of James draws again upon my essay "The Akedah in Four Traditions."

50. The relevant texts are Sir 44:20 and 1 Mac 2:52.

51. Contra Edward Kessler, who, in his otherwise insightful book, *Bound by the Bible*, remarks that James evidences no "association between Genesis 22 and salvation through Christ" (61).

52. See *b. Sanh.* 56a. Rabbinic literature actually evidences the existence of a more diverse and contentious argument over time than the notion of the Seven Noahide Commandments, despite its eventual normative status, can accommodate. On this, see Marc Hirshman, *Torah for the Entire World* [in Hebrew] (Tel Aviv: Hakkibbutz Hameuchad, 1999).

53. Gen 22:18. I have changed the NJPS wording so as to bring out Rashbam's point about the use of the identical Hebrew phrasing.

54. The textual variant is found in an interpolation into the Safed manuscript. See Bernard Mandelbaum, *Pesikta de-Rav Kahana* (New York: Jewish Theological Seminary of America, 5722/1962), 203. The biblical passages from which the midrash adduces the commandments operative before Sinai are Gen 2:16, 9:4, 17:9, 21:4, 32:33, and 38:8. For a list of parallels to this text in rabbinic literature, see Schultz, "Two Views," 51.

55. "Heaven" in this saying is a euphemism for God. The immediate context here is the study of Torah. The same statement, with the same underlying theology, appears in *b. Menachot* 110a in the context of sacrificial donations.

56. See n33, above.

57. There is, though, some distant affinity to this passage in later texts of a mystical nature. On this, see Arthur Green, *Devotion and Commandment: The Faith of Abraham in the Hasidic Imagination* (Cincinnati, Ohio: Hebrew Union College Press, 1989).

# CHAPTER SIX

1. *The Guide of the Perplexed* 3:29. The translations of the *Guide* in this volume are taken from *The Guide of the Perplexed*, trans. Shlomo Pines (Chicago: University of Chicago Press, 1963) here, 2:515.

2. Abraham's Path, http://www.abrahampath.org/about.php.

3. "Abraham Path Update—December 2007."

4. Bruce Feiler, *Abraham: A Journey to the Heart of Three Faiths* (New York: William Morrow, 2002), 11.

5. Ibid., 148.

6. Ibid., 130.

7. Ibid., 175, 181.

8. Bruce Feiler, *Walking the Bible: A Journey by Land through the Five Books of Moses* (New York: William Morrow, 2001), 31. Feiler goes on to note that his familial attachment to Judaism was "one based on family, community, ethics, public service; not spirituality or mysticism."

9. Feiler, *Abraham*, 128. The immediate context is what Feiler calls "the dominant strand of Judaism by the Middle Ages," which, in his view, "held that Abraham was

no longer the figure who expressed God's universal blessing to humankind." On the survival of the universal dimension in the interpretation of Abraham in rabbinic and medieval Judaism, see chapter 1 in this volume.

10. See chapter 5, above.

11. Quoted from Heinrich Denzinger, *Enchiridion Symbolorum: Definitionum et Declarationum de Rebus Fidei et Morum* (Barcinone: Herder, 1967), 52–53 (my translation). I thank my colleague, Professor Kevin Madigan, for his assistance in matters of Trinitarian theology.

12. Ibid., 66.

13. Sidney H. Griffith, *The Church in the Shadow of the Mosque: Christians and Muslims in the World of Islam* (Princeton: Princeton University Press, 2008), 33.

14. On this, see G. R. Hawting, *The Idea of Idolatry and the Emergence of Islam: From Polemic to History* (Cambridge, U.K.: Cambridge University Press, 1999). Hawting argues that the primary target of the Qur'anic polemics against those who engage in the association (*shirk*) of other beings with God is other monotheists, not idolaters and polytheists.

15. See Qur'an 22:78.

16. See Peter Schäfer, *The Jewish Jesus: How Judaism and Christianity Shaped Each Other* (Princeton: Princeton University Press, 2012), 42–54.

17. *The Guide of the Perplexed*, trans. Shlomo Pines, 1:111, 1:178. Whether the views of Maimonides and other Jewish polemicists against the Trinity do justice to the plurality within the Jewish God is another question. See Daniel Boyarin, "The Gospel of the Memra: Jewish Binitarianism and the Prologue to John," *Harvard Theological Review* 94 (2001): 243–84, and *Border Lines: The Partition of Judaeo-Christianity* (Philadelphia: University of Pennsylvania Press, 2004), especially 89–147, as well as Schäfer, *The Jewish Jesus*, especially 55–149. On plurality within God in Jewish mysticism, see Gershom G. Sholem, *Major Trends in Jewish Mysticism* (New York: Schocken 1961), 205–43, and Yehuda Liebes, "De Natura Dei—On the Jewish Myth and Its Metamorphosis," in *Maśśu'ot: Studies in Kabbalistic Literature and Jewish Thought in Memory of Professor Efraim Gottlieb* [in Hebrew], ed. Michal Oron and Amos Goldreich (Jerusalem: Bialik Institute, 1994), 243–97.

18. *Commentary to the Mishnah, Avodah Zarah* 1:1.

19. See also Jacob Katz, *Exclusiveness and Tolerance: Studies in Jewish-Gentile Relations in Medieval and Modern Times* (Springfield, N.J.: Behrman House, 1961), 34–36; and David Ellenson, "A Jewish View of the Christian God: Some Cautionary and Hopeful Remarks," in Tikva Frymer-Kensky et al., *Christianity in Jewish Terms* (Boulder, Colo.: Westview Press, 2000), 69–76, especially 70–71.

20. Katz, *Exclusiveness*, 36.

21. Siker, *Disinheriting the Jews*, 167 (*Dialogue with Trypho* 113:4).

22. See Jon D. Levenson, "Must We Accept the Other's Self-Understanding?" *Journal of Religion* 71 (1991): 558–67.

23. Gen 18:16–33, especially v. 25.

24. 1 Cor 15:21–22; Rom 5:12–21.

25. Gen 17:6–8 and 17:18–22.

26. Later narratives will further narrow down the range of heirs to the full reality of the blessing, promise, and covenant to Isaac's younger son, Jacob, whose name is changed to Israel. See Gen 25:19–34 and 27:1–45.

27. Feiler, *Abraham*, 148.

28. Rom 4:21–5:1.

29. On Paul's ambivalence on this, see chapter 5 in this volume.

30. See 1 Thes 4:13–18.

31. Karl-Josef Kuschel, *Abraham: Sign of Hope for Jews, Christians and Muslims* (New York: Continuum, 1995). As I was finishing the writing of this book, I received a booklet containing a symposium inspired by an article of mine that makes, in briefer form, the argument of this chapter. The article is Jon D. Levenson, "The Idea of Abrahamic Religions: A Qualified Dissent," *Jewish Review of Books* 1:1 (Spring 2010): 40–42, 44. The booklet is "The Faith of Abraham: Bond or Barrier? Jewish, Christian and Muslim Perspectives," and the main article in it is the annual spring McGinley Lecture at Fordham University for 2011, given by Patrick J. Ryan, S.J., with brief responses by Rabbi Daniel Polish and Professor Amir Hussain. Although Prof. Ryan describes his piece as a "dissent" from my article (p. 1), our positions agree more than they diverge. See especially his remarks on p. 19: "Irenical trialogue between Jews and Christians and Muslims would be better served by our frank recognition of the different ways, based on our historical experiences of faith, we think of Abraham," and his endorsement on the same page of the idea of "the polyvalence of Abraham, the polyvalence of great concepts like faith and revelation, community and the path of righteousness."

32. Kuschel, *Abraham*, 196.

33. Ibid., 204–5.

34. With the possible exception of one half verse, Gen 26:5b, as discussed in chapter 5, above.

35. See the discussion of *Pesikta de-Rav Kahana* 12:1 in chapter 5 in this volume. Note again that the Torah-observant Abraham may possibly have made his debut in Gen 26:5, as discussed in the same chapter.

36. Compare Hans Küng, *Der Islam: Geschichte, Gegenwart, Zukunft* (Munich: Piper Verlag, 2004), 82, in which the well-known dissident Catholic theologian (and mentor to Kuschel) maintains that unconditional trust in God is more important for Abraham than circumcision, which, following a respected position among biblical scholars, he sees as a product of the Babylonian exile and thus late (Kuschel voices the same view in *Abraham*, 25). The very notion that one must choose between faith and circumcision (or any other commandment), however, is altogether alien to the Hebrew Bible and derives, in fact, from the New Testament (especially Galatians).

37. See also Gal 6:15. Paul seems to backtrack on this a bit in Rom 3:1, but never wavers from his association of Abraham with the state of not being circumcised.

38. For example, 2 Mac 6:10; *Mekhilta de-Rabbi Ishmael*, bachodesh 6.

39. The statement refers to Gen 17:1, "Walk in My ways and be blameless."

40. Qur'an 2:125–29. But note that Jubilees has the patriarch speaking about a "house of Abraham" (Jub 22:24), though not, as in the Qur'an, in the sense of "the sacred site of Abraham" (3:97). On this, see Bat-Sheva Garsiel, "Quran's Depiction," 49.

41. Note Garsiel, "Quran's Depiction," 48: "Another indication of the Quran's perception that Islam preceded Judaism is that according to the Quran, Abraham built the Ka'ba together with Ishmael even before the Pentateuch was delivered to the Jewish people."

42. Kuschel, *Abraham*, 203.

43. See chapters 3 and 5 in this volume.

44. See the close parallel in Luke 3:8–9.

45. See introduction, note 4, above. As noted in chapter 5, Paul sometimes vacillates on this unqualified disinheritance of the Jews.

46. Kuschel, *Abraham*, 203–4.

47. Tim Winter, "Abraham from a Muslim Perspective," in *Abraham's Children: Jews, Christians and Muslims in Conversation*, ed. Norman Solomon, Richard Harries, and Tim Winter (New York: T&T Clark, 2005), 30.

48. In common with most Christian thinkers, here Kuschel loses the sense of the immediate points at issue in Paul's polemics and creates an abstract dichotomy of law and faith. Elsewhere, though, he shows some awareness of the situation in which Paul wrote (for example, *Abraham*, 78–85).

49. Kuschel, *Abraham*, 54–55. On these traditions, see our chapter 5.

50. Ibid., 65.

51. Gal 4:21–5:1.

52. Kuschel, *Abraham*, 85. The citation is from Gen 17:5, which Kuschel then explicitly connects to Gal 3:14. See also Michael A. Signer, "Abraham: The One and the Many," in *Memory and History in Christianity and Judaism*, ed. Michael A. Signer (Notre Dame, Ind.: University of Notre Dame Press, 2001), 204–12, a response to Karl-Josef Kuschel, "One in Abraham? The Significance of Abraham for Jews, Christians, and Muslims Today," in the same volume (183–203). Signer faults Kuschel for deploying the concept of "legalism" against Judaism. " 'Legalism' hearkens back to the supersessionist rhetoric of the superiority of the gospel over the law, of Christ over Moses," he writes (205–6). That very rhetoric, however, underlies Kuschel's discussion of Abraham in Judaism, and it recapitulates a deployment of Abraham in Christian anti-Jewish discourse that is at least as old as Galatians.

53. Kuschel, *Abraham*, 181, 182. What Kuschel seems to mean by his unfortunate term "Orthodox Judaism" is rabbinic Judaism in its broad outlines and not the modern religious movement that goes by that name (a modern coinage).

54. The word "pagan," with its connotations of barbarity and perversion, is unfortunate. All that is meant here is that those in question were neither Jewish nor Christian.

55. See Jon D. Levenson, *Sinai and Zion: An Entry into the Jewish Bible* (San Francisco: Harper & Row, 1987), 56–70; and *Creation and the Persistence of Evil: The Jewish Drama of Divine Omnipotence*, 2nd ed. (Princeton: Princeton University Press, 1994), 131–39.

56. Frank Moore Cross, *From Epic to Canon: History and Literature in Ancient Israel* (Baltimore: Johns Hopkins University Press, 1998), 8.

57. In the translation of Deut 32:6, I have changed the NJPS "created" to "begot," which strikes me as more accurate to the nuance of the Hebrew verb *qanah* here (see v. 18, which seems to predicate the same relationship between God and Israel), and added a question mark. On the adoption/begetting language in the New Testament, see the excellent article of Michael Peppard, "Adopted and Begotten Sons of God: Paul and John on Divine Sonship," *Catholic Biblical Quarterly* 73 (2011): 92–110.

58. For example, Jer 2:2; Eph 5:22–33.

59. Both of these texts echo Exod 19:5.

60. Martin S. Jaffee, "One God, One Revelation, One People: On the Symbolic Structure of Elective Monotheism," *Journal of the American Academy of Religion* 69 (2001): 760. The italics are Jaffee's.

61. Michael Cook, *The Koran: A Very Short Introduction* (New York: Oxford University Press, 2000), 56, but see Cook's qualifications on the same page.

62. On the question of descent and genealogy in earliest Islam, see David S. Powers, *Muḥammad is Not the Father of Any of Your Men: The Making of the Last Prophet* (Philadelphia: University of Pennsylvania Press, 2009).

63. Gen 17:19–21.

64. The statistic is taken from Reuven Firestone, "Abraham's Son as the Intended Sacrifice (*al-dhabīḥ*, Qur'ān 37:99–113): Issues in Qur'ānic Exegesis," *Journal of Semitic Studies* 34 (1989): 99n17.

65. Kuschel, *Abraham*, xiv, xv.

66. Ibid., 29–31. The last quote is on p. 31 and refers to Ps 47:10. Actually, it is not so clear that Ps 47 propounds the exclusive Abrahamic identity that Kuschel ascribes to it.

67. Kuschel has more respect for particularism than Feiler and some of the other advocates of Abrahamic religion, but he still thinks the particularism must be directed toward universal blessing and salvation. See *Abraham*, 23, and for a critique of this thinking, see chapter 1 in this volume.

68. Alon Goshen-Gottstein, "Abraham and 'Abrahamic Religions' in Contemporary Interreligious Discourse: Reflections of an Implicated Jewish Bystander," *Studies in Interreligious Dialogue* 12 (2002): 165–83, here 172, 174.

69. See Kessler, *Bound by the Bible*, 33–36.

70. See Shari L. Lowin, *The Making of a Forefather: Abraham in Islamic and Jewish Exegetical Narratives* (Leiden: Brill, 2006), 39–86.

71. *Mishneh Torah, Hilkhot Nedarim* 9:21.

72. Against this exclusion of Muslims, some scholars point to Maimonides's view that "everyone who is circumcised joins *Abraham's covenant*" (*Guide of the Perplexed* 3:49, trans. Pines, 2:610, his italics) and his ruling in *Mishneh Torah, Hilkhot Melakhim* 10:8 that the Ishmaelites are obligated by circumcision on the eighth day. See Menachem Kellner, *Maimonides on Judaism and the Jewish People* (Albany: State University of New York Press, 1991), 82; Hannah Kasher, "Maimonides' View of Circumcision as a Factor Uniting the Jewish and Muslim Communities," in *Medieval and Modern Perspectives on Muslim-Jewish Relations*, ed. Ronald L. Nettler (Luxembourg: Harwood Academic Publishers in Cooperation with the Oxford Centre for Postgraduate Hebrew Studies, 1995), 103–8; Josef Stern, *Problems and Parables of Law: Maimonides and Nahmanides on Reasons for the Commandments (Ta'amei Ha-Mitzvot)* (Albany: State University of New York, 1998), 87–107, especially 97. Note, however, that Maimonides excludes Ishmaelites from the Abrahamic commandment of "circumcision" in the immediately preceding passage in the *Mishneh Torah, Hilkhot Melakhim* 10:7, and elsewhere forbids a Jew to circumcise a non-Jew unless the latter is converting to Judaism. See *Teshuvot ha-Rambam*, vol. 1, trans. and ed. Yehoshua Blau (Jerusalem, 1958), no. 148, 282–84. How we are to resolve this evident contradiction is unclear. I thank Professor Bernard Septimus for helping me think about this complex and nettlesome issue and its sources.

73. My discussion of Massignon relies heavily on Sidney Griffith, "Sharing the Faith: the 'Credo' of Louis Massignon," *Islam and Christian-Muslim Relations* 8 (1997): 193–210. The Abrahamic theme can be found in many of the works of Massignon, especially "Les trois prières d'Abraham: Père de tous croyants," in *Parole Donnée* (Paris: Éditions du Seuil, 1983), 257–72, reprinted as "The Three Prayers of Abraham," in *Testimonies and*

*Reflections: Essays of Louis Massignon* (Notre Dame, Ind.: University of Notre Dame, 1989), 3–20. The essay dates from 1949.

74. Griffith, "Sharing the Faith," 198, 204.

75. Massignon, "Three Prayers," 6–7 (translation of "Les trois prières," 260).

76. Quoted in Griffith, "Sharing the Faith," 202, which gives the reference as L. Massignon, *Rythmes du monde* 3 (1948): 53.

77. Maurice Borrmans, "Aspects théologiques de la pensée de Louis Massignon sur l'Islam," in *Louis Massignon et le dialogue des cultures*, ed. Daniel Massignon (Paris: Les Éditions du Cerf, 1996), 130 (my translation).

78. Griffith, "Sharing the Faith," 204, translating Massignon, "L'Islam et le témoignage du croyant," in *Parole Donnée*, 241.

79. See Borrmans, "Aspects," 132.

80. See the contemporary counterstatement in A.-M. Goichon, "Attitude du chrétien envers l'islam," *Études* 257 (1948): 38–51.

# Index of Primary Sources

# Index of Modern Authors